WWII LIBERATOR'S LIFE

AFS AMBULANCE DRIVER CHOOSES PEACE

Norman C. Kunkel

Georgie Bright Kunkel

Seventy-five years ago, shortly after the outbreak of World War I in 1914, a group of 15 Americans living in Paris volunteered to drive ambulances for the American Hospital there. The group soon became known as the American Field Service, which operated a civilian mobile medical unit in France for several years before the United States entered the war militarily. The group finished the war under the U.S. Army Ambulance Service. By then, their number had grown to 2,500 volunteer drivers. ★ Supported by private contributions, the American Field Service was later active in World War II on a much broader scale. Its members, all civilian

ambulance drivers, were stationed in Europe, Syria, North Africa, Burma, and India. They carried only a passport and a Geneva card for identification. They were there to help. ★ Between the two wars, the members decided to use surplus funds to set up AFS-sponsored fellowships for French and American graduate student exchanges. This was before anyone had thought or heard of Fulbright scholarships. After World War II, in 1947, AFS members again were determined not to let the tradition die, but to do something more and something more lasting to hasten the postwar healing process. It was their personal declaration of peace. ★ They started mod-

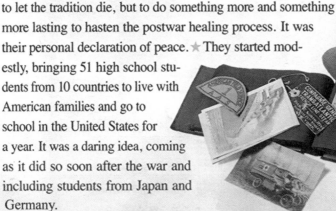

estly, bringing 51 high school students from 10 countries to live with American families and go to school in the United States for a year. It was a daring idea, coming as it did so soon after the war and including students from Japan and Germany.

Printed: 1989

WWII LIBERATOR'S LIFE

AFS AMBULANCE DRIVER CHOOSES PEACE

Norman C. Kunkel

and

Georgie Bright Kunkel

WWII Liberator's Life: AFS Ambulance Driver Chooses Peace
Norman C. Kunkel and Georgie Bright Kunkel

Library of Congress Control Number: 2005910547

Cover design by Jennifer Shontz, Seattle, Washington

Printed in the United States of America

Published by Bright Kunkel Books
March 2006
First edition

DEDICATION

This book is dedicated to the memory of our son N. Joseph Kunkel and to our grown children, Stephen Gregory Kunkel, Susan Ann Kunkel, and Kimberly Jane Waligorska, who were the first reviewers. Our children have kept us centered in our lives and we continue to learn from them.

This is the end of an elephant tusk that I traded my best pipe for in Manipur, India on the Burma border.

After many years, I had it inscribed and mounted to leave to my oldest son. Instead, I decided to give it to him as a present. It was not long after this that my son was killed in a traffic accident. I was so pleased that he was able to read the manuscript and have this memento before his death.

ACKNOWLEDGEMENTS

There are numerous people to credit with influencing my life and the writing of my World War II memoirs. Certainly this book would not have taken form without Georgie Bright Kunkel, my wife, who saved all my letters written to her between 1943 and 1945. Some years ago she prepared a four-hundred-page document consolidating my wartime diary and letters, a copy of which was donated to the American Field Service (AFS) Archives in New York. The letters and diary, along with Georgie's letters written to me, provided not only a wartime memoir, but a story of courting by letters that took sometimes months to arrive.

Sherrill Carlson served as first run-through editor. As a gift to me, Tom Spohn scanned in the photographs and Susan Thompson, a dedicated AFS participant, completed the preliminary editing and formatting. Jan Foster completed the final polishing, editing, and formatting for publication. Numerous friends and acquaintances helped to review the book at various stages. Eleanora Golobic of the AFS Archives facilitated my purchase of numerous photographs taken at Bergen-Belsen, Germany, and helped locate other relevant material.

Washington State Governor John Spellman established the first Commemoration of the Holocaust where I met survivors of Bergen-Belsen Concentration Camp. One of them, Laura Varon, has been instrumental in my telling of the Holocaust story along with Stella de Leon, also a Bergen-Belsen survivor now deceased. Washington State Holocaust Education Resource Center in Seattle supported my talking about the Holocaust. Warren Eisenberg, who helped to collect memorabilia for the expanded exhibit at Bergen-Belsen site in Germany, personally received my World War II uniform to place in this exhibit along with the Bergen-Belsen chapter.

Hugh Gemmell, son of an AFS Ambulance Driver, urged me to attend the Commemoration of the Holocaust in the Portland, Oregon, area at which time I posed beside the AFS ambulance that he refurbished. At this event I met another Bergen-Belsen survivor, Alice Kern, who presented me with her book from which I have quoted.

AFS made it possible for me to present the story of my AFS Ambulance Corps experiences at the Brazil AFS conference in 2000. There I met Paul Shay, then Executive of AFS International and the Brazil AFS Executive Eduardo Assed. I also took part in the

AFS Northwest Conference in Seattle, at the invitation of Floyd Van Weelden, and the AFS national conference in San Antonio in 2000, where I met the president of AFS U.S.A., Alex Plinio. Others who provided comments were The Rev. Dale Turner, who has served as minister for the University Congregational Church and Henry Friedman, early president of Holocaust Survivors and former Chair of Washington State Holocaust Education Resource Center.

Some years ago, a now-deceased AFS driver, Chan Keller, sent me *The History of the American Field Service 1920-1955* written by George Rock. It has served as an encyclopedia of AFS Ambulance Corps history, listing all those who served with AFS (1939-1945). Howard Mayhew and Thomas Hale, whom I met at our AFS Ambulance Driver reunion in Baltimore in the fall of 2002, provided me with further information about Bergen-Belsen Concentration Camp.

It was an acquaintance in Seattle who said to me in the early 1940s, "You ought to be attending the University of Washington." Two teachers at the University of Washington, Frances Hueston and Agnes Colton, gave me the courage to break out of the insecurity I felt at being the first of eight children in my family to strive for a college degree. Then it was the AFS recruiter John Burgess Whiteside who recruited me for the AFS Ambulance Corps in 1943.

Throughout my life I had family and friends who conveyed to me the values that I live by. My mom was an independent woman, honest and caring. My dad cherished the earth and all it produced. My seven siblings stimulated me with their curiosity and eagerness to learn. My wife interviewed six of my seven siblings who provided information about my parents and their early life in Missouri and South Dakota where I was born and about my childhood.

Chet and Betty Dutcher and Lewis and Evelyn Brownell have been close friends throughout the years. The teachers who were my colleagues in the education field reinforced my goal of lifelong learning and sharing what I have learned with others. The Saltwater Unitarian Universalist church community nourishes my spirit and allowed me to become a continually growing person finally willing to share an intimate look into my past.

Our four offspring: Joe (now deceased), Steve, Susan, and Kim have always offered me the support that a parent needs when opening up a story like this. Our nine grandchildren and our four great-grandchildren will now learn of their family heritage.

Norman C. Kunkel

TABLE OF CONTENTS

TABLE OF CONTENTS (continued)

TABLE OF CONTENTS (continued)

PREFACE

Adding one more account of World War II may seem superfluous. What more can a participant in the so-called GOOD WAR bring to the table? Having served as a non-combatant in the American Field Service Ambulance Corps, I was able to view war not as a warrior but as a rescuer—of men from the battlefield and, at the very end of the war, of women from Bergen-Belsen Concentration Camp in Germany.

I could not let all my letters and diaries and memories of my World War II experiences lie idle and so I made the decision to bring them to life in this book. Along with my letters and journal are two years of letters written to me overseas by my then sweetheart and now wife, Georgie. I managed to save these letters throughout my two years of service. They provide the other side of the war story—the story of connection to someone back home who bolstered me at the front and who promised to wait for me. We shared our parallel lives during World War II and came together afterwards to marry, raise a family, and finally come to terms with the horror of war, which I had buried inside me for many years.

It was AFS that worked to gain recognition for drivers as veterans. I was granted veteran status in 1993 after proving that I served the required time with the U.S. forces overseas. It was too late to receive GI Bill perks but I received the following: U.S. WWII Medal, European/African/Middle Eastern Campaign, Army of Occupation, AFS WWII, and the Good Conduct Medal. I have also been honored by AFS International for having been a part of its history and received a letter from the British Consolate thanking me for serving with the British Army.

The transformation of my life from one, who desperately wanted to be a part of fighting Hitler to a pacifist who realized that war is anathema took place gradually over time. The horrible sights at the battlefront and the concentration camp were buried deep inside me for many years. It took several decades before the story of the war in India/Burma, Italy, and Germany including the Holocaust was to pour out—one agonizing memory at a time.

I must remind the reader that the wartime section of this book was taken from my letters during a youthful, exploratory period in my life—wondering whether I could meet the manly challenge of war and the personal challenge of courting a young woman waiting at home for me. Much of the terminology I used then I would not use today. For example, using the term "Jap" for the enemy in India/Burma would not be tolerated now. Also, since I was overseas years before the women's movement of the late 1960s, 1970s, and early 1980s, I used the term "girl" for the young women that I met overseas. I also used "Kiwi" for New Zealander. I asked a woman to dance in this way, "Care to dance, Babe?" Words that are clearly derogatory are common in times of war and certainly during times of cultural bias and discrimination. I admit that I used the terminology of war and the terminology of a man in a man's world before the women's movement made us all aware of sexist language.

The last section is written from a more experienced, mature view, expressed by a person in his eighth decade of life. That I literally faced my own death numerous times in serving overseas cemented my resolve to return home to become an active member of society. This included choosing marriage, raising a family, finishing my studies at the University of Washington and becoming an educator, an environmentalist, and an equalitarian activist.

Just before publication of this book I suffered a devastating brain bleed and am slowly gaining back my strength and looking forward to this story being read by family, friends, veterans, those interested in World War II history and the Holocaust, and AFS people around the world.

Norman C. Kunkel

PART ONE:
A POOR KID GROWS UP

Born in South Dakota

If you had been at the train station in a certain little farm town in Missouri in the summer of 1918, you would not have been able to ignore a tall, striking woman of forty, my mother, Winnifred Blanche Kunkel. She was noticeably pregnant, rushing along the platform as fast as an awkward woman soon to give birth could move. "We haven't much time," she called as she led her gaggle of young'uns toward the train, still puffing as it stopped for five minutes to allow boarding. Frances, eleven, was carrying Josephine who was just a little past one year of age, and the other five trailed behind.

You may wonder how this mother with seven children and another on the way got from the farm to the station in St. Joseph, a good thirty miles away. Uncle Ame had just bought a brand new Ford and was anxious to show it off to the family that he would not be seeing again for a long time to come. Ame, his brother Lafe, and sister Cora couldn't imagine their sister making such a journey, but they knew they had to help in any way they could. Winnifred was determined to join her husband in South Dakota where he had gone ahead to find a farm with better prospects than working under the miserable taskmaster he had left behind.

And so the family of eight piled into the car and called out to Ame as he leaned over to put in the crank, turning it until he heard the motor engage. When he was finally sitting proudly in the driver's seat, he heard a commotion as his nieces and nephews pushed and shoved to find a place to sit. "What a fine new car," Winnifred remarked, and soon they were starting their drive to the train station. And what about baggage? There were baskets of food for the trip and the clothes on their backs with a couple of quilts in case it was cool on the train.

After all the goodbyes, it was time for the train to come puffing into the station. "Mom, I hear the train whistle." It was Mabel, then aged seven, who always noticed everything first and had to announce her newfound knowledge for the benefit of her

1

siblings. Mabel's loud message alerted her mother who gathered her children, all seven of them, so when the train made its stop there would be no straggler left behind.

Then one would notice Frances, the firstborn and the one who would need to help her mother with the new baby when it arrived. Lawrence, ten, the next in line, was still very young but strong enough to help with the few belongings that had to be stowed on the train. Shirley, three, and Emil, five, had stopped their bickering for the time being. They were so enthralled at the oncoming train that they stayed close to Mom while Ethel, nine, ran to catch up with Mabel just as the engine hissed to a stop and the conductor appeared, lowering the steps to enable Mom and her brood of seven to board.

As she herded the children up the steps, she used her skirt to wipe one dripping nose and called to Ethel and Mabel, "Hurry or we'll be late."

Ethel and Mabel spied a big black man, the first black person they had ever seen. They were frightened at first so they ran to hide under Mom's long skirts. After awhile they became accustomed to seeing many more people like this man working on the train helping passengers and handling baggage. My sister Ethel often remembered stories of this trip. Mom had prepared several baskets of food to feed her hungry brood.

Emil recalls that when the family had to change trains, Shirley began to cry out, "I don't want to ride on that black train. I want to ride on that pretty yellow train." Mabel told me that Shirley was such a cute little thing, always laughing and talking, but the strain of this long trip was becoming evident at last.

This was no ordinary trip for a woman pregnant with her eighth child. The children often heard Mom dreaming out loud about better times. "Someday I will have a new home with running water and electric lights and a built-in bathtub." Thoughts of what the new place would be like filled her mind, already cluttered with apprehension. Would the house really keep out the cold during the winter months to come? South Dakota was freezing throughout the winter. Would there be room for this newcomer soon to be born?

You may have already guessed that this newcomer was to be named Norman. Even though none of my three brothers had been named after my dad, I was not to be his namesake either. It was to be another generation before Joseph Edwin Kunkel would have another Joseph in the family.

Of course I have no memories of this trip, as I lay insulated in the womb. It was Mabel who remembered traveling in a big wagon to Wessington. Evidently, there were two Swedish women whom Dad had told about the family's arrival. They found a little shack in town, barren of furniture, for the family to move into. The neighbors brought pots and pans so that at least meals could be cooked, but the first night the rain came down and the family had to use the pots and pans to catch the drips that came through the leaky roof.

There was not nearly enough room for everyone to sleep comfortably. It was an old place with only one bedroom. My brothers and sisters were cramped, two or sometimes three to a bed. There was an artesian well that produced rusty, stinking water that gave everyone "the runs" from drinking it. Mom would mix up flour and water to tighten up the bowels until the family eventually got used to it. The locals drank rainwater collected from the downspouts on the roofs, but our family could not wait to accumulate a supply.

While Mom worked to get the house livable, the kids got acquainted with the neighbors. My sister Ethel remembered that all the girls in town wore black satin bloomers while she and her sisters wore flour sack bloomers. When the other girls would slide in the dirt it didn't show, but when she and her sisters tried it they would get paddled for dirtying their underpants. Their school lunch consisted of big crackers that came out of a big barrel from the general store, spread with peanut butter dipped out of a large container and packed in a carton.

My family then moved to the pink house in town, which my sister Fran described to me as a tiny little house with only one bedroom, room enough for two beds. There wasn't enough room in the kitchen to eat because of the bed in there, so the family ate in the living room. There were never enough chairs for everyone to sit down to a table, so meals were eaten on the run.

Grandma Wright came to visit us from Missouri just before I was born. In Mound City where she lived, she would hitch up the horse and buggy and head out to assist in every birth. Grandma kept a spotless house with a white bedspread. She would take a broom and draw it across the bedspread to level it as it had a feather bed underneath which had to be pressed down to look smooth. Ethel said, "Us kids would go by and just touch this bedspread to make a dent in this smooth surface and she would give us heck." Underneath that fussy exterior, Grandma was kind and thoughtful. Every winter she sent a twenty-pound sack of dried apples, which was a godsend when there was nothing fresh from the garden to be had.

On her first trip to our new home, it took Grandma no time at all to discover that in our house of nine people there was no place for her to be alone. After finally getting settled in following her long road trip, she was feeling rather grimy so looked forward to a nice cleansing bath. While all the children were out playing one day, she began the chore of heating the water. She placed the washtub in the middle of the kitchen and began filling it with buckets of hot water. No sooner had she removed all of her clothing and begun washing under her arms and her breasts when suddenly Ethel ran in and said, "Why are you doing that, Grandma?"

"Well," Grandma retorted, "If you don't clean under your arms and your tits, you're bound to stink."

After assisting Mom with my birth, Grandma stayed a while longer before returning to Missouri. After I was born, I slept with my sister Josephine in a crib until I was almost five years old. You can imagine what it was like after Grandma left Mom and Dad with this gaggle of eight children, none older than eleven years of age.

One of Lawrence's most traumatic memories of our family was on Thanksgiving Day. Evidently, we were considered the poorest family in Wessington because on that special day some women came to our door and presented Mom with a huge basket of fixings for dinner—including a wonderful turkey. My older brothers and sisters crowded behind Mom and peered around to see this special holiday treat that was being offered. They, I expect, were salivating over the thought of sparring for the drumsticks, eating the tangy cranberry sauce, the mincemeat and pumpkin pies, all of which would have fed our whole family with a little left over.

Their fantasies were quickly interrupted by Mom's voice saying deliberately, "Thank you for offering, but we do not need to take charity. We have always made do and we will make do this Thanksgiving." As she shut the door leaving the women standing there holding the big basket full of food, Lawrence was heart broken at the disappointment of losing this sumptuous meal, and he said he never forgot that moment in his life. I have a brief remembrance of this family story told to me when I was older. To me it was only a secondhand story of disappointment. But to Lawrence, who had at that time spent ten years in poverty, it was a personal tragedy.

It was the winter of 1918-1919 that the flu epidemic hit everyone in our family but me, probably because I was nursing at the time. Mom was so sick and yet had to brace herself for the chores of taking care of all the others. Josephine had double pneumonia and almost died. Mom, Dad, and my older siblings had to take turns staying up with her as they were all so frightened that she might die in the night. Fran said that she just fell over on her bed one evening and didn't remember anything for several days. Lawrence was determined not to get sick, but the inability to function came over him as well. Mabel said some had whooping cough along with the flu, and they were lying moaning and coughing and spitting onto papers placed by their beds on the floor. The neighbors, who were not ill themselves, would come in and help us when they could, relieving my ill Mom of cooking and other chores.

After weathering that terrible winter, my dad, who had worked for a boss on the Wilson place even before I was born, had a chance to move our family to a house on that farm. The farm owner didn't agree with Dad when it came to using humane methods of working the horses. The farmer would bring out his horses after a winter of rest and expect them to begin heavy plowing without a period of breaking in.

Dad finally quit after several months of working in this environment of disagreement with the owner. We moved to a place called the Franklin House in town. Mabel said the children brought their pet badger with them. He lived under the house and would come and go as he pleased. Life with this pet was short lived, however, as some fellow shot him and the kids were brokenhearted about it.

For some reason Shirley disappeared right after this move and no one could find him. Mabel even went to the outhouse and looked down to see if he had fallen in. Finally, everyone went downtown looking for him, and Mabel spotted him down the street surrounded by people calling to him and giving him nickels and dimes because he was lost and they wanted to cheer him up.

In the Franklin House, Mom and Dad slept in the living room, and I continued to sleep in the crib with Josephine, whom we called Jopey, or sometimes with Mom and Dad. I loved getting into their bed and pointing to the prettiest colors in the patchwork quilt that Grandma Wright had made.

Emil said that our place was the only one in town that had an apple tree, so my older siblings kept a close watch over it when the apples were ripening because all the kids in town wanted to share in our harvest. I still recall the sound of that apple tree limb being blown against the window after I had gone to bed at night and leaving me in fright as it scratched eerily back and forth against the window pane.

We pumped water from the well in the back yard. Dad had to dig a tunnel through the snow to get into the front door of our house. Once one of our hens was brought into the kitchen in winter, and I marveled at the hen laying an egg in the nest Mom had made. While Mom worked to get dinner after a hard day, I would take out the button basket and play for hours. I put all the gold buttons in a row and

I was almost 4 years old.

all the white buttons in another row, then counted them all. During warmer weather I could watch the English sparrows picking off buds from the lilac bush out front.

Later in the summer the tumbleweeds rotted off and were rolling about in the wind like huge gym balls. I tied a rope to one and in a high wind it pulled me along so I could pretend I was driving my buckin' bronco through the street. Sometimes we would get inside old tires and ride down Minnik's Hill. We had our own outhouse, and when the dust had piled up around the hole, I cleaned it off by peeing on it but got in trouble for that when I got caught.

Dad took any job he could find, sometimes doing part-time work on the railroad, probably as a Gandy dancer which was hard labor putting in railroad ties and laying down track. It seems the term Gandy dancer is related to the Gandy Manufacturing Company of Chicago that made tools. If you observed a Gandy dancer at work, you saw that their motions required the use of tools to pry up the rails and replace them. Their body movements were similar to that of a dancer.

My Dad, Joseph Edwin Kunkel, b. 1872–d. 1951

Dad loved the outdoors in the garden or observing the wildlife that he knew so much about. Many times he would read some expert's statements about birds or other wildlife and say, "They have never lived with wildlife like I have or they would know that what they say is not true."

I never went hunting with Dad, but once he let me tag along when he went with Jack the veterinarian to a farm outside of town to help him kill crows. They would get an old animal that had died and put strychnine on it knowing that the crows would feed on it. Farmers hated crows that would descend upon their corn crop and eat it before it hardly showed above the ground. (Later in life I would find myself feeding crows that raucously scolded me if I was late throwing out scraps from our deck. Our old neighbors next door remembered their own Midwestern roots and scorned this practice.)

Jack, whom everyone called a drunkard behind his back, was Dad's only means of transportation on these jaunts out in the country and especially out hunting as he was the owner of a Model T, something that we could only dream about owning. Dad made extra money trapping muskrat, skunk, badger, mink, and weasel and would do most of the skinning. I remember holding the animal by the legs while Dad used his sharp pocket knife to peel off the skin. In the spring, he could sell each dried hide for a little more than a dollar, and in those days that could buy some needed staples such as salt, sugar, coffee, and the like at the general store. We put the scent glands from the skunks into the toilet hole and burned the carcass, which had lots of oil and made a roaring fire in our heating stove.

When Emil was about ten, he got his first gun, a .22 rifle. It took many a Saturday setting pins at the one-lane bowling alley to pay for it. He could then tag along with Dad, who hunted with his shotgun. Emil said that Dad was a deadeye shot and never missed, even a bird flying high above. Too bad that he wasn't able to take advantage of the Old West traveling shows featuring such shooting experts as Annie Oakley. As it was, he never quite found an occupation that could supply a living for our family. He lacked any formal education and did not have an inheritance leaving him enough farmland to produce what a family of eight children required, so in the early days he had to work for other farmers.

It wasn't often that I spent time with my dad. My older sisters and nieces have more memories of him than I do because I was always tagging along after Mom. Fran told me that once she got into some stinging nettles when she was out looking for berries with Dad. She never had good eyesight and could never avoid such pitfalls so when she cried out that she was hurting, Dad knew what plant could be crushed and rubbed on to ease the pain. When Fran had children of her own, this remedy came in handy. She didn't remember Dad ever reading very much so my mom would read out loud to him in the late evenings after all her work was done. Fran wanted to hear the stories that Mom read so she would try to stay awake and listen.

I was surprised at learning of my dad's temper as he never became angry with me or laid a hand on me in punishment. Once I learned that he really was pushed too far by my brother Shirley who was a fuse easily lighted. Dad was preparing to set the garden sprinkler and suddenly threw it at Shirley. The spike under the sprinkler pierced Shirley's biceps. Dad calmed down enough to call for someone to get the turpentine bottle, which was our stock treatment for wounds. Luckily I never pushed Dad that far. It was Mom who disciplined me. When she thought I needed a paddling, she would send me outside to cut a switch and she would switch my legs. I don't remember suffering greatly from it but I certainly didn't like having to be switched.

It was Mom who was the organizer and coordinator of the family household. Mom did not sew very well, so Fran made all our clothes on the cabinet sewing machine. She called the girls' dresses butterfly dresses because that is what they looked like when she cut them out from the material she sewed together—two pieces sewed up on the sides. She even made me shirts and short pants. But it was difficult making her own bras. Mom never wore one, but Fran was well endowed and was determined to have adequate support, so she figured out how to make one for herself.

Fran had to be responsible for so much that she would escape up into the big pie cherry tree to read for a while and not be bothered by all the younger children. She said later that not many of the household chores were delegated to the younger children, who not only were free to play about, but they often upset her with their pestering. Mom and Dad also needed to escape from time to time so they took turns getting out. Mom went to church occasionally or drove the horse and wagon to town and Dad went hunting.

Once Fran said I was mad at being left home when Mom got out and I filled my pants instead of going to the outhouse. She stripped off my dirtied pants and put me into a big washtub in the pump house

Brothers Emil and Lawrence revisiting the abandoned Farron place after more than sixty years.

to soak, which resulted in my screams and cries. So that there would be no difference of opinion on what happened, she dutifully reported this incident to Mom after her return.

I remember one spring, after a winter of eating mostly potatoes and lard gravy, that I ran out into the yard when the first shoots of grass appeared. I actually picked them and ate them as one would eat salad greens. Later, Mom would send us out to pick dandelion greens so we would all have something fresh on the table at dinner. Sometimes she would heat bacon grease to pour over them before serving this original wilted-lettuce dish.

Then Dad got work sharecropping on the Farron place. In the fall, he would call all of us kids who were old enough to pile up manure all around the house to keep the extreme cold from coming up under the floor. We all helped spread straw on the floor before winter set in and Mom would sew strips of cotton carpet together to cover it. We could romp about on the soft floor and never hurt ourselves when we fell down.

In the spring we would shovel the manure into a cart and empty it on the fields we plowed up for the garden, which produced all the fresh produce we ate including tomatoes and rhubarb. I remember picking potato bugs by the hundreds off the potato plants. We also went up and down the cornrows pulling weeds. We never heard of spraying to kill insects. I loved it when Mom would gather up the dead ripe tomatoes, bring them in, cut them up, and put sugar and cream on them for a special treat. Although we could have a garden, the country was drier than Missouri and there were no paw-paw trees growing wild as my family remembered them.

THE PAW-PAW TREE

I still nurture one paw-paw tree that came from a seed brought from Missouri by one of my older brothers who had taken Dad and Mom back to see the old home place. You probably have heard the song, "Way Down Yonder in the Paw-Paw Patch," but you probably haven't ever tasted this fruit. It is a member of the papaya family, but without any amount of flesh on it to make it sought after in today's market. For my older brother Lawrence, there was something nostalgic about picking this meager fruit and tasting its unique flavor as his memory drifted back to good old Missouri.

Several family members have made the trek back to Wessington in recent years and found the town about the same size. The only difference, even after sixty years, was a bigger graveyard, new paint on the water tower, and the disappearance of all the houses that we had lived in.

We had a white pony, a scrawny animal with bad teeth that a neighbor gave us. My older brothers loved to ride him, although they knew he was a poor excuse for a horse as he couldn't run very fast and couldn't even seem to eat properly. One day we realized that the pony had disappeared. We looked everywhere and asked all the neighbors if they had seen our pony, but no one had.

After winter was over and we were out in the pasture playing, Shirley called out, "Hey, come look what I found." There was something sticking out of the straw stack. Barely visible were the feet of our white pony. He had eaten into the straw stack and it had caved in, suffocating him. My older brothers spent much of the day digging a grave for him. It was a sad day for all of us.

At last I was old enough to attend school in the old wooden building called the sheep shed. It was right beside the brick high school from which Fran and Lawrence graduated. There was an old wagon pulled by two horses that would come by and pick us up. On the wagon was a kind of box shelter with windows in it where we could sit and be protected from the cold, our feet warmed a little by the heated rocks in the straw on the floor. We still felt cold when we arrived at school, so we would stand over a grill where we could look down and see the red-hot coal furnace underneath. We even had a school-lunch program serving tomato soup, with chunks of tomato floating around in it, and hot cocoa, which was a treat that I had never tasted before going to school.

We had slates and special slate pencils for our practice in arithmetic and penmanship. When the slate was full, we took a cloth that each one of us had to bring to school with us and cleaned the slate to make way for our next lesson. We were supposed to wet our cloths in the pail of water outside the school door, but some of us got lazy and just used spit.

I had barely experienced my first days in school when a life-changing accident happened. I was just six years old when Dad, who was working in the harvest, was driving a wagon loaded with bundles of barley. I had been allowed to be part of it for the first time. While Dad was waiting in line for his turn at the thresher, Josephine had already climbed up onto the wagon, so I grabbed hold of the side and attempted to pull myself up, too. Immediately I found myself tumbling back onto the ground. Sharp pain threw me into a panic of crying after I landed on my left elbow, smashing it. Emil picked me up and took me to the house and yelled for someone to take me to the doctor. Fortunately, there was an old Model T truck there, so I was taken to the doctor and treated. Even today such an injured elbow cannot easily be reconstructed. In this little farming community, the best the doctor could do was to put it into a cast and just let it heal as it would. I remember it was a very heavy cast that extended down to my fingertips causing me to fall frequently when playing at school.

Jopey declares that she was blamed for my accident. She said, "You were always pampered by Mom and you could do no wrong. Not even when you were mean to me." It wasn't until she began reading to me after she started school that I stopped teasing and taunting her.

That Thanksgiving and Christmas we had snow on the ground. The guinea fowl were roosting out in one of the sheds behind our house. I don't know how Dad got them in a pen because they were quite wild in nature, but he managed to corral them and cut off their heads. I still have a vivid memory of the heads landing in the snow and making blood spattered patterns against the glaring white background.

After my first grade in school, we moved to what we called the stockyard house. There was no way to forget that we lived in this neighborhood because the fresh manure odors wafted down the block to our house. We kids would walk the railings around the stockyard, watching pigs and cattle being loaded on trains for Chicago. Sometimes we entertained ourselves by wading in water and mud after a rain or bumming rides with anyone who would take us along. Dad used to drive a team of horses with a wagon that he loaded with sand to take to the railroad and unload into the stock cars so the animals wouldn't slip and slide and fall down. I often rode on the wagon with him. Once when fooling around by the grain elevator near the stockyard, I stuck my finger in a hole where I saw a mouse go in and got bit. I was learning much as a young animal nosing about alone and investigating everything in sight.

Our house had a second story where I slept with my oldest brother Lawrence on a straw tick mattress in the loft room where all of the kids slept. Before I would go to sleep, Emil would teach me to spell words like "mattress" and "Czechoslovakia." Then Lawrence, whom I called Orency, would pinch me because I wouldn't go to sleep and kept him awake. I would say, "Let's go to sleep, Orency Bumblebeep." He would counter with, "Well, then go to sleep right now!"

Mom managed to raise a pig that she called Simon Peter, and I was sent out to pull pig weeds for it to eat. When I came in one day, there was Shirley, naked, getting painted with gentian violet for scabies (itch). Dad always had potions or ointments for anything that needed doctoring.

I always went barefoot in the summer, so it was inevitable that I would get slivers and be cut by glass. Once I was running around in the lumberyard and ran a big sliver up under my toenail. Dad took his knife and trimmed my toenail back as I yelped in pain, but it was the only way he knew to pull the sliver out. That same summer I was watching a blacksmith and was standing pretty close. He had been pounding on a piece of iron that was pretty hot. He threw it down on the dirt floor, but I didn't realize what he had done and stepped on it with my heel and hobbled all the way home. Mom put cold water on it right away.

They say that one remembers extreme pain and pleasure. During my early life, the stress of being poor in a large family sometimes overwhelmed the pleasure. But there were simple delights in being free to roam about the countryside as I got a little older, helping Dad trap animals, being with Mom who took me almost everywhere with her, and having the companionship of so many siblings. Boredom was not something one ever complained of. I don't remember saying, "I don't have anything to do, Mom."

At school we had an old phonograph with a horn out of which the sound emerged. I couldn't figure out how this band music could come out of this contraption, and I kept looking into the front, where the two doors were open, to try and see the people who were playing the horns. This was the first time I ever remember hearing music as we didn't have anything that made music in our house.

Even though Wessington was a small town, there was a rodeo every year and a theater, on Friday nights only, where black and white movies were shown. Fran remembered performances by Clara Bow and William S. Hart. The Chautauqua, a series of performances usually held in a traveling tent, also came to town, and Fran and Lawrence recall seeing Harry Lauder, the famous Scottish entertainer. They wouldn't have been able to attend such functions if they hadn't found out about getting free tickets for handing out handbills. There was even a swimming pool built in town, but after a while the dust that blew into it made a layer of mud on the bottom of the pool.

Fran finally got her first pair of glasses and was even able to play on the basketball team until her precious spectacles were broken, halting her involvement in sports. She worked in a restaurant even before graduating from high school and roomed with the cook, a big Norwegian woman, who located a room in a big house in town with three bedrooms upstairs. They even had an indoor bathroom. Fran would get up early, go help make breakfast in the restaurant, and then leave just in time to get to high school. She returned to the restaurant at noon to serve customers and again after school to work through the dinner hour.

When it was forty below zero, if one didn't have a horse to ride, it was sometimes impossible to get into high school from out on the farm. Sometimes the schools were closed until the weather improved. As Fran put it, anything above twenty below was considered "tolerable." Then she added, "Some people would think we had a hard time but that is all we knew."

Eventually, Fran moved into the home of the editor of the town newspaper so she could help with the babysitting. Mom worked at the restaurant and did laundry for people in order to make ends meet. I loved to go down in time to lick the spoon and clean out the bowl after Mom poured the batter into the pans for the pink-colored cakes that she made.

When Ethel was sixteen, she went to live with a doctor's family in town to help with the children, do the dishes, and clean the house. This was the first time in her life she had lived in a house with running water and inside plumbing and electricity. When she was at home she had to carry water buckets a whole block, then had to heat it in the boiler for the washing.

After Fran graduated from high school, she worked full time in the little restaurant downtown owned by the Watsons. We loved it when Fran would bring leftovers home for us to share—pie, cake, and sometimes stew dipped from the huge cooking pot into an empty jar. It was not long after Fran got acquainted with Mick Watson that they were married and she had her first baby, Faye.

I idolized my brother Lawrence because he was working at the mercantile store downtown and bought me my first pair of jeans that I could wear without galluses (suspenders). I was so proud of myself. I often went down to the store and bought a penny's worth of candy, usually a peppermint stick, not only because I loved candy, but to be near Lawrence. He sensed that I needed some extra attention, being the youngest of eight. All this came to an end, leaving me with a feeling of abandonment, when that spring he caught a freight train across the country when he was only eighteen. His friend had told him about jobs picking apples in Zillah, near Yakima, Washington. While riding the rails through Montana, he fell and hit the back of his head. The injury was severe enough to require a doctor to sew him up. Luckily he never suffered the fate of so many hitching such rides—those trapped in cars locked after they boarded them or being killed when jumping off a freight moving through a town. At least he was in famous company as William O. Douglas also rode the rails to get to places where he hoped to find work.

Going West

Over the years our family was to be uprooted numerous times, finally moving in 1926 from South Dakota to Yakima, Washington, where Lawrence had settled. As I said, Lawrence was the trailblazer, having gone west earlier, urging us to follow. He earned enough money for Dad to buy the old Model T truck that was our ticket west. It was Fran's husband who had the responsibility of driving us all the way.

We didn't know it then, but we traveled in a manner resembling the so-called Okies and Arkies who were routed from their farms by devastating dust storms throughout the Midwest. I relive this trip every time I see reruns of the classic black-and-white Henry Fonda movie *Grapes of Wrath*. This is the story of the Joad family going west to live in what they thought would be the land of milk and honey in California. Believe me, any privileged landowners who dominated the land of milk and honey probably wouldn't have been willing to share their harvest with the likes of people like us! But I didn't know that then. We had to come west. It was the only hope we had.

So there we were, with Mick sitting up front driving with Fran holding baby Faye beside him, as the rest of us crouched underneath the canvas providing shelter from the elements. We kids ranged in age from my age, almost eight, up to Ethel who was about sixteen. Mabel would later characterize our covered Ford truck as the "first-ever motorhome."

Looking back on it all, it doesn't seem possible for that many people to have spent their waking and sleeping hours together for several weeks. Fortunately, the truck made only twenty miles an hour. I say fortunately because when a tire would blow out at that speed, it wasn't too dangerous. Mick was the only pilot and mechanic on board, keeping very busy driving and taking out the tire mending kit whenever our truck jerked and swerved in pain, so to speak. I say tire mending kit, but, in truth, there was only patching material and glue of some sort.

One had to be creative when doctoring an old truck expected to last hundreds of miles on the road. Ethel later recalled her husband's method of fixing brakes. He would shout, "Ethel, go buy some bacon with a thick rind. I can use the rind to line the brakes." Ethel swears that their old car went many more miles with this repair job.

I overheard Mick say he was tired of driving. He tried to get Fran to learn how to drive, but she wasn't interested. Most of the trip was on a dirt road with two ruts, and if you met somebody, you backed up to a wide spot or they had to back up. Mick then made Ethel get up front and try to drive. She thought she was pretty grown up until she met a car coming toward her and realized she didn't know how to stop the darned thing—but with coaching she made it.

In Montana, we broke down and had to wire Grandma, on my mom's side, for money so we could continue on over the mountains. Up to this point, Mom had not parted with her most prized possessions—a sewing machine and a set of encyclopedias. But one day, after living on potatoes, bacon, and flour until even she couldn't stand the sight of another potato without any butter to put on it, she called to Mick who was driving, "Stop at the next farmhouse. I want to see if I can trade my sewing machine for butter and eggs." Mom was able to get a little money besides eggs and butter. With this money, we had enough to last for a few more days on the road.

Fran, Mick, and the baby slept under the truck, but I remember lying on my back alongside the road looking up at the stars at night and wondering what it would feel like to someday fly up to the planets that I was just learning about. I was curious about the rocks that we found at each stop and the changing scenery as we neared the desert and started up over the mountains. I saw a sign that said "Continental Divide."

"Fran, that sign says 'The Continental Divide.' What's the Continental Divide?"

"That's the line dividing all the rivers that run east on one side and west on the other."

We were actually seeing our vast country, which previously I had only seen in geography books: yellow for desert, green for forest areas, and blue for rivers and lakes. This was the real thing—mountains, valleys, desert, rivers, lakes and the plains. There were plants I had never seen before and red and gray rocks. There were jagged peaks that seemed unreal to a South Dakota farm boy. Fran seemed to be the one who knew about everything.

"Fran, what kind of tree is that?" I would ask.

She answered back: "That's a pine tree. They are usually found at a little higher elevation or a dryer climate than the firs that are on the western side of the United States."

I had to know the names of them all. No one in our family had aspirations of graduating from college in those days, but I wanted to learn all I could about the world. Geography was to be my favorite subject.

Once in Idaho we found some wild berries that Mom cooked up into a sauce. Did that ever taste like ambrosia compared to perennial potatoes! Day by day, we repeated the ritual of making a fire, shoring it up with rocks, cooking our meal, and keeping the fire going so we could keep warm after the sun went down. Then we sat around our campfire and shared stories about the old days. Fran once admitted that she used to believe that cows didn't have any legs.

"Why?" we asked.

"Because I could not see clearly before I was able to get my glasses." It was quite a revelation when she could look out across the fields and see cows and for the first time note that each one actually had four legs!

One evening Fran was telling about her early life back in Missouri. She said that one night Mom whispered to her that it was time to go fetch Grandma. Every time my mom was due to bear a child she would send Fran to bring Grandma who served as midwife.

Fran really didn't know where babies came from. She said she thought to herself: "Maybe if I don't go over and get Grandma this time, there won't be another child for me to wash diapers for. We only get another child after Grandma comes to bring one into the world." But she had to go and bring Grandma anyway.

We were always on the lookout for anything we could eat so when my sister spied berry vines along the road she yelled for Mick to stop. When we were fortunate enough to pass an orchard of any kind we stopped and picked up fruit off the ground so it wouldn't be considered stealing.

At one stop, Mom bought herself an agate ring, which she really cherished. She bought me some new pants called "Huskies from Mackintosh." Josephine was always jealous of me, so when she saw me trying on my new pants, she taunted me with this ditty:

> *A Husky came cross the mountains*
> *to see what he could see.*
> *Then when he got over the mountains*
> *all he could do was pee.*

Each time a tire went flat, we spewed out onto the side of the road. Shirley and Emil had more room to resume their fighting. Once, Emil chased Shirley out into the desert, and Shirley stepped barefooted onto a cactus, shrieking as he hopped about and requiring a whole evening to pick the spines out. Then at our evening stop we would start a fire and fry potatoes and boil coffee, which Ethel once spilled onto her legs followed by screams from the scalding pain.

"Try and find some branches for kindling," Mom would say as she climbed down from the truck and began getting the food ready. She would dig into the potato bag and pull out one for each of us. If we were spending the night at a campground, Mom would usually fry the potatoes, but when camping on the side of the road we knew that we were to tend our own potatoes over the fire until they were done the way we wanted.

When our brakes went out on the west slope of the Continental Divide, Mick yelled: "Hang on. The brakes went out. I'm going to head into the bank to stop us." We all had to get out, even our three-legged dog Brownie. We didn't know how long it would take to get to the bottom of the hill but we had fun on foot as we had been riding for many hours and needed to stretch our legs. As we made it to the bottom of the hill we spied a farmer coming along the road. He offered to take Mick into a nearby town, then called Cabin City, where he could get what he needed to fix the brakes. Mick had his work cut out whenever the old, worn out truck stopped running. There were no garage mechanics at most of our stops. Even if there had been, we didn't have any money to pay for truck repair.

We were all tired that night. Emil cried out, "Brownie's gone. We can't find him anywhere." It was too dark to go looking for him so we began our ritual of bedding down. Dad and Mom went to sleep under the cover in the truck, while we kids slept alongside the road after locating a level place to lay our heads.

The next morning Mabel and Shirley went back up the mountain to look for our three-legged dog, and there he was, running back and forth, probably wondering where we had been. So we were all united once more. We were to spend three nights at a campground we found while waiting for the truck to be repaired. My brothers found a little creek and were able to catch some carp, while we explored along the creek and ran about playing with children of other campers. The campground had shelters with bedsprings on legs and foam mattresses but no bedding. There was a place we could wash clothes by hand and a place to shower. Finally we had time to reorganize the contents of the truck.

Mom called out, "Where is the box of old photographs?" And then she let out a shriek, "I must have laid them on the truck fender when we broke down earlier and they fell off!" Mom never forgave herself for this loss.

Nevertheless, Mom was a true survivor as she demonstrated many times throughout this long, arduous trip. It took guts to head a big family that had made the decision to move from South Dakota to Washington State. Hadn't she gone clear from Missouri to South Dakota with my seven brothers and sisters when she was pregnant with me?

I didn't think anything could stop my mom. But on this trip, I learned that she was not prepared for traveling on steep canyon roads after living a life of farming where there were no mountains—just little slopes. When we got too near the outside of a curve on the way down, Mom's face fell as she envisioned every dangerous drop-off threatening to take us to the bottom of the canyon. Sometimes she would heave a big sigh and get out and walk when the old Ford sputtered slowly up the hill. She could then get a little exercise as she walked alongside the slow moving truck.

It must have been a strain on my mom to be cooped up so many hours of each day. She was used to being in her house washing clothes, cooking for the family, or outside weeding or watering the garden. It was truly a miracle that we sat confined in that old truck without terrible fights breaking out. Shirley and Emil had their brief altercations but nothing serious. When fighting would break out between them, they were told to get out and walk. Mick drove on ahead and then stopped to wait for them. By that time they got tired out and were ready to get in again and behave.

Ethel said she never ever remembered Dad speaking to Mick on the trip. They never said one word to each other. Dad was quiet anyway, but no one will ever know why that silence continued all across the prairies and mountains into Yakima. She said Mom bossed us around on the trip. Dad just seemed to be going along for the ride!

At last we arrived at the great Columbia River. We were astounded at this mammoth body of water stretching out before us. "Mom! Look! Look! How are we going to get across? I don't see any bridge." And there was no bridge. But soon Mick noticed a ferry coming from across the river to the little unpretentious dock. Cars in line would be motioned onto the ferry.

While we were waiting in line, Emil roamed the area finding some pear trees and brought some pears back. I had already found some ripe peaches but when I saw Emil with his pears, I begged for one. Emil said, "I'll trade you one of my pears for one of your peaches." It was a deal. But what I didn't know was that the pears were green. I started to bite into the pear but spit it out, sputtering. Mom, even as busy as she was with us kids, noticed what had happened and told Emil to trade back.

When it came our turn to drive onto the ferry, Mom refused to allow Mick to start up the truck. She wouldn't get on the ferry that was to take us across. It was very hot and we were all tired, but we just sat there with other cars honking and finally going around us because Mom wouldn't let Mick drive onto the ferry. "Mom, we are going to be left behind. Why won't you let us go? Can't you see, there is no bridge?"

Finally, with the pressure of the terrible heat and us kids beginning to get quarrelsome Mom gave in. "Well, Mick, I guess it is all in the hands of fate. We must trust that our old truck will not overload this ferry and that we will soon be on the other side." Mom probably closed her eyes all the way across the river as she often did when we were driving around the harrowing curves along the canyons as we came across the Continental Divide.

Once more we were on the road, and luckily we learned about a campground that we could reach by nightfall. Soon, we were all piling out and running about yelling and playing as Mick drove into a parking spot at the camp. We settled in for the preparation of the evening meal, our usual potatoes with whatever else we had scrounged on our trip.

Soon Mabel noticed a young girl coming from the next camping spot and peeking around the back of our truck. She spied Mom's encyclopedias and asked naively, "Are those real encyclopedias you have there? I have always wanted a set of encyclopedias."

Mom realized that her folks might give us money or food for them, so she asked the girl to have her mother come out and make an offer. Although the other family was almost as poor as we were, they did have some food they could trade. We were so tired of hard bacon and fried potatoes that any other food was welcome. As my brother Emil recalled, "They went away satisfied in getting this whole set of books, and we were delighted with our new cache of food which supplemented our fried potatoes until we reached Yakima."

We were nearing our destination. Mick had guided us from South Dakota across the vast plains, over the mountains, across rivers, and finally we sensed that the wonderful land of the Yakima Valley would soon be in sight.

Fruit Country

In August 1926, after weeks traveling from South Dakota, we arrived in the Yakima Valley in Washington State. On our first night in this new country, we camped alongside the Yakima River. But the summer night air was filled with pesky mosquitoes, which didn't have any regard for a poor, stranded family. Morning found us a sorry sight, crawling out of rain-soaked bedding. At first light we youngsters ran about to find the wonderful fruit trees we had heard about. We helped ourselves to fruit that we "borrowed" until we could find a way to coat our stomachs with hardier fare. Shirley told me that the green peaches I was eating would make me sick. He was right.

No one seems to know how we located our first place in Yakima, but soon we were pulling in on Fourth Avenue in front of an old rental shack. We kids found it strange to sleep indoors after being out on the ground during our trip west. Since it was still summer, we would often wake up and drag our comforters outside to curl up under the stars. When the weather got bad, we slept on the floor indoors. We still did not have enough chairs to sit on during mealtime, but it wasn't long before we collected apple boxes and barrels, enough for us all.

Dad was never very well, and all the rest of the family had to pitch in to make a living. He had never learned to drive, so Mick was the only one who could drive to get groceries or to work. Mom said that during the deepest of the depression, people would read the obituaries and hurry down to stand in line for the job that the deceased had left vacant. People who had been well to do but had lost their money didn't know how to cope. But we had been in hard times all our lives. This time, however, we were in a new town clear across the country from where we grew up.

There were jobs picking apples for five cents a box, sorting fruit in the canneries, and a few jobs of pruning the fruit trees in the off season. Finding work for all of us who could do a full day's work took all our energy for the next few days. When summer was over and the fruit was picked, sorted, and canned or dried, our family was out of work and had to find whatever was available—babysitting, housework or pruning in the orchards.

Entering Columbia Elementary School in the fall was a disappointment. I was behind in all of my subjects. The kids teased me about my last name. The first day one of the kids had an epileptic seizure and the teacher dragged him out into the hall until he became calm again. Since I was the new kid, I was baited to go out and ring the hand held school bell, which was rung by the custodian. I went to the front door where it was always kept and picked it up and shook it good and loud. The principal gave me a whipping with a small rubber hose for my trouble.

My folks were contacted halfway through my first year and told that I had not kept up and would have to repeat my first half-year again. So, in addition to Mom feeling sorry for me because I had suffered a crushed elbow, she now felt badly that I had to repeat a half year of school. Besides that, I felt left out in other ways. I had never learned to sing. I couldn't carry a tune, as they say. One day, before our school program, the teacher came by and whispered to me, "When we have singing, you don't need to try to sing. Just move your lips." I can't say I blame the teacher. Even in those days teachers were expected to perform miracles in the classroom. My off-key performance could have ruined my teacher's rating if I were allowed to sing in the school program.

At noontime I rarely had any lunch from home. I envied the kids who brought fried chicken and chocolate cake. They would often trade with each other, but I had no lunch, let alone something extra to trade. One day when I was walking down the alley to school, I found something wrapped in newspaper on top of a garbage can. I picked it up, unwrapped the bundle, and there was a bologna sandwich, a sugar cookie, and an apple. I felt fortunate that I could bring a lunch to school at last. During that year I often found this wrapped package waiting for me. I was so naive that I didn't realize that the woman who often looked out at me walking by without any lunch pail and wearing the same clothes every day was the one who left this surprise for me. I had seen her once or twice but didn't think anything of it. These lunch "finds" ended when we moved.

In the summer months I was still too young to get a real job, so I played with my friends, sometimes staying away all day without anything to eat except for fruit we were able to pick up in orchards. We went swimming down by the mill pond at Shiner's Hole, Mill Ditch, and Crystal Pool with my friends Chet, Leonard and Harold, always swimming naked. We passed the time having mud fights and lying in the sun from early in the morning until four or five in the afternoon without any lunch except for fruit we could take without getting caught.

All of us poor kids made the rounds of garbage cans behind stores. There we could find overripe bananas and sometimes oranges and other food that could no longer be marketed. I remember people hawking watermelons on the street for a quarter of a cent a pound so we could find good buys in this fruit country.

When I got really hungry, I watched for the bakery truck that made deliveries to restaurants and when the driver stopped to take in an order, I would hurry to take bread from the day-old bin. It didn't seem to be stealing to take from the bin that didn't hold the fresh bread. I suspect that the driver knew my plight and looked the other way. I hadn't heard about Jean Valjean who was imprisoned after stealing a loaf of bread, but I am sure if I had, I would have felt empathy for him.

After we moved to Selah outside of Yakima, we would climb up the hill and pick up Ellensburg Blue agates, which are now rare finds and much more costly to buy. My sisters collected arrowheads and would arrange them on cotton in interesting patterns and frame them to hang up so that we could admire them. We had no pictures on the wall until my dad came home one day with a picture of a wolf with his head raised as if howling at the moon on a snowy hill above a snow-covered village. It was not the original painting, which was by a rather famous artist, but it represented the rural life my dad had lived in Missouri and South Dakota. He missed the trapping of animals and selling the hides. Now we hunted for jackrabbits up in the hills surrounding Yakima, but it was just for sport as the hides were worthless and the meat not something you would eat unless you were starving.

I managed to earn a few pennies selling newspapers downtown, buying each for 3 cents and selling them for 5 cents. I could usually sell five papers before 6 p.m. One of my best customers was a madam in the red-light district, who always seemed to have enough money for the daily paper and even the more expensive Sunday edition. As she opened the door to hand me the money, an enticing odor of incense overcame my senses. I didn't really know what a madam was, but she was really nice to me, always giving me a little extra for the paper. I remember the paper that announced that Herbert Hoover was elected president. He served during the depression years.

On Saturday nights we kids would hang out on the streets, lagging pennies, fighting, and horsing around until midnight. When the Sunday *Seattle P-I* came we were able to buy papers from a dealer for 5 cents and sell them for 10 cents to people coming out of movies or pool halls. We never bought more than we thought we could sell as we couldn't turn them back in. We also sold the *Seattle Star*, but only made one penny on each one sold. We used to watch the bootleggers hide flasks of whiskey, and when the coast was clear, we would get them and sell them for 25 or 50 cents. The empty ones we sold for 1 or 2 cents.

In the bad winter of 1930-1931, we lived in what we called the Fulkerson house, a dump with two shacks behind the house. There were three bedrooms, a kitchen, and dining room. The cook stove had coils that heated our water and it provided heat to keep warm, as well as for cooking. Mom and Dad had one bedroom, Jo had a bedroom, Emil and Shirley slept together in a bedroom, and I slept on a divan in the dining room. That winter the pipes froze and I was sick a lot. I finally went out and stole bread, but my mom would not eat it, which made me feel very bad. The Boy Scouts brought us a Christmas tree, but we didn't have any decorations to put on it so we just threw it out into the back yard.

Next year wasn't so bad. Lawrence bought us a carom board that had a checkerboard on the underside. I was better at checkers than Shirley, who rewarded me after I won by smashing my toe with the heel of his steel rimmed heavy shoes. My toenail got all black and I couldn't wear my shoe for quite a few days.

Again, I got hungry and stole pies and doughnuts from a bakery but didn't bring them home this time because I knew my mom would refuse to eat them.

Mabel and her husband Ray moved into one of the shacks back of our house in 1930 after the mill closed down in Onalaska. Ray and Ethel's husband Clyde hunted for magpies that spring and early summer. There was a bounty on the eggs and the heads of magpies that were considered pests because they robbed other birds' nests.

I was the one who was sent across to Carmichael's Creamery to get the half-gallon pail of skim milk. Mom hated it as she had been raised on a farm where the milk was rich with cream and not this pale blue-colored stuff.

That year I got my first toothbrush. Someone told me that brushing with ashes would make my teeth white so I tried it. It had an extremely nasty taste so that was the end of my tooth brushing until I was grown.

My Mom, Winnifred Blanche (Wright) Kunkel, b.1880–d. 1964

Christmas was usually a rather sad time for us kids. One year I saved enough pennies to buy Dad a stick of peppermint candy and Mom a candle. I don't remember getting a present of my own that year. Mom was so afraid that she wouldn't have enough money to bury her and Dad, so she scraped enough money together to pay for an insurance policy. In those days, the insurance representative would call at the house and collect pennies each month to keep up a plan that later I learned would probably never return even what had been paid in. I can still hear the words of this salesperson, "Madam, you don't want to be buried in a pauper's grave or see your children go without if anything should happen to you, do you?"

Today the fear is not the expense of burial, but the worry of being faced with thousands of dollars a month for care center costs, unless one can spend down to qualify for Medicaid. In those days there was no Social Security, Medicare, Medicaid, or Unemployment Insurance. You were on your own and lucky if you had some family member who would care for you in your old age or when you were unemployed.

As Mom got older, she would often take care of Fran's children. As I was the youngest and spoiled by Mom, I probably experienced my first taste of sibling rivalry when I had to share Mom's attention with my nieces. Geraldine, Fran's third child, remembers how she hated the way I treated her and did everything she could to pay me back. Once she said I got her to eat a whole tablespoon full of horseradish for a nickel. Teasing was the Kunkel family's pastime. As I grew up, I developed a wry sense of humor that stood me in good stead through tough times. I learned my Missouri colorful language from my mom. Mom always referred to someone who put on the dog, as they say, as Mrs. Gotrocks. If a family was poor, she would say, "They don't have a pot to pee in or a window to throw it out of."

School was something I didn't always look forward to. I do remember having to memorize a poem called "Flander's Field." It was about poppies growing in the graveyard where soldiers of the First World War were buried. I was supposed to learn a song called "The Volga Boatmen" about the boatmen who pulled the boats up the Volga River with long ropes. From that day, I wanted to see the Volga River. (In the 1980s, my wife and I took a cruise on the Volga and actually took a swim in it.)

In the fall of 1931, we moved to the Stone house where there was another family living in the basement. The upstairs, where we slept, never seemed to get above forty degrees so we heated rocks in the oven and took them to bed with us. There was no warm comforter but only denim quilts made from patchwork pieces of old jeans. The more quilts we piled on, the heavier it got; we could hardly turn over.

The people in the basement butchered a hog in the backyard, cutting its throat and holding it down until it bled to death. Dad was appalled at the cruelty. He could not stand to watch an animal suffer.

That year it snowed in November and lasted through March. For school Mom bought me a pair of rawhide shoes. Since I was growing so fast, she bought them two sizes too large for me as she could only afford one pair for the winter. Naturally, I developed painful blisters. I finally stuffed the toes with rags and the blisters healed up but the shoes leaked water when the snow thawed.

Dad worked all night at an apple drying plant that winter, feeding three peeling machines. We had plenty of apples to eat that winter, and Mom made lots of applesauce, but we all got cabin fever. Emil was always teasing me about something or other and I had had enough. I hit him in the nose and thought I must have broken it as it looked crooked after that—it worked, he stopped teasing me.

It was time to move again, just a block away, into a big house with three bedrooms and a cellar for potatoes. Early in May we would get wet mill scraps, which we would dry out for winter. If we ran out of dry wood, we would put the wet wood into the oven, leaving the door open, filling the house with a god-awful smell. The only hot water we had was heated on top of this old stove.

One advantage was that we had a large garden plot and, at last, had corn, beans, peas, cabbage, onions, cucumbers, carrots, ground cherries, and on the back half we grew dry beans. I helped Dad make sauerkraut and several kegs of dill pickles. When spring came, Mom would feed us molasses or syrup mixed with powdered sulfur. It was pretty awful and was gritty on our teeth. Mom said it thinned our blood and made it pure again.

An old shed served as a chicken house where we kept about a dozen hens so we could have fresh eggs. We raised rabbits as well. Our plum trees were no asset as they were of a variety that was inedible. However, on the way home from Franklin Junior High we knew where there were two English walnut trees and we could get all the nuts that fell on the sidewalk every afternoon on the way home. They were husked and kept for Christmas.

To supplement the wood supply, my brothers-in-law would ride the freight train to Ellensburg and then catch another train going back to Yakima, riding on the coal car. They would pile chunks of coal on the edge of the coal car and wait until they were near a good place to dump it out onto the tracks near our house and then push it off. Later they would come back and fill gunny sacks with the coal and carry it home.

As we got a little older, we would go to the YMCA to play ping pong. We had to deposit a dime for the ball. When we didn't have a dime we had to leave our cap. If the ball wore out or cracked, we had to go home in the winter night when the temperature was down to twenty degrees without a hat.

The summer of 1933 changed my life in many ways. Ethel and her husband took me to Starbuck, Washington, where Clyde was working for a farmer in the wheat harvest. Ethel and I stayed in town while Clyde worked on the ranch. It was a carefree month of swimming in the Tucannon River, helping to milk cows after bringing them to the barn from the pasture, and being invited to my first party. I remember that I only had two shirts and two pairs of pants for that month, but Mom finally sent me a pair of 49-cent sneakers, which arrived in time for the party.

The son of the farm owner made my acquaintance. He talked to me about his plan of going to college and that he had a brother, who was a teacher. I am reasonably sure this association had a big influence on me. I had never had a chance to be the focus of attention without all my brothers and sisters being around. It was just my big sister taking me under her wing and having a friend all to myself for a change.

Most of my summers growing up I stacked boxes for the box makers on fruit row. All the wooden boxes were made by hand. I was paid five cents per hundred. On good days I made as much as $1.50 for nine hours work. I usually gave most of the money to Mom for food and other expenses.

My Yakima High School graduation picture.

When I was big and strong enough to carry a twelve-foot ladder, I picked cherries or pears. One summer I made $15 and spent it all on getting some dental work done—at the urging of Mom I am sure. I thought it was a waste of money at that time. Another spring I worked trimming cabbage that had been stored all winter, making about $7.50 which I used for a new pair of slacks.

I didn't do well in my studies until my senior year. My class in psychology was my favorite. I got a higher grade than the valedictorian of our class, and she didn't like it at all. She was a straight-A student and wondered how I could muster this kind of grade after not making much of a mark throughout my earlier school career.

All during my growing up years my parents never came to any of my school functions, probably because they didn't have any good clothes to wear. At my own high school graduation I wore a suit and new shoes that I

25

saved up $35 to buy, once even staying out of school to work for two weeks picking apples. I got up at 5 a.m., walked or hitchhiked to the ranch, which was six miles away, worked ten hours and then returned home. I was hauling apples out of the orchard on a sled pulled by two horses. I learned all about harnessing horses and driving them.

As I was almost late to graduation, I ran much of the way, slipped on the ice, and fell, tearing a hole in my pants leg. You can imagine how I felt, limping the rest of the way to school and trying to hide the tear in my pants. None of my family came to see me graduate, so I sat there bemoaning my ruined suit of clothes as I waited for the head of the school board to call my name so I could go up on stage to receive my diploma. Since I was one of five in our family who graduated from high school, my parents must have been proud that their youngest had made it. I don't remember them ever praising me for anything that I did, however. Their lives were so stressed with just making ends meet that they didn't have much praise to spare.

Dad, even though ill much of the time, managed to maintain a garden and even raised some poultry that attracted attention in the local paper:

BANTAM AND PHEASANT CROSS SHOWN IN EXHIBIT

A cross between a Golden Seabright bantam chicken and a Chinese pheasant, shown at the Central Washington District Fair was raised by Joe Kunkel of Lower Naches. A young male pheasant came into the yard last spring and made itself at home with the chickens, so Kunkel raised it along with the young bantams. Later he penned a pheasant up with the bantam hen resulting in the hatching of three birds. Their feathers resemble the bantam but their tail length and body conformation are like pheasants.

Later on, when Mom was older, she had to rely on a meager pension and the money some of the older children brought home to help pay the bills. There were times when we went without electricity because we couldn't pay. Luckily for us the city wasn't allowed to turn off our water!

Emil was gone before I finished high school. He had decided to hop a freight train with a friend to try to find work. They went to Seattle and down to Los Angeles and all through the Southwest. When he returned to

In the Lower Valley Sagebrush with my Shotgun and Emil's Pickup Truck

Yakima, the economy was still in deep depression. He learned about the Civilian Conservation Corps (CCC) and soon became a forest fire lookout. After he left the CCC, he went to Alaska in 1938 and spent a summer in Skagway. He returned to Yakima, but again jobs were scarce, so he returned to Alaska.

While Emil was having his adventures, I was still at home living with my folks in the first house they owned, on an acre plot of ground in Selah across the street from my sister Fran. I was the only one of the kids at home so I had the attic bedroom all to myself. It could be entered by way of a crude stairway built on the outside wall of the house. Nowadays it would be considered inconvenient, but I always felt it was an adventure to climb up into the loft, which was all my own.

I followed Emil's footsteps and joined the CCC near Yakima where a lot of poor kids like me went to work for room and board and little else. Before the Great Depression, our government did not subsidize the poor. Government was to provide money to support the armed services and provide seed money for building dams and bridges and highways, and subsidies for farmers and certain business enterprises. But with vast numbers suffering from unemployment, the government's New Deal programs provided support for hard-working families who could no longer work hard since there were simply not enough jobs.

Kunkel Family Portrait When I Was in High School
Front row: Shirley, Dad, Mom, and I. *Back row*: Emil, Frances, Josephine, Lawrence, Mabel, and Diane (Ethel)

So here I was, taking advantage of one of the new programs provided for people who wanted to work but could not find work. If anyone had known how to assess my interests, they would have offered me a cooking job. But instead I was put into the office as a typist where I pecked away at twenty-five words a minute. I was soon moved to the garage for truck maintenance, but didn't fit in there either. Then I did fieldwork, using pick and shovel making terraces for conservation. I realized that I was not going to find my niche and quit after two months. There were few young men there who had interests like mine. Even with my poor economic background, I had been raised in a family that reinforced learning and exploration. I was not able to communicate my own feelings and desires at this time. Neither was there a counselor who could help me find my place.

After I quit the CCC, I got a job in the fruit warehouse loading refrigerated boxcars with boxes of cherries and later plums and apricots. In the fall I packed apples—Red and Standard Delicious that were sought after for their beauty, Winesaps that would keep longer, Rome beauties for baking, and Yellow Newtons, which were good for baking into pies.

I was now back home trying to find some other way to survive since the CCC didn't solve my employment problems. Emil was already in Alaska working as a Gandy dancer out of Skagway. I decided I had to go up and find work. It cost $40 one way to sail on the S.S. *Alaska* to reach Seward. That meant I had to work in the autumn of 1938 for 22½ cents an hour and ten-hour days at the South Selah evaporating plant, which dried apples, to save enough money.

With Yakima Pal Bill Miller and his '28 Ford Model A Roadster

In March, Lewis and I took the S.S. *Alaska* to Seward stopping at Ketchikan, Skagway, Juneau, Cordova, Petersburg, and Valdez. We went steerage, sleeping in bunks down in the hold on sleeping bags that we brought along.

We arrived in Anchorage, then about two thousand in population and with only one main street about two blocks long. The liquor store advertised, "Yes, Another Liquor Store." Every steamship that docked in Juneau would blow its deep-sounding whistle and many of the townspeople would come down to the dock to greet the passengers getting off. There was even an old dog that met every ship. Even though he was deaf, we were told the dog could feel the reverberations of that steam whistle and then would come bounding down to the dock.

John Herman and I decided to ride the blinds to Fairbanks, meaning we got on the back of the engine where the coal was kept. The others didn't want to because they had already experienced the flying sparks and soot of this method of train travel and chose to wait for a freight train that came along later. They managed to keep warm in a flatcar carrying an empty tank they crawled into.

We stopped at Curry in the Mount McKinley National Park overnight. There were no restaurants along the way even if we had had money enough to buy food. At each train

Lewis Brownell and I in Alaska

stop the train crew called out, "Come have some coffee and sandwiches." This was an unusual luxury. Our only problem was that we had to chase moose off the tracks. The next morning we were on our way riding on the coal car behind the engine. It was snowing and cold. The train stopped and we saw two minors get off the train. One handed a large sack of whiskey bottles to the other, and since they were both drunk, the whisky sack fell with a crash of breaking glass.

What spectacular scenery—at Mount McKinley, standing majestically alongside other snowcapped peaks. Near Nenana a railroad cop told us he was going to have the sheriff meet the train and put us in jail for hitching a ride. We told him that was okay with us as we had little money and no job. So the cop let us alone.

After arriving in Fairbanks, we did not have any place to stay. Of course, the rest of the passengers stayed in the hotel. We slept in one of the machine repair shops where it was warm. We were given some dinner rolls by someone who felt sorry for us. There we stayed for two nights until Lewis, Leonard, and Emil arrived.

Lewis and I joined the CCC, which had a contract with the Alaska Road Commission. After painting one of the buildings we were sent to Standard to cut trees for poles. Lewis felled trees, and I worked in the kitchen as assistant cook. After years of helping Mom in the kitchen at home, I was finally in my element.

We lived in railroad cars on a siding. There were a dozen cars—cookhouse in one, dining hall in another, and the rest were sleeping quarters. Two or three times a day I would climb on top of the railroad cars and run the length, jumping from one to the other.

After coming back to Fairbanks, we were put to work at Ladd Field digging trenches in the muskeg to drain the water off. It was obvious that they were shoring up for involvement in the impending war. The head of the road crew then sent us out to 33 Mile Road House, an isolated rest stop on the way to Valdez on the Richardson Highway. We stayed there for a couple of months. On June 21 we attended a baseball game starting at midnight and then went on to a dance, but the women were all taken by the locals. No fun.

In the middle of August or so we left Fairbanks, paying $15 apiece to ride in a three-ton truck with open sideboards and benches to sit on. Imagine trying to balance when we were being thrown about by chuckholes caused by frost bubbles that shook us until our teeth rattled. I stood on my toes and bent my knees to lessen the shock over the 370 miles we covered in less than ten hours, arriving in Valdez with no more money than we had when we came.

At last, we were billeted in the forward hold of our ship, which would take us back to Seattle, in bunks three high. The rest is a blur interrupted by our arrival in Puget Sound around 3 a.m., anchoring in Elliot Bay looking directly at the big PORT OF SEATTLE sign. At 6 a.m. they put us off without any breakfast. Once more we were out of work and had to find a way to get back to Yakima.

PART TWO:
BECOMING AN AFS "CHARACTER"

Joining Up

In 1941, after traveling to Seattle with Chet in his 1926 Oldsmobile two-door sedan and moving in with friends, I worked first as custodian at the Roosevelt Hotel and then for Sears Roebuck. I was picking items in the mail order department and bringing them to the place where they were wrapped and shipped. War industries were working around the clock, so when one of us got up to go to work another fell into bed. During this time I introduced Lewis to my friend Evelyn, and they were soon married.

In September I worked in the woodshop at Boeing building a wooden, full-scale mock-up of the B-29 bomber. Then I transferred to Shop 302 as a shop clerk, which was final assembly for the B-17 bomber. The mechanics would come to my cage and present a tag with their number on it for every tool they requested. I would take down a drill bit or a drill, for example, and I would replace each tool with their tag. At the end of their shift, they would bring back the tools, and I would give them back their tags. War was declared in December, and since so many men were going overseas, it was easy to get a job.

During this period of not knowing what my future was to be, I met a fellow studying sociology at the University of Washington. He convinced me that I belonged at the University of Washington (UW), so I signed up to attend summer and fall of 1942 and winter and spring of 1943. Before I ran out of money, I found a job at Sea-Tac Shipyard as a scaler, the dirty job of cleaning up or cleaning out anything that needed cleaning. When I didn't have anything to do, I was told to hide out somewhere, and so I climbed into the double-bottom (inside the skin of the ship). You cannot imagine my tall, gangly frame wedged into this cramped hiding place.

At the shipyard I met my lifelong friend Brent Milnor, who influenced me in many ways. He was a natural for sailing as his Dad was a ship captain, often bringing his family on board to sail with him. Brent still recalls the distant ports he sailed into with his father at the helm.

I was most interested in how I could be a part of serving my country because it was wartime and all my friends were either being drafted or were joining up. I could not be drafted because of my childhood accident leaving my left arm without full mobility. After finishing spring quarter at the UW, I was recruited by John Burgess Whiteside of the American Field Service Ambulance Corps (AFS) based in New York City. It was after my decision to join the ambulance corps that I met Georgie Bright at the Trianon Ballroom. She was working for the Federal Housing Administration during the summer months and staying at her brother's apartment in Seattle. This particular weekend she had come to the dance with her friend, Rachel Smith. Georgie and Rachel were both teachers in Centralia.

I found Georgie sitting alone in a dimly lit area under the balcony. The large, mirrored ball hung high in the center of the ballroom, lighting up the area with reflections from the mirrors and letting me see her dark brown hair and flashing dark brown eyes. I approached her and said, "May I have the pleasure of this dance?" She admitted later that she had hidden farther away from the dance floor than most of the

Trianon Ballroom in Seattle, Washington, Where I First Met Georgie Bright

single women there because she had just danced with one fellow who was reeking with cigarette smoke and alcohol breath. That she changed her mind and said "Yes" provided an aura of serendipity during this evening, which was the beginning of a whirlwind dating period. I was committed to leaving in a little over a month for New York City. Without much money and no car, dating consisted of riding public transportation whenever I could save enough money to take her out.

As we finished our first dance to the swing music of the forties, Georgie's friend Rachel came over to us and announced, "Georgie, I have met someone and will be going out with him, so I will not be going back with you." That gave me the opportunity to offer myself as her escort. Before we said goodnight, we agreed to see each other again.

Once I traveled to Chehalis, nearly a hundred miles south of Seattle, to meet Georgie in her hometown. I walked from the bus, down Prindle Street to her home, and as I approached the house I could see her mother, her graying hair piled up on her head, tending her roses in her big yard. She looked at me, a tall, skinny guy with dark eyes, and after I introduced myself she announced, "Georgie is not coming home from Seattle this weekend." Later I heard from Georgie's sister that her mother was thinking how much I looked like her husband when he was young. Right there, I had my foot in the door but didn't know it.

Instead of Georgie introducing me to her folks, I met them without Georgie being present. I always kidded her about learning more about her from her mother and sisters than she probably wanted me to know! And yes, I saw her baby picture in her sister Sarah's photo album, the one taken by a roving photographer showing Georgie in her plump stage sitting up in the baby buggy with the top down.

After a trip to Yakima to spend time with my parents and other family members before leaving for New York, I headed back to see Georgie in Seattle, carrying a large box of cherries. Most fellows would bring candy and flowers—my finest gift was the fruit that I loved.

A very special date was an evening I planned for us at Laurel Hedge, a small restaurant in a large home probably once owned by an early lumber baron. Georgie discovered I was not used to dating when I neglected to put money into the fare box for her as I followed her onto the bus and she took her seat. The driver called out, "Do you intend to pay for the lady?" Georgie told me years later that she was pleased that I didn't turn out to be a slick Casanova who was used to squiring lots of swooning lady friends.

Laurel Hedge was characterized in its brochure as:

An attractive private home where good food is served, large living room with tapestries, carved woodwork and huge fireplace. The dining room and sun room have tables at the windows with a view of the city, lake and mountains.

Dinners for 4 to 7	$1.00, $2.00 on holidays	Served on the terrace or
Sunset suppers	85 cents	inside near the fireplace
Afternoon tea for 4 to	50 cents to $1.25	or west windows.

Georgie told me later that she had never been escorted to a fine dinner house in her life, a realization that caused her so much stress that her stomach did flip-flops. I took great pride in introducing her to the finer things in life, my last and only splurge before leaving. For once I could overcome the gnawing feeling in my own gut that she had everything—a completed college education and a career—and I was leaving to go overseas without having yet achieved any of this.

Our summer relationship was cut short when I received my orders to report to AFS Headquarters in New York City. On July 29, 1943, I left my home state and boarded the train in Yakima headed for the largest city I had ever visited. After three nights in coach, you can visualize what I must have looked like, tired and sweaty, as I checked in at the AFS Headquarters at 60 Beaver Street in lower Manhattan.

I knew very little about the AFS before I made my decision to join. I was told by my recruiter that students from the U.S. who were in France studying when World War I broke out offered to drive ambulances for the American Hospital serving the French. When World War II started, those involved in the AFS organization decided to organize and fund an ambulance corps and once more served the French. When France fell, they offered themselves to the British. It was when the British were involved in the jungle fighting in India/Burma that I was in New York signing the papers to join up. I became one of the AFS characters, so named because they were a varied lot, most of them having no extensive training in ambulance driving or medical corps involvement.

So here I was, with very little money having to wait out my call to enlist. (As my wife now says, I would not have married her if I had stayed with one of the well-to-do AFS families in New York City and had met a wealthy heiress.) As was my way, I did not tell the officials at the AFS office that I came without any money for housing or food as I awaited my orders to leave for my AFS assignment. I paid for a room and some meals at the YMCA by bussing tables there and then got a job at a hole-in-the-wall deli serving meat pies for lunch and rolls for breakfast. I was intrigued by a food automat that I walked by on the way to work. How interesting to put in money for a sandwich and then open the door and take out the food chosen. I was as curious as any hayseed staring up at all the tall buildings! I did that too!

Front: Ball, Burgess Whiteside, Donald J. Bragg, Norman C. Kunkel, and Michael S. Cheney. Back: Frank Dignam; Robert Wilson; Shirley W. Hendryx, Jr.; F. Mitchel Smith; Robert Waterbury; and William L.B. Eggleton, III.

Every day I checked in with AFS and had time after work to see some of New York. I had my bathing suit so I headed for Jones Beach where I learned about the great surf on the Atlantic side of the U.S.A.! I turned my back and was wiped out by a huge wave, which covered me with sand and knocked me down. Later, I found my way to the ferry that takes visitors over to the Statue of Liberty, and from the top I could see the skyscrapers of New York. I explored the Bronx Zoo, Harlem, Jones Beach, and Columbia University.

One evening I was looking around town in the theater district and came upon quite a crowd of people standing waiting. Suddenly a large limousine drove up to the stage door and who should appear but Frank Sinatra. The crowd came alive as they saw him step out of the limo with his bodyguards. I couldn't afford to attend his concert, but I can say that I saw the Rage of New York.

Finally, orders came for me to travel back across the country to Los Angeles with Don Bragg, Burgess Whiteside, Robert Waterbury, Shirley Hendryx, and Mike Cheney. We reached San Pedro where we embarked on a Liberty Ship with eighty people on board. I had little idea of what was in store for me, but I did know that I was to be involved in a new contingent of AFS Ambulance Corps drivers attached to the British in their fight against the Japanese in the India/Burma campaign.

So here we were on board, living in a small deck house eight feet by fourteen feet, which we appropriately named "The Brig." There was no complaint about food since we ate with the officers. Meat three times a day and plenty of fruit. We took advantage of this sumptuous fare, because we had heard rumors of the stark rations we would be served in India where we would be eating with the British soldiers at the front. To earn a little money, some of us decided to start a barbershop, laundry, and pressing service. After a clever bit of advertising under the name of Ratsnest Enterprises Inc., we were swamped with work. I made about $1 an hour, because I had the distinction of being better at using the scissors than my partner.

Crossing the Equator

I was no longer a pollywog as they call those who haven't crossed the equator. I was now one of forty "shell-backs." It was a rough initiation paralleling that of a college fraternity hazing. Our commanding officer managed to get his camera out of the hold after an endless amount of red tape and took pictures of the king and queen and the baby who was the chief engineer. Some baby! He weighed about two hundred pounds and was so homely only his mother could love him. The gunnery officer was the king, and the third engineer was the queen. I could then carry a certificate signed by the captain stating that I had crossed the equator.

Since we were in dangerous waters, there was a blackout effective every night requiring that every porthole and door in the ship be closed. After getting a headache from all the smoke and foul air inside, we came out on deck to get air. I watched the stars—the constellation Orion and the Southern Cross, which were very beautiful. We could also see the rays of light reflected by the sun at the South Pole. It was similar to the aurora borealis, but was actually light reflected from the ice.

One of the gun crew shouted over the telephones to the rest of us, bringing our attention to a bright light on the eastern horizon. We jumped up and saw what looked like a burning ship. After about a half-minute of watching, we realized it was the moon rising. Slowly the stars lost their brightness as the light from the moon spread across the sky. The night was still very beautiful so we sat there for an hour or more before hitting the hay.

The next day we saw huge albatrosses, each with a wingspread of about eight feet. Most days we saw flying fishes. One day something came up on the horizon. We were only a few miles from Pitcairn Island where Fletcher Christian and the other mutineers sailed on the ship *Bounty,* which they commandeered from Captain Bligh. Bligh had been on an expedition to get breadfruit trees to take to the English colonies. Christian put the captain and those loyal to him into a small boat and set them adrift. Miraculously they managed to get back to England. It was exciting to realize that I was so near to the scene of such an historical event.

After awakening early for church service on board, we looked out across the water, which was smooth and glassy as far as the eye could see—not a ripple to mar the surface. I had to stay inside much of the time because my warm clothes were stowed in the hold and all they would let us bring topside was a musette bag which held about as much as a large handbag.

Water had been rationed so we got only one shower a week and no water to wash clothes in except salt water and that requires soap, which we didn't have. The day we finally got extra water we shouted "hooray," but we were soon back on the once-a-week shower routine.

I got up and looked for penguins every day but didn't see any because we changed our course to the west. Otherwise, we would have ended up in Little America in a week or more. The captain spread rumors as to when we would tie up. Our menu for the day that we lost on the dateline was a silly one listed as inebriated prunes, hominy grits, flapjacks, and jazzed-up sugar syrup! Humor helped ease our minds about being out in the open ocean with a long journey still ahead of us.

It didn't take long for the heavy weather to materialize, waves breaking over the deck and forecastle. Dishes were rattling and sliding as mess men tried to carry three cups of coffee at one time while walking down the narrow companionways as the ship rolled as much as thirty degrees. There was nothing to do but to stand in one place only to be thrown against one wall and then the opposite wall.

In the rough sea, the propeller came out of the water and the whole ship shook like a dog that had just gotten out of icy water with a duck in hunting season. Since the rough seas prevented us from making port as soon as we expected, we had time to get acquainted with the boatswain when the weather calmed. This fellow with a sea-beaten face and tattoos covering his body had seen forty years of service including the sailing of the seven seas more times than he had fingers and toes. He could name all the ports of the world as well as the names of bars and pubs and sporting houses. Over the years he had learned to be amused by everyday happenings. Even with all his gray hair he hadn't lost any, so I earned the fee I charged him for cutting it when he was getting ready to go ashore to assuage his mania for tassel dancers.

We had time to whale watch, but at the same time we were in a state of anxiety because the harvest moon made us visible for many miles to the submarines and enemy airplanes. Although we all acted nonchalant about it, we managed to tie our most valuable possessions to our life preservers.

With the storm and the delay in arrival, we were all getting cabin fever. The mess man and the radio operator were at each other's throats. The passengers and the chief engineer were not on speaking terms since everyone learned that the water rationing was not necessary but was just a way of showing his authority. Knowing that we would be sailing by the place where the mutiny had occurred, I guess he wasn't taking any chances.

Tasmania

At last, after thirty days, we had twenty hours in Hobart, Tasmania, where people could not believe the way we spent money. There, the average wage for a waiter was two pounds a week (about $7 U.S.). Tasmania was noted for its ABCs: apples, beer, and plenty of women. Now, how does the C in ABC become women? Well, you must extrapolate to the term men use for women when only men are present. In my youth, using the term for the female's sexual anatomy as synonymous for female was "man talk" and hidden from the so-called "fair sex." Although I overimbibed in my attempt to release a lot of excess energy, I still had my virtue although many of our unit did not.

Tasmanians knew more about our country than we knew about theirs. Before reaching Hobart, I certainly did not know about this prosperous city of 64,000 people. I met a "girl" who had been the beauty queen of Tasmania, or so she said. She even gave me a gorgeous color portrait of herself, which proved her point. I intended to carry on a correspondence with her, my stated reasons being to learn more about the Australian people. At least that is how I rationalized it. But after a few letters, I was distracted by what was to be my fate after reaching the battle zone of the India/Burma campaign.

Besides the original five AFS fellows who came to L.A. with me, there were Lawrence Eggleton, III; Bob Wilson; Frank Dignam; and F. Mitchel Smith. On board we joined the Air Corps Lieutenants Vincent Seranni, Richard Griffith, R. E. Alexander, Alfred Bosnos, and a fellow named Jack. There was also a General Motors fellow, Henry M. Canal.

Sunday dinner was roast chicken with lemon pie and Indian tea, a far cry from the rations that we were to live on in the jungle. We crossed the Indian Ocean during the monsoon season. Everyone slept fully dressed because any ship on the horizon might have been the enemy. Our shoes were under our pillows and life preservers on top of our beds. Instead of a full meal we got sandwiches. The song "You'd Be So Nice to Come Home To" started us all reminiscing about those we had left behind.

Another terrible storm almost washed our shack off the deck. I stood there talking to one of the gun crew and all of a sudden the bow would hit a big wave and start rising and then plunge down sending a wave over the top of it. It felt like we were dropped down in a fast elevator about six floors.

It was now September 17, 1943, my birthday, and I was running around the ship singing "Happy Birthday" to myself. It's silly I know, but nobody else would do it. I didn't feel any different than I had the day before—or for that matter a year before.

[From My Diary]   POTENT MIX

Sergeant Smith, the nearest to a doctor that we have, just mixed some kind of drink from his medicine cabinet this afternoon and is as stiff as a board now. He studies pharmacology in college and he knows what to mix and what not to mix to get drunk and not get sick. He offered me a drink as it was my birthday but the smell was more than I could stand. The concoction ran something like this: a tablespoon of mineral oil, denatured alcohol, phenobarbital, cough syrup (75% alcohol), sugar, lemons and oranges. I was satisfied eating the great ice cream that we picked up at the last port.

(This recipe is not to be taken seriously. Don't try this at home!)

We ran into one storm after the other. During a calm period I watched Larry, our resident artist from Philadelphia, paint with watercolors. What talent! I started reading *War and Peace* by Tolstoy and *Ulysses* by James Joyce in between watches to supplement the gun crew's watch for subs, planes, and raiders. As one AFS driver once said, "We are continually waiting between duties or waiting for orders to move from one station to another so we learn to pass the time creatively." I made myself a ring out of a florin, an Australian piece of money worth about 33 cents. Before I had finished it I had cut a big gash in my left forefinger, but at least I felt I had been productive.

[From My Diary]

Whiteside, Lt. Seranni and I had a midnight snack of fresh lobster that we bought at the last stop. The other fellows had all gone to bed. To stir up things the next morning we told Hendryx, from Indiana, that if he would keep quiet and not say one word for 12 hours, we would give him $20. He was glad to accept the challenge and we were glad that he did because all day long we had been hearing "Indiana this" and "Indianapolis that" and what he did in the frat house he belonged to when he was in college.

The fun started when everyone who had anything to say about him let it all out. He was cussed and discussed, ribbed and ridiculed, teased and tormented. But he wouldn't talk. In desperation I started to bounce him up and down on his bunk. He got mad but he wanted the money and didn't say anything as he jumped down and piled on me to try and keep me from bouncing his bunk. Someone heard him talk but they said they would forget it. Then during his watch, he burst out with the song "Old Black Joe." He claimed that wasn't talking but the rest of us knew better because we heard him try to sing and everyone agrees that it wasn't really singing! No matter. He won the money but is not on speaking terms with any of us now, just sitting around writing and sulking.

While I was getting up nerve to actually write a poem of my own up on deck, a flying fish jumped so high that it flew up on deck beside me. This was my first chance to examine one—a fish about eight inches long, colored a beautiful blue and with large fins resembling wings.

There was nothing but food to distract us from the war zone we soon would be entering. It was agreed by everyone that it was better to be shipwrecked with a full stomach. Just think what mental torture we would have gone through in a lifeboat after having had only a bowl of soup and a cup of coffee when we could have eaten a huge meal. After reports of submarines in the area, we checked and double-checked the lifeboats.

Since our trip was nearing its end we were all getting channel fever. The captain said he would rather do the whole trip over again than go through the last stretch that was so dangerous. We each had our gun station and got to shoot five rounds a day. Our armed guard fired the guns before we got up one morning and scared us to the point that we were all running for the lifeboats. I was sweating like I once did after having danced about four dances at the Trianon Ballroom in Seattle.

We heard that the people in Calcutta were rioting in the streets because of lack of food. I wondered if I might grow cynical and become callous with all the suffering I would see. It was time to mellow out and write down some poetry for Georgie.

The ship's prow pointed to the west
We sailed into dusk's deepening blue
My heart beat dully with unrest
The sea was taking me from you.

I looked across the lonesome scene
Dreaming, dear, of past delights.
Mulling o'er the might have been
Of cozy rooms and low turned lights.

The water seemed a loathsome thing
To me and in my troubled heart
I knew what sadness it would bring
By taking us so far apart.

As days crept by a gradual change
Took place and then it seemed to me
That all your moods, of widest range
Were part, too, of the sea.

Your gladness and your sadness
Your depths of deep despair
Your joyful, carefree madness
Were all reflected there.

When roaring winds their anger vent
Upon this restless moving shroud
The waves leap high with vain intent
To grasp aloft a moving cloud.

The quickly folding colors change
From deeper green to coldest gray
From valleys to a mountain range
Whose snowy crest is blowing spray.

When in this angry mood the sea
Brings to my mind another frown
Who so in anger looked at me
With flashing eyes of lovely brown.

Then like a living thing, it seems
The anger slowly fades away
And as in quickly changing dreams
The water sprite decides to play.

The wavelets leap and dance and pose
Their varied forms in colors rare
In gay abandon, shy repose,
Like elfins in a wooded lair.

Their pranks I watched in rapt content
The twinkle of reflected rays
Convey the wink of sunlight sent
To me from you, in other days.

Sometimes in warm murmuring night
Illuminated by the moon's soft glow
The lonely waters know my plight
Of loneliness, and whispers low.

They whisper of our wondrous love
Of all our smiles and hopes and tears
And promise me that we will move
Together, through the coming years.

And so at last I know the sea
And understand each changing hue
In all its great complicity
It reminds me, dear, of you.

I must admit that I had help with this poem from Vince Seranni, who had already written one to send to his wife. But even if I did not write it all by myself, the excitement of being aboard ship out on the ocean along with flashbacks of being with my love would have been enough to stimulate my writing a poem all on my own. Not only did I show an interest in poetry for the first time, but I was to learn that I was not truly finished as a person. I still had many new experiences and accomplishments before me in my life. What I yearned to do, I might someday do, even write poetry or even sing if Georgie would someday teach me how.

Near the end of this voyage food was accumulating around my rib cage. Tea was our main beverage. I suspected we were being prepared for a time when we wouldn't have a good cup of coffee for a long time. Too bad we weren't heading for Rio de Janeiro where the coffee was abundant.

Our little artist, Eggleton, had time to carve a nude out of a piece of two-by-four with a big knife. Baumgartner, who was on the gun crew, came walking by and after he watched for quite a while suddenly said, without any reference to the nude, "Gee, where'd yuh get the big knife?" in a John Wayne kind of drawl. The rest of us who were standing watching could hardly suppress our laughter until he had gone.

Colombo, Ceylon

We were nearing the port of Colombo, Ceylon, as evidenced by a rumble of voices all declaring that they planned to look for an air-conditioned cocktail lounge where they could each just sit and drink a Tom Collins. While the boats were lowered for us to go ashore, I spent the last few minutes ironing a shirt for shore leave where I hoped to find precious stones such as sapphires, topazes, aquamarines and garnets. But only twenty-four hours was allowed, and the American Consul told us not to buy anything there because we would get gypped. (Actually, that is a discriminatory term downgrading gypsies, but in those days we didn't think of it that way.) Before leaving the ship we were cautioned not to eat anything and not to drink anything but Scotch whiskey. With our meager $20 a month it wasn't easy to part with the $17 it cost for a fifth of Scotch, difficult to find in any case.

The allied ships and submarines docked here were serious reminders of what we fellows were about to engage in. Pity the "characters" who thought serving in an ambulance corps would protect them from being killed or wounded in battle. For now, I just wanted to let off steam.

[From My Diary]

Drank too much and after being tagged by rickshaw coolies saying, "rickshaw, American gentleman, rickshaw," Dignam and I rode a rickshaw with Abdul who could speak fairly good English. He took us all over, tirelessly running in a dogtrot. The thing I didn't like was the bargaining. We knew that 3 rupees were worth one dollar and we also knew that when our coolie named a price it was three times as much as he would finally accept. It took five minutes to come to an agreement. I had been paying the rickshaw driver 2 rupees to take me from the dock to the European section of the city. According to his license he was only supposed to be paid 4 annas, which is one fourth of a rupee, for the first hour and 3 thereafter. It didn't take me long to catch on to the system.

Abdul worked so hard pulling us up hills but we had been warned that we had to bully the coolies or they would take us into dark alleys. We didn't want to end up being robbed so I grabbed him by his sheet and told him I would kick his teeth out if he didn't go where I wanted to go. We were told to say insults in their language which would keep them in line. Not a pleasant way to communicate but otherwise we would have been taken advantage of.

At one location a "blind" man was calling out to me "bhakshee," which means to give him something for nothing. I thought I would see if this man was for real and handed him an English three pence, which is about the size of a dime or a 4-anna piece. The "blind" man quickly put on a monocle and looked at it and said "no good" and started his pitiful begging again. I then cried out saying "puh" as loudly and as harshly as I could and he left. What we were told about this word was true. It worked wonders.

We finally ended up in a brothel. Object for going was to see what a native prostitute looked like. I agreed that they were not great looking and that they probably had every disease known to man. (After reading this comment in one of my old letters, my wife wondered what I would have done if the prostitutes had been gloriously beautiful!)

It took me a while to be able to face the poor, destitute natives. If you showed sympathy for one, you found twenty or more hanging around you. We were constantly followed by children who had been taught by English-speaking soldiers to say, "No mama, no papa, no extra-curricular activities, Sahib, bhakshee." Amongst all this poverty I was suffering a sort of poverty of my own. Coming from fruit country I longed to taste the wonderful fruits I found in the markets but didn't dare because of the risk of getting cholera or dysentery.

Bardu, our No.1 boy, had been evaluating stones that one of the Air Corps fellows bought in Colombo. It seems Griffin bought what he thought was a genuine pigeon-blood ruby for 90 rupees and Bardu said it was only an imitation worth not near what he paid for it.

We anticipated our next stop, which was to be Madras, India, where I was anxious to purchase some precious stones at a place that was more reliable than Colombo.

PART THREE:
MUD AND MELEE IN INDIA/BURMA

Buying a Ceylon Sapphire

On October 5, 1943, we stopped in the much cleaner city of Madras, India, but only for eighteen hours. There were still beggars and natives all trying to cheat foreigners by giving less than what was bargained for and even by stealing. I felt sorry for the rickshaw coolie and even felt the urge to get out and help when the going got tough for him, but at the same time I had learned how tough one has to be when dealing with the coolie. I enjoyed shopping at Spencers where I got knee pants, long stockings, and a Frank Buck hat. I felt at last comfortably cool. It was in Madras that I felt safe in purchasing a Ceylon sapphire, a blue-white stone, which I carried with me until I arrived at our Headquarters in Poona.

We sat in the river channel waiting for high tide so we could go into Calcutta. It seemed like a great waste of time to take two whole months to get to our destination, but I made many friends and proved to myself that I could take what was pushed my way and all without cracking up. There were native boats alongside to barter with us as soon as the ship dropped anchor. Lots of trading was done, and we were ready for bartering this time. I bought coconuts without knowing whether I would be comfortable eating such rich fare. I suspected that I had dysentery even before beginning my service.

Calcutta, India

Here I was, looking at the Ganges for the first time. It was not a romantic spot, more like the old muddy Missouri River. As we experienced the quietness of the ship, we almost missed the motion we had lived with for so long. It was rumored that only 50 percent of ships would survive this trip so it was a miracle that we made it through. Instead of the rocking of the ship, we were bombarded by the noise of unloading in port. At last I set foot in Calcutta where I would be on solid ground for a year in a country that was strange to me. It was so hot and humid that I felt suffocated until we moved into the

Hotel Grand with good food and service. I was not used to being waited on with servants bringing me breakfast in bed and doing anything that I wanted done. What a place—a hotel with an outside garden seating four hundred and an orchestra playing every night.

I went to the American Red Cross dance and was initiated by dancing with "23:59s," Anglo-Indians, for the first time. The Navy, which counts time up to twenty-four (midnight), came up with this title meaning not quite as "black as midnight." Their descriptive title is "part Tamils from southern India." In every country there is the so-called favored race, and those who are of mixed heritage are not offered the same dignity as those in power. No matter that the favored race is one part of the mixture. Sounds and sights of this shocking cultural environment were to close in upon me time after time. As I walked through the streets, there were small children begging, some holding their bloated stomachs. It made me feel ill to pass them by, knowing that all that I could possibly do would not be nearly enough.

In my favored status I had what was called a "No. 1 boy" who brought me afternoon tea and cake. I couldn't enjoy it entirely as I knew that just outside this wonderful oasis was a sea of poverty. What I saw in my first few days in this place was like a very bad dream softened by my isolation from the street and its vicious level of degradation. But even that isolation was penetrated as I glanced through the large arch window, which had no glass in it, and watched the swarm of beggars, the untouchables. Women with matted hair held babies in their arms while toddlers clutched their mothers' filthy clothing. One woman was chanting and the police officer chased her off. It made chills run down my back.

Pondering our status here in the ambulance corps, I felt I was in luck. I could go to enlisted men's clubs or officer's clubs of either the U.S. or British armies. We could also be civilian if it suited us. So far, the British had been treating us with great respect. However, I had little money since we had to wait to get our allowance. All I could afford was a ticket to the cinema which was showing *Random Harvest*. I had wanted to see this in the states but could never find time. So here I was, seventeen thousand miles away, seeing it at last.

Waiting for our baggage took another two or three days, enabling us to live in the Hotel Grand a little longer. While waiting, I bought some small, carved ivory animals: a lion, a camel, a water buffalo, and an elephant—all with money I had made cutting hair on the way over.

At last, we were on the move toward our destination, Poona Headquarters. Whoever was in charge of getting us there didn't bother to explain our tickets, which we certainly couldn't read. We overrode our train stop. Luckily someone on the train noted our predicament and explained that we needed to get off at the next stop with a five-hour layover and take a train going back to Poona. With five hours to kill, we took a taxi to the hotel where we spent the afternoon bathing in a nice, white-tile bathroom. We must have been black as coal as we left a dingy rim around the tub. We ate lunch while looking out at the harbor and the different uniforms and headdresses of people walking by. One was a "lady from Hell," which was the name the Germans hung on any soldier from a Scottish regiment who wore beautifully pleated plaid kilts.

When we walked about town, we were followed by shoeshine boys who had a way of coming back at our feeble attempts to shoo them away by saying, "You mean get the hell out of here?" We were more interested in the snake charmer that turned the snake and the mongoose loose and let them fight until one was killed. Between three of us fellows, we forked over $1 to watch this. As we expected, the snake was killed, since a mongoose is seldom ever killed by a snake. I was told the reason is that the venom is removed from the snake. It was easier to replace a snake than a mongoose.

Poona Headquarters

Our group arrived at Poona on October 17, 1943, several days later than planned. We had hoped to get a tonga—a two-wheeled conveyance that is pulled by a small, scrubby horse—to take us to Headquarters. It swayed from side to side and jerked us back and forth like a small rowboat in the wake of a ferry in Puget Sound waters back home. We lucked out by getting a ride with a sergeant driving one of the ambulances we would soon be driving. After reporting in, we all found that our enlistment officially started the October 15. We thought that we had already fulfilled several months of our first year overseas, but instead, we had been credited with only two days.

After the outbreak of war with Japan in December 1941, the first AFS unit, which had been en route to Libya, was rerouted to Bombay. Not many people in the United States were aware that part of World War II was seriously fought in India/Burma against the Japanese.

The Allied Powers created the Southeast Asia Command with Admiral Lord Louis Mountbatten in charge. The British 14th Army was under General W. J. Slim. It took a good deal of time and effort for the AFS leadership to establish AFS motor units in India after the British Army accepted the ambulance corps.

Major C. B. Ives was in command of this new AFS service in India/Burma. Not only were ambulances and support equipment needed, but also training for our drivers and orientation to a climate and culture unfamiliar to most of the volunteers. This required meetings with department heads. Major Ives described the conditions of these first meetings as follows: "We thrashed around in 115-degree temperatures trying to explain who we were and what we wanted. General Headquarters was friendly, but busy and overheated."

Among other things the British suggested that each MAS (Motor Ambulance Section) be issued an emergency pool of rifles. After consideration of the lack of training and the consequent possible danger, the British were pleased to recommend that the unit should not be armed.

On May 29, 1943, Colonel Richmond and Major Ives left General Headquarters to go to the Eastern Army front in Burma to see the conditions under which the MAS would be expected to work. Ives wrote:

> From Delhi we went to Calcutta and then to Imphal by two different gauges of railroad and by the tarmac road that the army built up into the hills. The Army supervised the building of it and used it. The actual building was done by families of Indians and Naga hill people. . . .They hoed the dirt out of the side of the mountain, piled it in bags the size of potato bags, and then carried the bags across the road and dumped the dirt down the khud. [The word is pronounced the same as the word that means what a cow chews. It refers to the side of the road that drops down as distinguished from the side that goes up.]

> The road to Imphal was a twisting tarmac all the way. From Imphal there were two roads—one that went south to Tiddim and the other that went southeast across the valley around Imphal and then east across the mountains to Tamu. The Tiddim road had been a mule track, then largely changed into a jeep track, then a road, all muddy and greasy. It went up into the mountains after it had crossed the big valley around Imphal, much like the Tamu road.

Colonel Richmond and Major Ives were given a station wagon with a mad British driver, who seemed to have no fear of sliding over the khud (hill in India). They did not want to show this Tommy that Americans were afraid to die, but they were actually very afraid. Ives felt particularly unwilling to die in a way that seemed trivial and lacking in significance. Afterwards,

The Naga Women by Larry Eggleton

the Colonel said that he had felt more comfortable under mortar fire. They tried to get the driver to be more careful. The driver smiled but didn't change his driving pattern. They sideswiped three other vehicles and bumped against the mountainside of the road twice. For the record, Colonel Richmond did not return to India after this inspection trip.

It took four months to organize the new command in Poona. Lieutenant John Patrick was one of the early officers taking on the responsibility of public relations as well as supervision of personnel, along with Lieutenant Craven in charge of finance. I was not personally involved with Lieutenant Patrick, but I heard much about his skill as a playwright and in later years read his play *The Hasty Heart*. He undertook the publication of *The American Indian*, to which AFS members were invited to contribute lighthearted writings and drawings. Larry Eggleton contributed many paintings, including a full-page watercolor of the Naga women whom I was to meet later on.

A great deal of preparation took place before AFS established the new command. Getting acquainted with India took more time than the orientation to any other area of operation. The establishment was similar to that in the Middle East except that the MAS included Indian sepoys for sanitary duties and batmen who served the officers. They also enrolled Indian personnel for cooks, water carriers, sweepers, and washermen. It was specified that fifty to fifty-five AFS drivers were to be assigned to each section of twenty-five ambulances—but this affluence was seldom maintained.

There were sixty-nine men in Unit India/Burma 1 who were sent to Poona on July 4, 1943. Their training was begun immediately. Drivers were divided into groups and given training in maintenance of the ambulances. Some attended lectures while others went to the training field where they were given lessons in driving the hospital ambulances.

We ended up living in a regular hospital ward where we had showers and plenty of good drinking water and sleeping in beds made with rope stretched across a frame, really quite comfortable. But, we were cautioned to look into our pants and shirts and shoes before putting them on in the mornings—seems as though snakes like to curl up in warm clothing.

Frank Dignam and I became friends, sharing the settling-in process of emptying duffel bags and locating places to store everything. I managed to bring in ten cartons of cigarettes (each package would sell for 90 cents) and pipe tobacco without duty. Thinking about the time ahead and wanting to assure that I had boots that could withstand slogging about in the monsoon-created mud, I decided I might sell my cigarettes in order to buy a pair of mosquito boots for $12 and a pair of shoe moccasins. I planned that I might have enough

Frank Dignam and I in India

money left over to buy two tailored bush shirts for $5 each. These shirts could do double duty—work and leisure.

After settling in, Dignam and I were just entering the "out of bounds" area when a Sikh M.P. gave us hell in English that we pretended was unintelligible, and we kept on walking. We found that the natives who were doing business from little shops also slept there. Mangy and flea-bitten dogs ran about along with goats and cows and cats. The smoke was nauseating. The state of undress was startling.

We were beginning to experience the first shock of any Westerner facing extreme heat, winds and rain, along with the Indian caste system and the bombardment of our senses with the smells and sounds created by camels, cows, beggars, dogs, goats, people sleeping in the streets, spicy foods, and more. Dirt, poverty, and disease were prevalent. I realized later that there was good reason for such "out of bounds" areas throughout the war zones where the bubonic plague was rampant. There were also safety issues when going into the extremely poor areas of a town or city.

[From My Diary]

My account of all this will seem ordinary at times, but at other times almost anyone could identify with the fear and terror we were about to face. It was always a balancing act—self preservation on the one hand without forgetting our basic duty to save lives.

I was intrigued by the occupations displayed: sewing, shoe making, silver-smithing and dyeing. I have been contemplating the caste system here. There are hundreds of them with Brahman being the highest. I figured out that it is a way of accomplishing the division of labor in the country as each caste has certain duties, the lower castes doing the most unwanted jobs. Certain caste members called Dung-wallas do nothing but sweep dung from the streets, pat it out into flat pancakes, and after they are dried sell them for fuel.

It is no wonder that those Indians who were serving us wanted us to take them to the United States after the war. I do not know any AFS fellows who actually took their bearers back with them, but some did get to the U.S. on their own.

Here I must explain that although I was serving the British in the India/Burma campaign, I never actually served in Burma proper. The crucial turning point in that campaign was carried on in Manipur, which was an area of India very close to Burma. The British describe that campaign in their "Victory in Burma" information service pamphlet. In the following chapter is a description of conditions in Burma which relate closely to my experiences in the jungle in India.

Monsoon

The jungle is often so thick that it looks from above like a bed of parsley. A reconnaissance plane can fly five hundred feet above an army corps without seeing a single human being. To hack your way through the bamboo, you have to relieve your machete squads every four minutes, and you are lucky sometimes if you make two miles a day.

The monsoon, a wind of cyclonic character, which blows for five months, will toss a big transport plane around like a leaf or rip it to pieces in the air. The monsoon also brings the rain from the Bay of Bengal, and the mountains precipitate it. During the monsoon soldiers were never dry for months on end. Roads, which yesterday carried tanks and guns, will tomorrow be either thirty feet under water or simply washed off the side of the hill (called the khud in India). If you leave a road alone for two weeks the jungle will have moved back and obliterated it.

The damp and heat bring malaria, sprue, dengue, dysentery, and jaundice. If you try to march in a mosquito net it is ripped to pieces by the undergrowth. If you cover yourself with anti-mosquito cream, you are ready to burst after one hundred yards, for it clogs the sweat pores. So you eat anti-fever atabrine tablets, which turn you yellow, and salt tablets to put back what you lose from sweat, and you trust the medics to get you back to duty from the malaria in three or four weeks.

Meanwhile you are bitten by leeches—they go in an inch deep and the only thing that gets them out is to apply a lighted cigarette. You are bitten by bugs and ticks and ripped by thorns. You suffer from "Naga sores," great poisonous holes which spread like wildfire all over you. And you march, with or without your mules, up gradients of 45 degrees in temperatures ranging up to 105 degrees and a humidity of 95 percent. At night in the jungle the darkness is so intense that you can't see the end of your rifle; and during the monsoon the driving clouds and mist make the day almost as obscure. The British fought in this for nearly four years.

When I thought about the British Tommy going through this torturous life, slogging through mud and sleeping wherever he could rest his head, I counted myself lucky. I could drive in my ambulance to pick up casualties and sleep in it at night, even if my long legs hung out the end of the stretcher that was my bed.

The Allied forces in Burma made their way on foot the last two hundred miles to the Indian border, where they took up positions in the jungle, weary but prepared to repel any attempt at invasion. By June 1942 the enemy had taken all of Burma but a fringe of mountains in the north and bits of jungle swamp to the west. They might have brought off a successful invasion of India at that time, but with the coming of the monsoon they halted their attack. Again in 1943 the monsoon season stalled activity.

In December 1943 the Allies had grasped the initiative, and the campaigns, if small, were going well. Because of the terrain and the enemy's tactics it was far more of an infantryman's fight than the AFS was to know in any other theatre. The enemy had developed a strategy for jungle fighting—infiltration and a tactic of slipping around through the jungle to reappear behind established British posts, upset communications for a few days, and then slip away into the jungle again to reappear no one could guess where. Patrolling, therefore, was constant.

The fighting was as nasty as it was intimate in scale. Patrols were in almost as much danger from mines and booby traps set by their own side as from enemy activity. These and the many jungle diseases provided a steady stream of casualties for evacuation. The greatest number was caused by dysentery, while at other times of the year malaria was the chief cause of sickness. In 1944 the sickness rate was 100 percent though there was only one battle casualty for every twenty sick. There was plenty for our AFS ambulances to do. During the 1943 monsoon season, however, there was only patrol activity at the front. Behind the lines both sides were busy building strength for the winter campaigns. At the end of the monsoon season the Japanese renewed the offensive in western Burma, pushing north from Akyab toward the Indian border. A British counterattack pushed them back, but its gains could not be held and the Japanese pushed up to the frontier.

Consider Yourself Engaged

The monsoon season was ending and there would soon be active duty for all of us. While waiting, I packed and sent to Georgie the ivory carvings, two hollowed-out beans with miniature elephants inside, and the ring I had purchased in Madras along with a note saying, "Consider yourself engaged." I was ready to stand firm in my assurance that I would come back from the war and that Georgie would be waiting for me. I suggested that she read *India Without Fable* so she could keep up with what I was experiencing. (It took a long time for this to reach Georgie and to receive her reaction to this gift and message.)

Meanwhile I was becoming accustomed to a schedule, which included guard duty from 2 a.m. to 5 a.m. and staying awake for a class at 10 a.m. We had no previous training, so it was essential that we learn about the care and repair of our vehicles, learn to ride a motorcycle, and become familiar with Urdu, the most widely used language.

Meals consisted of bully beef (corned beef) for breakfast and dinner. Good thing I made the most of the meals aboard ship as I expected to lose pounds in the frantic life I was soon to live in the jungle. While we could, we took advantage of the servants we hired to do everything for us. Four of us hired a bearer for $4 a month who made up our beds, shined our shoes, put our clothes away, and put our mosquito nets down at 6:30 p.m. Since the bearer didn't wash clothes, we hired a dobiewalla to wash and press our clothes for $4 a month.

Every night we were supposed to light a match and see if there were mosquitoes within the net. One night Paul Clark, who had a terrible hangover, crawled out from under his mosquito net. Finally we told him, "You know malaria is around here." Paul's reply was, "Yeah I met him, he's a fine fellow."

The day our unit was on ration detail we went to the quartermaster depot to get two truckloads of food. We also had time to fix up our Café La Trine with grass matting, nice chairs and tables and curtains. Lieutenant J. K. S. Fearnley wrote about the decorating of this club:

> The walls of La Trine have been painted by one of our manic young artists with a defiant attitude toward art—Eggleton. Along one wall, life-size angels float in flimsy streamers, angels whose symmetry does not quite correspond with what I have gleaned from morphology and personal experience. The upper portion . . . reminds me of the oncoming view of a Pierce Arrow, while the hips are Russian, ponderous and pear shaped. The expression is angelic. On the opposite wall is painted a life-size giraffe eating roses with a look of gleeful idiocy. Its playmate is a fat-bellied horse with a bloodshot eye painted on its side. This Dali touch might be intended to represent the watchfulness of God or a warning to be kind to your stomach—I don't know. Our British friends don't quite know what to make of it. Neither do we.

Café La Trine became the light side of our very serious introduction to the India/Burma campaign. It even produced a new mixed drink they called "The Blue Nile." I hadn't had one yet and didn't think I wanted one because some of the guys drinking them started seeing black and pretty soon they just ceased seeing for a while.

I drove about fifty miles in the countryside looking at castles. I found a coffeehouse where I purchased a half pound of cashews for 11 annas, about 22 cents. A dinner and movie *Between Us Girls,* with Kay Francis, Robert Young and Diana Barrymore, in town cost 3 rupees, 8 annas. A rupee was approximately a quarter in U.S. currency. There I learned that the lizards running up and down the walls were welcomed as they eat the pesky insects. This was only one of my learning experiences connected with living in a tropical climate.

We simply waited to head out cross-country. A description by Lieutenant Patrick sums up the down-to-earth experience traveling by convoy:

> Some of the cars had been stuck in river-crossing on the first day, but no one was on hand to get pictures of the men struggling in the mud with natives and cows trying to pull the ambulances out. Lt. Willson returned after the first day, leaving the convoy in charge of Sergeant Parker, so that the men would have experience in taking care of themselves in the field.

> After traveling all day, the convoy pulls off the road at night onto a field the pre-scribed distance from a village or river. They drive in and quickly park beside each other, forming a closed square, covered-wagon fashion. The cook truck, under Spencer, promptly begins to prepare the night's meal—tea, bread, bully beef, onions. In the meantime, the men get into overalls and take care of their cars, doing the tasks and checking the motors. If an ambulance has been having trouble, it is tested on the road by the sergeant and men from the Light Aid Detachment truck. The men are issued their daily allotment of one quart of water, which is all they get for the next day's washing and drinking. They clean up for the night's meal. After dinner they sit inside the circle, talk for a while, and turn in early. Most of the men sleep inside their ambulances on stretchers under mosquito nets—in about as much space as you would find in a good-sized coffin. Some sleep under the cars, with the mud of the undercarriage a few inches from their faces. It rained nearly every night. Night guards are posted. The cooking is done on a small sort of blowtorch cylinder, which never seems to work. Nothing tastes quite so good as that hot tea as we stand in the drizzle watching the sun descend on a part of the horizon where it isn't raining.

> In the morning, it is reassuring to wake up in the blackness and hear Spencer roaring at his native cooks (Indian soldiers) to get the fires started. Then the horn on one of the ambulances is sounded to wake the unit. They stumble out in the wet darkness and quickly shave and dress and get their gear packed before breakfast. They stand in line by the cook truck as it is growing light and are served hot tea, steaming mush, and bread. When they have finished. . .they line up and draw their rations for lunch—a can of bully beef (sometimes cheese), bread, and dried fruit or an orange. . . .

> The cook wagon begins packing. The ambulances file past the petrol truck to fill up. Olmsted and Forman have this hard, thankless, dirty, greasy job. The perspiration rolls off them as they try to speed the line onto the road. . . . Checked and tanks filled, the

ambulances drive onto the road and take their positions in the convoy line to await the signal to start. A motorbike is at the head, and one brings up the rear. The petrol and Lad trucks are usually the last to take their places. The station wagon leads the convoy—the rest follow 50 yards apart, stretching over a distance of 2 or 3 miles. . . . The men did a hell of a good job according to any standards. . . .They drove through rivers and mud, heat, and rain. At night they were tired, filthy, and cheerful. The first section is ready to move.

Captain Pemberton wrote, "We have come a long way from the time when we used to look at a new guy, ask him if he'd ever driven before, and then turned over an ambulance to him. . . ."

Now it was October 27, 1943, and I had drawn barracks guard duty interrupted by one-and-a-half-hour breaks. Krusi and I went to the bazaar festival for the Hindu New Year (Denali), which a Hindu told us would last for three or four days. This fellow asked us if it was true that 75 percent of the people in our country got divorces in just a few weeks. He had many more questions that seemed to reflect perceptions he gained from watching U.S. movies.

The streets had designs all over them of different colored chalk. Along the way we saw papier-mâché idols and dolls, candles in the windows and in front of their shacks and stores. The air was also delicately scented with incense. Women were wearing their best saris and all seemed to be in a good mood.

Speaking of high spirits, I must tell you about a native who worked in our canteen. We named him Mystery because he never wore shoes and so crept about noiselessly. His eyes had a mysterious look adding to his seeming clairvoyance. Whenever he got a two or three anna tip, he would come to attention and salute. He dressed in a white uniform with a white turban and sash of orange and yellow cloth. He was always smiling. I didn't know whether it was to show his gold tooth or whether he was happy to be working for Yanks or just proud of his uniform. (Can you imagine having a foreigner living with you and taking pictures of you and writing all about your looks in a diary? At the time, I didn't realize how my curiosity might offend someone.)

Now came some serious preparation for marching. No telling when we would be forced to go cross-country if something happened to our ambulances. We left one morning intending to go four or five miles, but actually went nine. Most everyone came back with sore feet breaking in new Indian army shoes. On the way back we had some glorious scenery along the canal—palm trees and small green birds that looked like parakeets, as well as blue and yellow birds. There were many nests hanging from the trees. One looked similar to an oriole's nest. I had heard that there were quite a few orchids growing wild, but it was against the law to pick them. Many people grew them in their yards and gardens, however.

A Kashmir merchant had been coming by our barracks to find someone to pay his full price for his merchandise, which provided him enough profit to live for a month. They all thought that we were rich. One special item was a white, woolen, silk-lined evening jacket, all handmade. It was embroidered in bright mustard yellow on the front flaps where it was buttoned, and then around the bottom, collar and cuffs. I planned to wait for him to bargain with me so I could get it for a much lower price.

A mad bull broke the quiet of the day with his bellowing. He was being held in tow by two natives who had put a ring in his nose and tied it to hobbles. This caused the bull to thrash about, letting us all know of his misery. Meanwhile, I had misery of my own with my infected knee from a spill I took. I wanted to get cleaned up and go to the bar at Café La Trine, but it wasn't open that night so I couldn't drink to Dignam's wedding anniversary.

[Letter to Georgie]

While on guard last night (10 to 12 and 4 to 6) I had time to learn the words to the song "The Dreamer." I wish I could hear the music while I am on duty. It would make the time go faster.

It was a beautiful night—a night typical of the tropics starting with a long-lasting sunset giving way to the moon setting in the west as the star of Bethlehem came up over the mountain. It looked like a big bright jewel within arm's reach. All the pictures you have seen of the morning star on Christmas cards were not in the least exaggerated.

Bob Wilson and I took a long walk. We sat on a bridge in the bright moonlight and talked. The air was heavy with tropical fragrance resembling the smell and taste of hard Christmas candy with the stripes on it. Later I learned it was called "lady in the night."

We lost 3½ hours sleep because some of our fellows came in blind drunk and caroused without regard for those who were sleeping. Then an oot came in and started crawling on our beds. An oot is a small animal that has a long tail and a fox-like face. If you have seen a mink, just add a long tail and change the mink's color to a dirty black.

Bombay

When I was attending the University of Washington, I lived at the YMCA with my friend Bill Hoekendorf, Eduardo Calas from Cuba, and Royal Bisbee whose father was a missionary in Bombay. Since Bombay was only about forty miles from Poona, I had some time to visit there before we moved on to Calcutta. I contacted Reverend R. D. Bisbee and his wife who invited me to a dinner of fresh fruit cocktail, fresh fillet of sole, chicken soup, roast beef with seven vegetables, followed by fruit gelatin pudding, coffee, sweets, and nuts. Reverend Bisbee filled me in on many native customs and special words I needed to learn. "Buhut uchchha" is Indian for "very well" and "khurab turuk" is bad or no good. I also learned another expression, "mah-ah-lish," which was brought from the Middle East, meaning "So what? Does it make any difference? I don't care. What the hell." That's what we felt about our limey legs. You got limey legs from wearing knee pants and long, knee-length soxs so your legs became striped.

Later, Dignam and I walked around the Gateway and saw many ships in the harbor. We admired a beautiful young Hindustani girl wearing a luxurious sari. Her hair was carefully done up, and she wore silver bracelets and silver toe rings. We were commenting to each other about her beauty when suddenly, just as she was about to pass us, she turned her head and spit out a large mouthful of cherry-red betel nut juice all over the sidewalk. We were dumbfounded. I wrote to Georgie that she didn't have to worry about competition from the Indian girls. However, we took advantage of every opportunity to dance. There was a big celebration for Armistice Day in one of the nicest clubs in India with the proceeds going to charity. I had a few drinks, enough for me to buck up against the majors and captains who dominated the scene. Every time I found a dance partner, someone would tag me. I left early as I was on guard duty that night. At least I told myself that was my reason for leaving early.

We talked about getting to the front and then coming back home again. We all seemed to take it for granted that we would be coming back and carrying on from where we left off—that is until we began to see casualties in our own ranks. Wilson came down with dysentery and was taken in an ambulance to the hospital. Burgess Whiteside had malaria and was taken to a Calcutta hospital. I had my black plague shot as a precaution. All this signaled what was ahead for me.

Everyone anticipated our move to Calcutta so we prepared our gear and clothing. Our bearer had not been very reliable and came late saying, "Wife sick, gonna have baby," with the most pathetic look in his eyes. The way he said, "Yes, sahib" you just couldn't be mad at him very long. I ordered boots that would fit me from a moochie walla (shoemaker) and had to sell my watch to pay for them. I could tuck my trousers into them and defy the mosquito. What a pleasure.

There was a rapid and enlightening conversation going on in the barracks. It was all about glass eyes. Two of the fellows in this section had one. Tom Burton was telling how Crowley would take his out and then put it in upside down. When he would do this he had no muscular control of it, and when he would roll the good eye, the glass one would have a cocked fixed position. "Sister" LeRoy Krusi's reaction to this talk was terrible groans and moans. "Oh, my God! How horrible" is all he could say. We always called him "neon" because of his many ribbons. He never went anyplace without all of them pinned on his chest. He tried to be British in everything he did—clothes, speech, manners—even though he was from the U.S. Next he planned to get a monocle.

TEAKWOOD

I met a man who had been in Burma in the lumber business for over thirty years. He told us all about teakwood. From the time a tree is felled until it is sawed up into lumber is seven years or more. They fall a tree of at least 150 years of age and let it lie for two years without touching it. Then they have an elephant drag it down to a streambed, which is dry because of winter. In the summer when the monsoon starts, the streambed fills up with water, carrying the log down the river to the mill. It lies there for five years in water and is then sawed into lumber. After that it has to go through the seasoning process of ordinary lumber.

Thanksgiving was only important to us AFS fellows from the U.S.A. Even so, the mess sergeant got some live ducks and we fattened them up on rice and bread, though that meant we had less to eat ourselves. Our dinner consisted of fresh onions and lettuce, roast duck with the feathers on, mashed potatoes and gravy with cornstarch pie for dessert. Besides this fabulous dinner, I got mail from home after waiting three weeks to hear from Georgie, wondering if she had stopped writing.

[From My Diary]

One of the many interesting sights we saw was a rajah's palace. It was said that he had 60 wives with eunuchs guarding them. On another day we rode bicycles up to the base of the mountain. We had no guide or interpreter but some Indian boys who spoke English were coming down the elephant steps. An old legless beggar guarded our bikes so we could go up to the castle and the two temples. At last we completed the ninetieth step to the top where we could see for miles in every direction. We were awed by the complexity in design and color of the temples, built before the year 1750. They were the homes of the rulers of India and had also served as a fortress where they made their last stand against the British. We were not allowed inside but we could see the god Shiva through the window. Shiva is a major Hindu god who, as lord of the dance, is god of creativity and is infinite and eternal. For over two thousand years sculptors and painters have brought to life the many manifestations of Shiva, as woman, as man, as youth or maiden, as cloud or sea.

When we came down, we got lost in the city. We didn't mind because we were seeing so many interesting sights. We would be riding down a street and either George or I would see a side street and then we would ride down it to see where it went. We soon arrived at a big square market place where we saw bananas (including Bombay green), papayas, mangoes, oranges, lettuce, eggplant, squash, okra, you name it.

Everyone was staring at us because we were both over six feet tall wearing shorts and Gurkha hats, which added more than three inches to our height. A tall man in this section of India is seldom more than 5 feet 8 inches so you can imagine how we stood out. A street photographer took our picture in front of a garish backdrop painted with tigers and other symbols of India. we rode down into Poona, which is out of bounds for us. it is not uncommon to see people excreting and urinating in the street so you can imagine that the stench was nauseating as it permeated the atmosphere everywhere.

A few days ago we went to Bombay to pick up a 4-wheel-drive Chevrolet that Frank Dignam and I were assigned to use as a petrol lorry. We were expendables. By that I mean, when you are driving with petrol and hit a mine, there is no getting out alive. Our petrol would have sent us up in flames. We worked hard getting the lorry ready for action, tightening nuts and bolts and greasing and oiling it.

After we washed up, we went downtown to the market and bought tangerines, bananas, and some onions to eat with our bully beef to make it almost palatable. We decided that we could trust the fruit if we peeled it. Little boys were tagging me around with baskets on their heads wanting to carry the things I bought. It was a good thing I grabbed onto one, or rather that he grabbed onto me, because he found two bad tangerines in the dozen and made the Indian woman give me two good ones to replace them.

There was a little monkey around camp that belonged to a British sergeant who tied him to a tree and fixed up a little rope swing for him to play on. Everybody left him alone all day and they didn't bother him much but just before dark some of the guys gave him some of this foul Indian gin to drink. He drank it and got "tighter than a tick." The poor thing was running around twice as fast as before and making all kinds of strange noises. It was fun to watch his crazy antics but when you thought about it, it was downright inhumane. I knew my Dad would have disapproved.

Traveling Back to Calcutta

At last we received the order to move. Some of our men had been rushing around, acting like Boy Scouts who had just been told that they were going on a two-week camping trip. I found it interesting how different things excite different people. I had been that way myself, packing and repacking, but eventually I never lost any sleep over it.

Being tired of waiting was nothing compared to traveling over roads

Beside My Ambulance in India

that would be considered almost impassable in the U.S., then stopping overnight and trying to see a little of the countryside as we prepared for the next day's trek. We were now two days out of Poona on our way to Calcutta. Diggie and I were delayed about six or seven hours due to a bad bearing, but we overtook the convoy at last. Budinger piled up Raache's ambulance forty miles from Nasik. Barrett and Sweetnam both broke axles on their fifteen-hundred weights because they overloaded their trucks.

We camped at Chalia, a strictly Indian town. I talked with some Indian children who saw a Ghandi follower coming toward them, and they said, "F--- Ghandi walla, no good. Me British. Me good." There weren't so many Ghandi followers around Poona because they were being arrested in great numbers so they did not knowingly expose themselves.

[Letter to Georgie]

I am writing this without artificial light—just the light of the moon. It is so beautiful that I just had to tell you about it. I'm sure that this is about the closest we will come to seeing a white Christmas. Everything is bathed in a soft light resembling snow in the early morning. I remember one Christmas back home I woke up early in the morning and looked out to see if it had snowed. I was completely fooled into believing that the scenery bathed in moonlight was snow. How beautiful and quiet it was.

Tony Bradley, our Sergeant Major, treated the Indians like they were dirt under his feet. He bullied them all the time. I was appalled but then I remembered how I had to treat the Indians when I first came here in order to get them to do what I needed done. It is easy to criticize when one is the onlooker and not the perpetrator.

Jeffries, our CO, was an eager beaver, trying to get us going before he even got out of bed in the morning. I decided I had to accept the judgment of my superior officers whether or not I believed they were right. Up to this point I had always done what I wanted to and relied upon my own judgment. I thought to myself, "Maybe I'll get used to it. If I don't, God help me! I'm only glad that I don't have to assume the responsibility for getting us all across India into Burma! What a hellish job."

We came 125 miles in one day and about 100 miles the next day. We didn't get into Shimpuri until late one night, reaching Mhow on December 21st and then came through Bioria but only stayed long enough to refuel. About dark I saw a lot of peacocks with tails six feet long. Stopped the truck and grabbed some rocks and started chasing them. I couldn't hit one of them even though the thought of one roasting on a spit started my juices flowing.

Shimpuri, a north central province owned by the Maharajah of Gwalior, looked the same as it had a thousand years before. It was Christmas Eve and we camped at Jhansi, which is quite a big British cantonment where troops from the U.S. were housed as well. By nightfall we reached Allahabad, which I was told was a hotbed for the Congress Party, where Nehru lived. The Indian National Congress, founded in 1885, served as a sort of political debating society where Indians could discuss their grievances. In 1919, Mohandas K. Gandhi attained leadership and it became a powerful political organization. As individual religious groups began to be given more voice, there was competition between the Hindus and Muslims as to who would control India after it gained independence. [It was not until three years after I came home that India finally became self-governed.]

It was in this climate of Indian political struggle that we found ourselves in the India/ Burma campaign. After leaving this geographical center of the Congress Party, we spent the evening cleaning our trucks. A harmonica was playing as we sat around in the late evening after a full day. It sure sounded nice in the dark with the stars in the sky like diamonds on black velvet. The air had just a trace of the fall weather that we have back home.

We had to leave James Baars in Allahabad because he came down with malaria. The rest of us left for Benares, the Hindu holy city. A temple is a bone of contention between the Muslim and the Hindu. The Muslims took over a Hindu temple and tore it down and built a temple of their own on the same spot with the same stone. Well, the Hindus built another temple as close to it as they could and when the Hindus and Muslims came to worship they got into fights.

On Christmas Eve, I was feeling very morbid and lonesome. I got drunk with Diggie, Brown, Gilliam, Fenn and Searles. Searles brought out his phonograph and we played his records with "White Christmas" getting the most requests. I got to feeling happy and forgot all about it being Christmas Eve. I hit the stretcher (bed) about 10:30 and remembered no more. Fortunately, G. Moon put my net down for me after he came back from Ghanzi.

On Christmas we arrived at Capor. It was dirty and stinky like Calcutta. Went to Bristols and had coffee with Beeber, Krusi, Hendryx, Brannan and Ainsworth. They had sold out of practically everything so we had to eat what they had left. Christmas dinner was a real letdown and the company officer had to take the rap for it.

To get to Begador, India, we drove over 200 miles. From a distance, the city of Benares was beautiful. Antasol, about 143 miles from Calcutta, brought us to the famine district where 50 to 75 kids were waiting for leftovers. They are all wretched looking little things, hardly like humans. I cut up half a loaf of bread that I had left over from lunch and gave it to the little devils. They fought over it like starving animals. I always shared whatever I could but it was never enough.

I forgot to duck when I went into a low Indian hut where our water tap was and ran into a sharp pole, seeing stars, and having to have the gash in the top of my head sewn up. Saw a large convoy of jeeps heading for the road into China. Reminded me of having to drive the petrol lorry being bounced about while always in fear of some Jap waiting in ambush till I've passed and then tossing a grenade into the back of the truck. Not a pleasant thought! But I decided that I mustn't think of such things with the beautiful new moon out and the stars so beautiful and bright. It was now a quiet New Years Eve.

[Letter from Georgie]

Dear Norman, I don't ever want to talk myself into any false hopes by writing down everything I'm thinking. Right now I'm hoping that you'll be safe and that you will feel that coming back is important. It rather startled me when you asked, "Will it matter if I come back?" Of course it matters very much. So don't talk that way about it. I must admit that you have made a great impression on me—in just the short time I've known you. Your sincerity and concern in matters that interest you, your vigor and energy in pursuing what you think is worth the pursuit is more than the minimum. But you're across the world and I have to go on every day with just a part of the vigor that you seem to have as you write. It's no fun to be left behind! I wish I wouldn't tell you all this but you've been so swell to keep your promises about writing. Such an interest in one so far away makes me glad that I met you for I was afraid then that you'd go away and something would keep you from writing, or that you'd cease to care so much.

Guess what your letters have done to me? The night after receiving so many I dreamt you had come back and that I was expecting you any minute to walk in the house and you did just that without phoning or anything! In case you aren't aware—you actually invaded my world. You were the unexpected person—someone I never dreamed of being a part of my life, so it took a little time to get used to the idea. But there was no time was there? You were here and gone before I had a chance to give you a definite place in my thoughts.

After receiving Georgie's letter, my romantic reverie was broken by the realization that we had finally arrived in Calcutta after our long trek from Poona, through Chalia, Shimpuri, Hhow, Bioria, Jhansi, Allahabad, Benares, Campor, Begador, and Antasol. This city of Calcutta would foreshadow the reality of moving to the front in Manipur: the jungles, the unpredictable perils of malaria, dysentery, monsoon rains, and mortar fire directed by the Japs at the British troops and in the line of fire ourselves.

We saw slums in Calcutta around the jute mills, the most appalling in which humans could live. The city was blacked out so driving was nerve wracking. With people, bullock carts, and sacred cows in the streets I still had a clean record with only two birds that hit my windshield.

I wrote home after taking time to feed some Indian children and then I said, "sub-chee-juldee jao" which means, "That's all, go quickly." I was guarding our vehicles as bedlam broke loose with wild dogs making a terrible noise, howls and yapping all at once. They just started and stopped like rain. Now they started up again, but I went to sleep even with the noise of the animals and the Indian drums thrown in.

On January 2, 1944, after we boarded a train for the front, we changed to the Bengal and Assam railroad narrow gauge, which is run by Yanks. Fenn, while moving a motorcycle, fell with it on top of him and lacerated his calf—just one of many little casualties as we moved toward the front.

By January 6 we left the train and hit the road driving twenty-one miles to a ferry, which took us to Goalpara, on the opposite side of the Brahmaputra River. We changed trains at Parbatipur where we took a case of canned pears from the dock. Later the Major and Lieutenant Jefferys "scrounged" a couple of ducks. On the train, the real owner of the ducks came over and told Lieutenant Jefferys that he was a disgrace to his nation and that he wouldn't take the ducks back, because they had been touched by white men. The major and the lieutenant had to pay for them, probably more than they were worth!

We advanced to Assam where the Indians look more oriental and have sturdy physiques. In the flat country the Indians seemed to be darker and thinner. For the next 115 miles the road was passable because big road gangs kept it up. I saw a woman cracking rocks as she sat by the road, wielding a large hammer with both hands and moving the rocks in front of her with her feet.

Manipur

To put all this into perspective, I must quote from George Rock's AFS history:

> Although by early 1944 the Allies were about to take the offensive, in the two years since Pearl Harbor the Japanese had earned the reputation of being invincible and had taken a great deal of territory. Between December 1941 and May 1942 the enemy had overrun the Philippines, much of Oceania, all of the Netherlands East Indies, the Malay Peninsula, as well as most of Burma. India was in danger. And the last supply route to China was cut.

> In January 1942, Japanese forces advanced west from southern Thailand to take Moulmein in Burma and then turned north. Rangoon, the capital city and principal supply port for the Allied forces in Burma, was taken on March 8th—overwhelmed by the enemy's superiority in numbers and equipment. The Japanese then advanced to the north and by infiltration and outflanking tactics, completed the conquest of southern Burma in two months, surprising the British by their cunning and jungle craft. . . . Mandalay was occupied by the Japanese on May 1st.

By January 11, 1944, I found myself in the area of Aguhati, Nowgong, and Imphal where we camped at Gauhati in the jungle after traveling 140 miles to Nowgong, passing many tea estates. Another 150 miles over very bad road brought us to the state of Manipur. I bounced along in my lowest gear for what seemed like ten miles averaging one mile per hour. I heard that the usual run with four stretcher patients was twenty-seven miles in nine hours. If there were battle casualties in the top stretchers, and they were badly injured, it would often take twelve hours.

My hopes were dashed by a deep gully that my truck would not go through. We piled out and started toward the timber with machetes and kukrees (Indian cutting tools which can be hung on the belt) until we had enough wood to raise the roadbed sufficiently for passage. Then another 130 miles to Imphal, the capital of Manipur, over a better road, reaching six thousand feet only to come back down to about two thousand feet.

That evening as I stood amongst the soldiers all dressed the same, waiting to get a ticket to a movie in town, I felt a lack of individuality. What a terrible feeling—everyone all the same. I used to feel the same thing when I was working at Boeing Airplane Company in Seattle. I was just one little part of something too big for my comprehension. It was difficult to realize the immensity of this war and the thousands and thousands of us taking part in it.

Ten Rupees printed by the Japanese Government in preparation for taking over India.

We lived in a little grass and bamboo hut called a "basha." I helped build a nice fireplace for warmth and had my little kerosene lamp for light. Very cozy, indeed, although only one side of me kept warm. It was peaceful and quiet. Most everyone was in bed, and there didn't seem to be many animals around this place to howl or make other strange noises. As I sat there, it was hard for me to believe that there was a war going on all around me and, for that matter, all over the world.

I had been assigned to an ambulance with lots of room in the back for my gear and clothing, giving me the evidence that I was actually ready to evacuate wounded when we reached the battle area. I had time to make a hospital visit to see Krusi who was bright yellow with jaundice and had lost a lot of weight. I think I was able to cheer him up considerably as he was smiling when I said goodnight to him, even though he was facing more than two more months being confined.

Strangely, the cause for elation and future hope can sometimes be sickness. Can you imagine that illness and injury could be something to look forward to? Well it is for some! Our fellows have to face the pressure of entering the battle zone in their own way. Some may welcome a trip to the hospital if it puts off the moment of truth—the life and death duty that we came here to engage in. You can understand why we made plans for a canteen, which we called "El Malaria." It is a place where we could relax, away from the hardships of driving ambulances long periods of time in battle conditions.

On a walk to explore the village, Morrill and I stopped at the YMCA where I dropped off some battle dress to be altered as everything I get is always too short. Being tall sometimes has its disadvantages, but on the plus side, not many people wanted to challenge me.

This village consisted of several shacks built around a square compound. Many of the little communal gatherings shared a common water hole (just a square hole dug deep enough to hold enough water through the dry spell) and a grain storage house. This grain storage place was usually just a roof held up by poles. The Indians usually grew enough potatoes, cauliflower, and cabbage to meet their own needs.

[From My Diary]

Yesterday I climbed onto the roof of one of our shacks to view the Indian houses. In the center of the compound there was an old lady pounding grain with a pole. She had a huge log with a hole in it and was raising the pole and letting it drop on the grain in the hole. Near the water pool was a younger woman with a child tied on her back washing some clothes in a small pan. In another part of the compound a very old and feeble woman was operating a small and primitive-looking cotton gin. It made a squeaking, screeching noise that sent shivers up and down my spine. On the porch of one of the shacks sat another old woman weaving cloth.

Soon the woman with the child tied to her back was giving it a bath in cold pond water. Her child was screaming at the top of its lungs but she didn't pay any attention. After she had finished, she ran after two small boys, about 3 and 5, who were running around as naked as little baby birds playing in the dust and the rubbish scattered around the edges of the compound. After she had finished bathing these two boys, she bathed herself. You never saw an adult bathe in the nude. They always left their clothes on and when they were finished they put on a clean, dry sari.

Later on they ate their cauna (lunch or dinner). A woman came out of one of the shacks with a large, flat, shiny brass pan heaped with steaming rice. This she set down on the ground and after much shouting, many women and children gathered around the pan, all sitting on their heels and began eating with their hands and fingers.

I always felt more comfortable when I had investigated my surroundings. Now I was ready to settle in and begin camp life. The mess sergeant Dick had a little problem, and I think he aged a little during that short interval. The problem: One Indian soldier attached with us to do regular camp work such as carrying water, etc. did something he shouldn't have, and the sergeant wanted to reprimand him for it. In order to do this he had to call in an Indian, who acted as interpreter, and the Indian corporal who disciplines the other Indians to assist him in bawling out this fellow. The sergeant told the interpreter to tell the corporal to give the offender Hades for the misdeed. This setup would have worked fine, but the corporal spoke a different dialect than the offender, so another interpreter of Indian dialects was located in order to tell the offender what the corporal was saying. Before it was over, Dick was tearing his hair—what he had left—and wishing he had let the whole matter drop.

Our dispatch fellow is in deep trouble because he hasn't brought us mail for two weeks. I was beginning to rely on Georgie's letters more and more as we got deeper into the Indian jungle. I passed the time and made a little money by cutting all of our IOR's (Indian Other Ranks) hair. There were about eleven in all. One wanted a Hollywood haircut, short on top and combed back on the sides. The Mohammedans wanted me to run the clippers right over the top of their heads. The Hindus only wanted a partial haircut. I had to leave a little pigtail. They believe that when they die they will be pulled up to heaven by this little wisp of hair. The Sikh's hair went uncut. They never cut their hair or shave but braid their beards and pin them under their chin. One of the outstanding things about our IORs is that they all get along so well. It is a little hard to understand when you consider there are Muslims, Hindus, and Sikhs.

One night I went down to an Indian burlesque show with the fellows. Even without a strip tease routine it was a bit risqué. We could understand only a little of what was said, but dancing is a universal language. Some of the fellows were making cracks about how buxom they were. I noted how thick-waisted they looked. Even though Barbie Doll hadn't appeared in the U.S. as yet, our male view of the hour-glass figure as perfection was always held up as the ideal.

With so much time to think about the next phase of this war, I talked with our commanding officer (CO) about getting transferred to Italy. I said I would sign up for another year if he would let me leave this God-forsaken place now, but he said it just couldn't be done. I wasn't the only one who was unhappy. Some time ago, our CO came up to Dewey Swensson and said, "Dewey, 90 percent of the guys in the AFS look unhappy 50 percent of the time, but you look unhappy all the time. Is anything the matter?" Dewey didn't know what to say because he always looked like he had lost his best friend, no matter what. My way of getting my mind off of it all was to attend what I called a concert, records playing Tchaikovsky's Piano Concerto in B Flat Minor.

Our dispatch fellow heaved a sigh of relief, as he was able to bring us eleven bags of mail. For me the bully beef even tasted better after receiving my letters from Georgie. Everyone shared Christmas packages in February! Some gave me candy or gum or wanted me to try some of their good pipe tobacco, which they knew would take that lump out of my throat that the English brand produced every time I tried to smoke it.

[Letter from Georgie]

Dear Norman, you're one ambulance driver that can't be worried about the front. Remember you've got a date for next year. Am beginning to count on it so don't stand me up. After they train you and you begin to be of great value in your work, they might not want to let you go next year. Then what? Oh, well, it isn't next year yet. A lot will be happening before then. I will have received hundreds of letters and lots of pictures and I'll just forget about the time. Nothing ever works out perfectly to plan but it is nice to plan anyway.

With Georgie hinting that I might stay overseas longer I thought, "Maybe I will stay a while longer so I can go to Italy for the next stretch. Who knows what I will do?"

Now I was writing to my love hinting that I could use a pair of all-purpose leather gloves, a waterproof pouch for my Geneva cards, and one or two combs, because I was tired of cutting my hair short for lack of a comb.

To come down from my daydreaming I started hauling rocks and gravel for our main compound so that it would be fit to walk on. I hadn't worked so hard in a long time. All this was getting me in shape for what was to come. Work was stepping up its pace so much that I didn't have time to tend the orchids I had been carrying in my ambulance.

Khongkhang, Palel, Tamu

We spent four weeks in Imphal and left February 7, 1944, with tank escort and got up to Khongkhang, which had just been bombarded by Japanese artillery. One night three Grant tanks brought back 110 men crammed in like sardines. They reminded us we were awaiting orders from the brigadier to move farther forward.

The Burmese evacuated through this area when the Japanese came. Many died and they have a place called "skull corner" where seven skulls were nailed on a board. A sergeant who had been traveling all over India looking for his unit stopped by. He had been working in Bengal in the famine area and could tell horror stories of what he had seen—starving people dying everywhere.

An Indian soldier was very sick and expected to die. As there was a latrine hole that needed to be filled in, they waited until the Indian died and disposed of his body in the latrine so they wouldn't have to dig a grave. Wartime was rearing its head and wiping out the usual protocol.

While the British were at the front facing the Japanese attacks, Albert Hill, DeWitt Morrill, Louis Kornbrodt, and I got up a rat brigade one night. With our lantern and clubs we managed to kill two, but that didn't scare all the others from climbing all over our mosquito nets after we went to bed. One ate the leather lining out of my felt Gurkha hat—

probably in a search for salt. I vented my anger in frustration, but it was short lived as I suddenly heard someone whistling "What a Friend I Have in Jesus." I couldn't believe my ears. Looking up I saw an Indian who began singing it in his own language. Later I learned that he was a Christian and had gone to school at a Baptist mission. I rarely heard anyone singing "The Road to Mandalay" because we will probably never get there.

That night I hardly slept because an Indian soldier, probably suffering with cerebral malaria, crawled into my ambulance going into all kinds of contortions and moaning terribly. He was shaking like a leaf on an aspen tree. I couldn't just kick him out, so I gave him some blankets and gave him a stretcher to lie on. There wasn't anything I could do for him but keep him warm. Come morning I turned him over to the medical officer and then began my day of hauling casualties, all seriously wounded. Once I got three at the same time: one with a battered hand, one with a neck wound, and the third with a piece of shrapnel in his side. Of the three, the one who had the least serious injury did the most hollering. He cried like a baby and kept repeating that he was going to die. It took two shots of morphine to quiet him.

The one with shrapnel in his side was quiet even though he was bleeding to death internally. We gave him morphine, and the medical officer said he wouldn't last until we could get him to a Main Dressing Station. I'd always heard that bleeding to death was painless and now I was convinced. It was touching the way he fumbled in his pocket and produced a wristwatch. It was new and looked as if it had never been worn. He admired it for a while, then slipped it on. He would at least have the pleasure of dying with it on his wrist.

Since I was not in command but simply carrying out orders from our AFS officers, I did not always see the big picture. Joseph Desloge, Jr. agreed that it was difficult to know what the military leaders had in mind. We were never let in on the battle plans. Our duty was to take orders, to go wherever a stretcher and an ambulance were needed. Desloge remarked, "The wounded were supposed to be handled according to a certain plan, doubtlessly conceived by someone who had probably never been in battle, and to which few of us ever strictly adhered." As with any well-laid plans, wartime skews the rules.

Generally, the AFS Ambulance Corps Medical Officer received the wounded by stretcher-bearers to the ambulance or dugout near Headquarters. They were given what assistance a single, harried medical officer and his orderlies could supply. Then they were taken by ambulance to an Advanced Dressing Station where better treatment might be administered, then sent on to a Main Dressing Station which was about twelve or so miles from the front. Here special treatment could be offered until a motor ambulance convoy transported them to a casualty clearing station and from there to a hospital.

On February 9 I made a trip to Palel to get some tents for the colonel of the casualty clearing station and rode back with W. T. Smith. He had a load of patients, all lying down, a rough, slow trip. Unluckily I lost ten tent poles on the way, but I now had thirty-three rounds of .303 cartridges, wishfully thinking I could have gone hunting in the jungle!

The airstrip at Palel on the Tamu Road was vital to the defense of the Imphal area. It received half the supplies brought in to support the large garrison. Whiteside, who had recruited me for AFS service, went up to take pictures of AFS work on the Tamu Road. An Indian driver had gone over the khud in his truck, which rolled over several times. We had a call to pick him up and bring him to the hospital to give him first aid and then send him for X-rays and a more thorough examination. Some ambulances that went over the khud were not recoverable, while some were eventually hauled back up. One fellow said he would face the bombardment of battle rather than slide into the khud where you might roll hundreds of feet without being noticed for a very long time—a concern reminiscent of the colonel who first assessed this situation.

WARTIME JOKE

Question: Ah my good man, and what were you before you entered the service?

Answer: Happy.

Question: And what would you like to be more than anything else?

Answer: An ex-serviceman.

[From My Diary]

As I was coming back last night after ten hours behind the wheel, I was tired, sleepy, dusty and all the while I drove over the road I was thinking of it being Saturday night and what I had done before on my Saturday nights. I tried to think about pleasant things. It worked to some extent but that last eleven miles seemed like an eternity. One of the fellows who was still up reading gave me a shot of hospital rum which soothed me to sleep in a hurry. Maybe that is why the next morning the song "I'm Getting Tired So I Can Sleep" was running through my mind.

Being so close to death as we were, the other fellows were all busy making out their wills while I sat looking at Georgie's picture in my billfold. If looking at a picture would wear it out, then it would have been worn out long ago. I wasn't making out a will because everything that I owned was right in my ambulance. My only concern was getting out alive.

After taking another load of patients, I spent the afternoon reading and realized that I needed glasses. When I joined AFS, I was never put through a very extensive physical exam other than getting a blood test to determine my blood type. So now I had been resting my eyes outside watching the bamboo leaves fluttering in the breeze. They were like the aspen in that it takes the minimum of a breeze to make them quiver. I really thought the bamboo leaves were prettier and that they provided a quick way of building a very comfortable little shack in a surprisingly short time. Sitting in the shade of this tree I got away from the flies. I heard the sounds of the four chickens that were not consumed in the officer's mess when there were officers in the hospital. They woke us up every morning and amused us by their fighting during the day.

I carried this picture of Georgie
in my billfold.

Nanda, one of our Indian cooks, went wild because the hen laid an egg. "After she lays about eight more," he thought, "she will begin to set." At least he had something to look forward to. Kanhai Ram, our new cook and mess boy, was the most jolly, happy, energetic Indian I had ever seen. If he couldn't make you understand his Urdu, then he acted it out. I had been teaching him to print his name but he had trouble with curved letters so he was still learning to make R's and K's. He got writer's cramp every minute or two and had to stop and shake his hand.

He told us that he was going home for two months and then get married and have a cheko (a child) so the cheko could take care of him when he got old. I didn't know how he could do all of this in two months, but he was optimistic.

[Letter to Georgie]

Received letters and began thinking of the seasons of the year and realized how much I miss them. A Washington spring with all the daffodils, rhododendrons, bluebells, and violets. All winter they have waited for the warmth of the spring sun to awaken them. Oh, yes, and the camellias. I had almost forgotten about them. Then summer with blackberries, strawberries, and huckleberries. Pie time. Usually when I think of pies I think of the good blackberry pie your sister Sarah made when I was in Chehalis. Then autumn with its Indian summer days. I always liked those clear, still days, when it would be almost too cool in the shade and almost too warm in the sun. Late fall brings the fine light misty rain. It is fun to be out in that kind of a rain because of the long time that you can stay out in it without becoming wet. When winter finally comes with its dreary days, you know that all the rainy days will be forgotten when the beautiful days of spring arrive. The rain in winter doesn't really seem so bad when you realize that you have to have it in order to have the flowers and beauty of spring. Seasons! How I long for them. I am always going to live where I can see the seasons of the year come and go.

[Letter from Georgie]

Dear Norman: here's a part of a song I have been singing lately:

> *No love, no nothin'*
> *until my baby comes home.*
> *No sir, no nothin'*
> *as along as my baby must roam.*
> *I promised him I'd wait for him*
> *that's a promise I'll keep.*
> *I'm lonesome that's sure*
> *but what I said still goes.*

You must be good at sending your thoughts because I certainly can't stop thinking of you. You're getting to be too important in my life. No sense in upsetting my equilibrium when you're so far away but there you are—all the time. Guess you'll just HAVE to come back right as soon as that year is up because I certainly wouldn't want to put off any longer all the things that we haven't done and the places we haven't seen. Just think of the time we have to catch up on.

To keep you posted on what is going on here—I've just seen the movie *Best Foot Forward* with Harry James and Lucille Ball. Just heard Fred Waring and his Pennsylvanians. Here's what Kate Smith says, "If you don't write, you're wrong!" I love to hear Jimmy Dorsey play "I'll be seeing you in my dreams" on his trombone. A little more upscale is Ferdie Grofe's *Grand Canyon Suite*. I listen to all the Saturday afternoon opera broadcasts on the radio, sometimes to the consternation of my sister. Even my Mom admits that she doesn't like Wagner's music. But I love opera. It brings it all together, the voice, the scenery, and the acting. Even if I can't see all of it on radio, I can imagine.

You know, the other day I was biking to my voice lesson and was joined by another biker, a young boy in Chehalis Junior High, whom I had often met on other biking trips. He said, "I suppose you're in senior high as I haven't seen you at school." Well, I hope that's not the impression you got when you first saw me, that I was some high school kid. I am really trying to act a little more poised and dignified but it's so much fun to wear sporty clothes and bike around. I never want to be too dead to bike or skate. I never want to think of the day when I have to stop dashing around.

Here I was nearing the heat of battle, and Georgie was home biking, taking voice lessons, learning all the popular songs, and, of course, lending me moral support with her telling me how often she thought of me.

Now I was involved with nine British Other Ranks in my ambulance headed for the hospital on bad road, a trip of twelve hours including a two-hour delay at Khongkhang and three hours waiting for a tank convoy, including fourteen General Grant tanks and some Bren gun carriers. Then I had to make up my bed from the pile of blankets and gear I had to toss out of my ambulance so that I could make the trip. I calmed down some after a shower with the Cashmere Bouquet soap my sister sent me.

Had another run for eighteen hours and was so tired I couldn't sleep until 2 a.m., so I started thinking about Georgie and wrote:

[Letter to Georgie]

I feel like crying tonight. I hate to say this but I think I have tossed away to the four winds 1½ years of my life and perhaps 1½ years of yours. I wish I knew. Your last letter came with that special valentine prepared on onionskin paper and was sealed with a real live lipstick print. I could even detect a faint scent and wondered what flavor it was, Max Factor, Richard Hudnut or Coty?

So your brother Norman is disappointed in not getting to go overseas? My own brother Shirley has probably left for overseas by this time. The new draft situation will take all my civilian friends so there will be no one left for me to visit when I get home. Some of our AFS men who went home after the end of their enlistment were reclassified under the draft and were sent back overseas. I would rather stay here until the war is over than to be sent back.

I am thinking about you, as you would look after an invigorating bike ride, in a big soft chair in front of your fireplace. Your hair has been blown by the wind and your eyes sparkle as they always do. Your cheeks are rosy. I don't know what from but they are bordering on bright red. Maybe you eat a lot of carrots but I think the rosiness is from the cool air of the outside or the heat from the fireplace you are looking into. Your clothes are comfortable. You don't look like you just stepped out of Bon Marché and neither do you look like you were dressed in clothes shown in Vogue magazine. You are very sensibly dressed. Last, but most important of all, you are relaxed. There is the slight trace of a smile on your lips as you look into the fireplace. You are reminiscing. Call it day-dreaming if you like. You are happy. That is the way I would like to see you, always happy! Are you happy? I hope so.

I must have a green thumb or something because I like plant life and especially the rare specimens. One of the captains and another British fellow have collected orchids and plan to sell them for $50 each since they are a light blue variety that are found in no other place in the world. As you know, orchids only bloom once a year. What a shame! Wouldn't it be grand to have a dozen plants all your own in a greenhouse? Then when you wanted a flower for a new gown you could just call up the caretaker and tell him you wanted one. Twelve large plants would give you orchids almost the year round. A wonderful thought.

I hate these jungle nights. They are so dark and mysterious. I hear all kinds of noises and can never tell what might be within "spittin'" distance of me. When I think about it I feel just a touch of fear. I'm not afraid of darkness, just what's in it. I can hear baboons hollering now. For the first few days up here I had an unholy fear of the road, not only the terrible driving conditions but also what might be lurking in the jungle as I drive. The fear has almost worn off now. I hope it doesn't return.

By the way, tell your sister Grace that it is a sin to have only one child. I think every wife should have at least three. Having brothers and sisters helps a child to develop character and personality.

As I sit writing this letter, one of the little Indians who does the camp work is watching me and he wants to see his name, Sher Mohd, in writing. Now Tohid wants to write his name. Now Alidad wants to write his. Surju Dom says he wants to be my bearer and he wants me to take him to America when I go.

I just gave my little lamp a shake and I can hear nothing swishing back and forth, which means I am burning wick only and am without oil so it is time to stop writing.

[From My Diary]

I had a corker of an argument with Dan Moor who seems to be the object of an over-doting mother. Although he was engaged, I wondered how he could find a girl he would really like. She would have to be much like his mother in character. He heartily disagreed with me. I kept on saying that his mother was so close to him that she might be reluctant to let him go and would probably do some unpredictable things to get her own way and remain the only object of his affection. He was furious at this and retorted that his mother was self-sacrificing and would do anything in this world to make him happy. I stuck to my guns that human behavior is unpredictable. No one can tell what a person is going to do, even if they have lived together 35 years. Neither one of us won the argument. I told him to let me know how his life turned out. I never found out!

[Letter from Georgie]

Dear Norman: My favorite tune for the moment is "My Ideal." Don't know why because I don't believe in an "ideal" man. Nice to think about, but never the attainable. You might as well be the ideal man—at least at this moment you are the most unattainable person I know.

Do you know how men in civilian clothes are regarded here? They are eyed by every draftee. Very conspicuous—that's what every fellow feels now if he isn't in uniform. I keep telling myself that you were right and that you must do your part but I don't believe myself tonight.

[Letter to Georgie]

You asked about Indian life here. The seasons have a lot to do with the work that people do. The men plow and plant rice and harvest it but not in the dry season. For now, they dress in bright colored loincloths and lead a life of leisure. The children don't seem to work now either. The women do all the wood chopping and other work. Think I'll get a woman to wait on me and take life easy. No, on second thought I don't think I could stand it.

I read whatever is available these days. I recently completed *A Tree Grows in Brooklyn, Congo Song*, and *Nana*. The *Reader's Digest* hasn't come yet. If you see spots on this letter where ink won't take, it is mosquito cream coming from my hands. As soon as the sun goes down, I have to use it even though it makes me twice as warm. Worse than that, it makes my clothes get dirty so much more quickly. And how I hate to dhobi (wash) my clothes.

On March 7, 1944, I took eight patients that were to be evacuated over to the airstrip. Stopped on the way back at what we called the San Luis Moreh Bridge and took a swim to lessen the terrible heat. Overhead there was air activity—bombers pulling gliders. Hill and Morrill picked up a Canadian that had bailed out of one of the gliders. He had sprained his ankle and had been wandering in the jungle for twenty-four hours, lost. Now he was in our hospital. Just heard there are five thousand British glider troops in Mandalay. All ambulances are in use.

REVERIE

Have been feeling terrible for the last few days—no appetite and little sleep. The moon is visible. Many times over the years the moon has seemed to upset me inside. But now that I have Georgie, the full moon has special meaning for me. If I could only be near Georgie! I want her so much for the comfort I would get out of just talking and being with her. I surely must be deeply in love with her or is there such a thing as love? I know I love Georgie.

Hope she hasn't changed her mind about me by the time I get back. I wonder if she will notice any change in me. I don't think an open-minded person ever stops growing and changing. Wouldn't it be a dull world if people remained the same all the time? I am aware that Georgie has changed. I can tell it in her letters. I'm not complaining a bit. I'm very pleased. She is now telling me in her letters what I wanted to know last July when she seemed to be more uncertain about us.

I wonder how I could ever marry her when I feel I have so little and she has so much. She has a profession and talent and what do I have? But if she wants me and loves me that will make no difference to her, I hope. I want her an awful lot and I am sure she knows it. I am just now beginning to feel how far I am away from her. It will be at least ten months before I'll ever see her. I wonder if I can bear up under it? Time will tell.

I met Jammy, a well-educated little Karen (Burmese), several days ago. He gave me the tip of an elephant's tusk so I let him choose which one of my two pipes he wanted. He picked my favorite, the one that my friend Chet gave me for Christmas, but after what he had given me I couldn't very well refuse him something special or I would lose face, as they say. He had his boys cook us dinner Burmese style—rice, roast chicken and curried chicken. I ate in their style of eating, with my fingers. Jammy said he knew Dr. Gordon Seagrave, the Burma missionary who wrote *Burma Surgeon.*

Encircled by the Japanese

On March 13, 1944, I was on the way back to Tamu where I liked to stop because it's the highest point on the road and it's usually cool enough to sleep well. At 6 p.m. a Japanese plane flew right over our camp. I was told by an MP that twenty more Federals (semis) were coming down the road and that I might as well stay all night because I probably wouldn't get through anyway.

Now I was stuck at Damphal. I ran into hundreds of mules and horses going away from the front and two large convoys going back. I ran into a mule and an Indian tonight, but only caused the Indian to suffer a scraped arm. It was a miracle that I hadn't been in a more serious accident in such conditions.

Everyone was breaking camp and moving except us. It makes an ambulance driver a little squeamish to be left behind in the fray, but our responsibility was to carry the wounded left at the front, retreat or no retreat. It was a nightmare of transports and troops pulling out from our area.

The final day came and I had a run back to the hospital. On the way back, I fought traffic for forty miles—mules, men, guns and trucks—coming in an endless stream. I finally arrived about dark to find just a skeleton of a force, eight of us plus a small medical unit with about thirty Indian Other Ranks with guns in the box (an area enclosed with barbed wire). We all got together for a conference. We agreed that two men should be on guard all night, working in shifts. The night was sticky and pitch black. It was too quiet. Everyone was jumpy and on edge. We didn't know what to expect as we were not in the most forward position and there were Japanese almost within hearing distance. We were encircled or cut off from Imphal. I heard that sixteen ambulances were cut off up Liddim way.

In wartime, expediency is the way of life. On these one-way roads if a vehicle stalled, it was just pushed over the khud to let the retreating troops get by. The shells were getting closer and closer. Buck Clay, Russ Knuepfer, Bob Wilson, and I played bridge at night to try and forget that the Japanese might be here any minute. I crawled down into the deepest dugout I could find and planned to stay there until my turn came for guard duty. I can honestly say that I was really afraid that night. It was awful and I will never forget it.

Some Indians were fighting for the Japanese—they were considered to be traitors. How could I tell a traitor Indian from one that wasn't? I would have had to wait until he started shooting—then it would have been too late. How I wished I had been back in Calcutta!

There were flashes on two sides of us now. I hoped they wouldn't get any closer. What's more, I got bit by an anopheles mosquito. I was sure because I saw his tail end sticking straight up in the air. My hope was that it wasn't THE one in a million that carries malaria.

On March 19, 1944, I got back from the hospital after being on the road over twelve hours and going about a hundred miles. The dust, which was three inches thick, splashed like water when we ran through it. Morrill made a pickup of three Indians that had gone over the khud. I went up to the front with Bragg and picked up five tank casualties. Some were very serious cases. We were supposed to have lost one to every one the Japs lost.

I saw the Grant tank that got knocked out. Three hits put it out of commission although it did limp back to camp. These Tommies were tough. When they got hit about all they said was, "The bastards got me," or "I've 'ad it." They didn't cry or make nearly as much fuss as the Indians did. After all, the British were the ones with the power and status. They had to show that they were fearless leaders. At least this was my take on it all. The colonel told us to expect a shelling by Jap artillery as they had moved within range.

On March 23, 1944, I got sick. Nothing serious, just a cold in my chest. Thought I had malaria for a while because I had a temperature and my back and head ached terribly. I had a blood slide taken and it proved negative. I remain a virgin. Anyone who hasn't had malaria is so honored!

I attended a service the chaplain held before supper. I expect the service was just preparing us, putting our souls at ease. There were quite a number of us there, and we sang two hymns and read some passages from the Bible. Too solemn for my taste.

Friendly Fire

You can imagine the problems with Indian guards. Instead of getting into a shadow where they couldn't be seen and yet could see everything, they stood out in the moonlight and sang, telling their enemy exactly where they were. Well, one night we had fireworks which woke us up in time to scramble around and crawl under our ambulances. I was so scared my teeth chattered. We thought we really had "had it." When we all came up for air, we learned the awful truth. The barrage was caused by an Indian who was on guard. He heard something and started shooting and then everyone else in the whole box started, too. Result, two killed and two wounded. There were no Japs around, so I guess they just started shooting at one another, not knowing whom they were shooting at.

Funny what a person does to escape from thoughts of danger. Just to take my mind off the gruesome reality, I started fantasizing a method of getting out of washing clothes. Start out with two shirts and two pairs of trousers. Wear the first outfit until it is slightly soiled. Then put on the second and wear it until it is dirtier than the first. Then put on the first outfit, and you feel as if your clothes are clean. Then wear them until they are more soiled than the second pair. Well, you can take it from there. It can go on, ad infinitum.

The night wore through only to bring a shelling about 6:30 a.m. One lit close to me, too close for comfort. An Indian eight feet from me was killed, but I only had dust and rocks showered over me. By the time the next one landed, I was on my belly next to the bank in a foot of powdery dust. Although the troops did suffer quite a few casualties, not one of our AFS men was hurt, and at least half of our number was right there watching the battle.

After the road had been cleared and we had picked up the casualties, we moved on. I took my load of patients in and came right back to be on hand in case any more got shot up. We waited on the road at Mile 66 for a company to retreat. We were supposed to pick up their casualties if they had to fight their way out. They had no fight, so we moved down to Mile 59 and stayed for the night.

> Want to hear something strange? There are some wild fowl that have feathers growing backwards. I am told that it is nature's protection for them against snakes. The snakes just couldn't swallow them. Strange thing, nature. Strange also are the things a person thinks about when death may be closing in.

[Letter to Georgie]

> I have been thinking how I will act and how I should act upon returning and seeing you. I wonder whether I'll timidly knock on your door without you knowing I'm anywhere near or whether I'll call you on the telephone first. Then what should I do when I really see you? Wonder if I'll say, "How do you do?" and be very calm and act as if I'd seen you just yesterday or grab you in my arms and kiss you, disregarding people and places. I'm sure I don't know now and only time will tell just what I will do. It will be hard not knowing just what to do.

> The other day one fellow asked how far it was between two towns on an ambulance run and the reply was—2,641 turns or about an hour and a half. I'm building up strong, arm muscles from turning the steering wheel. You need not be alarmed because I will take that into consideration when I hold you in my arms when I see you.

> I have picked up some orchids from the jungle. They are of a small type and should be in bloom in a day or two. Will send you some, pressed.

FOXHOLES

I decided it was time to dig a foxhole. I had to dig out six cubic feet more dirt than an average-sized man, but no matter. I needed it immediately. The HEs (high explosives) came whistling over our heads, and I got just as close to the bottom of that hole as I could. It is a funny thing but you can ask any number of people how they got into their hole when it was necessary and none of them can remember. They don't know whether they fell in, crawled on their hands and knees, or stood on the edge and jumped in. Here is one time where it doesn't matter how you do it, just as long as you do it. Needless to say, every night we counted noses to see that everyone was accounted for.

We dug a foxhole some time back that was called "Little Corregidor." It was dug deep and had long tunnels running into both ends. It accommodated three of us for sleeping and about ten otherwise. We had two or three feet of dirt and timbers on top of it. It was really a good thing we dug it because the tent we were sleeping in, which was about six feet from it, got 126 shrapnel holes in it one night while we were in where it was safe, although suffocating.

Recuperation at Imphal Headquarters

It is March 25, 1944, and I had been feeling ill. I was expected to stay at Headquarters to recuperate, but things were really happening and I felt as though I was going to miss something. One of the guys wondered if he would hold up physically and mentally until his year was up. I sometimes wondered that, too. Then again, I felt like Rhett Butler and convinced myself that I didn't really give a damn.

I saw our canteen, El Malaria, for the first time. The bar was made from split bamboo. There were green curtains at the windows and pictures on the walls. The floor was covered with woven bamboo matting. We had a radio and a phonograph with a few records—almost like civilization again.

Many jungle flowers were blooming as spring was in the air. Just two weeks before, all the teak trees were shedding their large leaves and the whole jungle looked bare and naked. Now the teaks were bursting forth with beautiful new, red-tipped green leaves.

Here at Headquarters I had time to drool over the pictures of delicious-looking food in an old magazine. I would have paid a chip (rupee) apiece for nice crisp carrots. "Must stop this. I'm just making it harder for myself," was my way of getting back to reality.

A Jap plane, a two-motored job, flew over twice dropping leaflets for the Indians in the area, trying to get them over to their side. Our ack-ack sent up a barrage but didn't wipe it out. It is said that the Gurkhas behead almost every Jap they catch. Guess that if you have to kill in battle, it doesn't really matter how you do it. Our road was still open, but we had to have an armed guard when we made a trip. Thirty Japs were killed on the road at Sibong.

F. Wilson Smith passed by shortly after and was afraid to stop and scrounge for souvenirs for fear that more would be nearby, waiting for a chance to carry off the dead. Yes, I got close to the Japs as well. I almost had a skull with gold teeth in it but I couldn't stand the stench. It was repulsive. If I had been there two or three days later the buzzards and jackals would have made a clean job of it all. (As I now consider this early diary entry, I realize how startling this must seem to a reader who has never known war close up. I consider myself to be quite sensitive to those around me and here I was considering bringing from the battlefield a skull of one of the enemy. Now I am glad that I couldn't quite bring myself to do it.)

[From My Diary]

Just had a choice story from one of the fellows who had been on sick leave, recuperating in a city that I could not name in my letters because of security. Two more of our fellows were there also. One was getting some dental work done and the other was having a cyst removed from his cheek. The two had been inseparable. Where one went the other went. They were starting to be called Mr. and Mrs. Both are referred to as J.R. Confusing, eh? At any rate, they were in this hotel and the conversation went like this. It was 2:00 a.m.

"J.R."

"Yes, J.R., what do you want?"

"Come over here."

J.R. crawled out from under his mosquito netting and went over to the other J.R.'s bed. "Feel my head, I think I have a temperature."

"Yes, J.R. I think you do have a temperature. Could I get you a glass of water?"

"Yes, please—thank you."

"Do you think I'd better call a doctor, J.R.?"

"Yes, maybe you'd better."

Well, the J.R. that didn't have the temperature called the hospital and asked for an ambulance. As soon as the ambulance stopped at the hotel, an orderly got out and went up to the hotel room to "collect" the J.R. who was the patient. The J.R. who had a temperature slowly dressed himself and walked down to the waiting ambulance!

Everyone who knew about this was madder than "wet hens," as they say. I think that was one of the reasons the major made the blanket statement and called us all "characters," with a capital "C." I was thinking that we would all have much to tell when we got back. I even predicted that some would probably write books. (Well, I never thought I would be one of them but here I am telling my side of the story.)

By March 30 I came back to my unit with a fever and headache. We had been completely surrounded and cut off in places and only a handful of us were left in this dangerous position: Fenn, Gilliam, Dignam, Ruppert, Waterbury, Horton, Wilhelm, and R. B. Whiteside, and myself. Whiteside reported:

Mayfield loaded up in the gray afternoon with the mortars whistling over and set off. All ambulances that leave today are not to return. The Royal Artillery below us, who defended our outer perimeter, rolled out at 1300 hours. The box (where we are holed up) is haunted now. We are among the last left except for the fighting troops, and we aren't even sure there are any of those. The Colonel ordered us to establish our own listening post this evening but under absolutely no circumstances to fire a shot. We drew straws to determine the sequence of the guard and then went to bed fully clothed. Word finally came that we are to evacuate at 0600 hours tomorrow morning, with the exception of Waterbury and Wilhelm who were assigned to the 38 Gurkhas, who would fight the rearguard.

That night, without question and by mutual admission, was the worst of our lives. It was filled with the noises of the forest, which gradually became indistinguishable from the noises a Jap patrol might make. Toward the end of my guard, there was the noise of something trampling the bamboo just below us by the creek. It was a cloudy night and impossible to see more than a few feet, which may have been just as well. Silence for a few minutes, except for the woods noises, and then the sound again. More silence, and the sound again. A mortar shell passed over. I woke Kunkel, told him what was happening, and then went to get Gilliam and his Tommy gun up. Gilliam and I sat for 15 long minutes and heard nothing more. I crept to Kunkel's dugout to find that he had heard nothing either. When Gilliam woke the camp at about 0440 hours, he said he finally had heard the sounds, as though someone were moving forward through the brush and then stopping to listen. A patrol was probably there. Whether it was our own or a Jap patrol we'll never know.

[From My Diary]

It's raining now and that may hinder our retreat. Slept in a dugout last night with Peter Stewart and Charlie Horton. We may have to walk 75 miles through the jungle yet. I have a compass so maybe I'll be able to find my way out if worst comes to worst.

The British opened up the basha (storage hut) where the dead soldiers' personal belongings were kept. They said that if there was anything that anybody wanted to come and get it. Whiteside scrounged a Remington portable. Everyone is scrounging now. What we can't take with us, we will burn before retreating. I would be rich if I could have one tenth of the equipment and war material that is being destroyed.

Six Jap planes flew over early this morning bombing our gun positions. Three nights ago when I wasn't here the barrage put sixteen holes through the tent I had been sleeping in. I don't have a gun yet but everyone else does. I plan on getting a Tommy submachine gun today. I can't see being unarmed in this jungle. The Japanese Indian fifth column is everywhere.

Had a letter from Georgie today and read it while the shells were bursting all around us. Charlie Horton cooked what may be my last dinner a few minutes ago. It was called "swim" which is made from scrounged peas, potatoes, and a can of salmon. Really good!

Slept next to a Jap last night. He was an imperial guard, beautiful specimen of manhood, 6 feet tall and weighing at least 185 pounds. He was wounded in three places and was in my ambulance where I also slept. Heard the road was cut at Kohima and 2,500 men were lost. Hurricanes from the RAF were still buzzing over our heads so I guess we were not altogether forgotten.

OPERATING IN THE FIELD

For the last two hours I have been assisting in a major abdominal operation. The Tommy had run into a minefield and a piece of shrapnel entered his abdomen about even with his navel. I watched the major pull out all of the small intestines looking for punctures. The patient had internal hemorrhages and his abdominal cavity was full of blood and it ran all over the floor. The doctor then looked over the entire length of his intestines and found about fourteen holes and expertly sewed them up, tying knots in the cat gut with one hand. After he had gone over the entire length twice to make sure, he pushed the intestines back in and sewed him up. It all took about an hour and a half. I didn't get sick or anything but it was intolerably hot wearing a mask and surgeon's apron and I left promptly.

It was a beautiful morning at 42 Traffic Control Point. We were about four thousand feet above sea level so it was nice and cool. The whole place was in the center of a big cloud formation with wonderful fog reminding me of Seattle. We had one chance. If the Japs didn't move in by ground we were told, "WE WILL GET OUT!"

It was during this precarious situation that I hunkered down in my foxhole and having no other outlet, I wrote a letter to my love. But I did not write it on my usual writing paper but wrote it directly into my diary because I seriously thought I would never get out to mail it. Here is the letter.

[Letter to Georgie]

It is March 31, 1944. I am writing you what might be my last letter, Georgie. The Jap artillery is laying them down all around us now. Any one of them might have my name on it. But thank God it hasn't so far. Went to 42 Traffic Control Point yesterday with medical supplies and was sniped at most of the way. Came back here to Moreh where shells have been whining over our heads every minute. Everyone has moved out but four ambulances and I am one of them. We will bring up the rear guard with the retreating infantry, carrying their casualties. We have been promised air support till noon tomorrow by the Royal Air Force.

As I lie in this foxhole, darling, I think of you and my thoughts are very vague. I haven't lived a full life like some people. There are a lot of things I haven't done and there are a lot of things I yet want to do. The one main one is to see my darling again.

We might have been made for each other. If we had, think of what we both would have missed if I don't get out of here.

It is hotter than Hades in this foxhole of mine. The sweat is running off from me in streams. My body is bathed in it. Darling, I love you and only you and I would forsake all others for you. If I am the lucky one and finally marry you, all my dreams in India and Burma will have been fulfilled. I can't write much more, my sweetest darling in all the whole, wide world. I'm choking. I want to cry. Everyone is a baby at heart I guess but they are not atheists. God, may I be spared so I can go back to my dear Georgie. She is the one and only one for me. Spare me, I pray. I love you Georgie darling. I love you. I love you. I love you.

Near noon the road was sufficiently clear to send traffic through. We had been saved. Once more we were on ambulance duty. I brought in a wounded artilleryman. Three supply trucks, Mayfield, Beeber and Devine, went through. As they passed under the Japanese positions, three tanks laid down a barrage of 75-mm and .50-caliber shells to discourage sniping. This move gave them something of a turn, as they had not been told the barrage was to be fired over them. Soon after they departed, I brought down three more casualties.

To quote further from Rock's *History of the AFS*:

April 1: Horton brewed some tea, which sufficed for breakfast. We could hear mortars where the road led out of the box. 0600 hours finally came, and our vehicles moved off, joining the convoy that had already begun. We drove and halted while the traffic straightened itself out, listening for the first hiss of a mortar. About ¾ of a mile out there was a long halt and the mortars found us. The first landed a few feet over the khud and directly opposite my ambulance. A piece of shrapnel bounced off my helmet. A few more landed among us, but they were small and the casualties were few. The convoy finally moved off again and we slouched in our vehicles trying to joke. Ruppert coolly loaded a bloody Tommy onto a stretcher and into his ambulance under fire. Horton took several more. A few yards past the shelling we picked up an officer who, in leading his marching infantry, had been struck by a car. We propped him in the jeep.

The place where the marching troops were to meet the convoy for transport was a few miles out of the box. Fenn was in charge of last guard casualties, so we had to wait there until the troops were loaded and clear. The mortars found us again, but were small and inaccurate. While we waited, Moreh behind us went up in a tremendous billow of smoke. It was raining, and the troops slogged up the long hill to the waiting trucks, glancing back over their shoulders at the smoking valley. Two RAF planes hung lazily over us, momentarily stopping the mortars, but they commenced again when the planes had gone and continued until we left.

As I have mentioned before, I did not know the big picture. We drove our ambulances where we were sent. We put blinders on and drove like hell over ruts and through mud and even in blackout conditions. It was the British Information Service pamphlets I read many years later, that provided the overall picture. Here I will quote excerpts from the pamphlet, "Victory in Burma."

In 1943, Field Marshal Wavell employed the principle that inspired the Commando raids on German-held Europe from 1940-43—the principle of constantly harassing the enemy while building up strength for the decisive assault. He set a comparatively unknown officer, Brigadier Wingate, the task of organizing and training a force to act on Sherman's classic proposition: "The enemy's rear is there to play hell with."

Wingate's reconnaissance in force carried out by his raiders in Burma caught the imagination of the whole world. His "Chindits," named for a fabulous Burmese animal, were mainly troops from the British Isles, but they included Gurkhas—those magnificent soldiers from the independent state of Nepal—and men of the Burma Rifles. Their marauding columns kept 10,000 square miles of the enemy's rear areas in a constant state of confusion, terror and disrupted communications for the better part of six months.

When they returned, after frightful privations and heavy casualties, Wingate's Raiders had done much more than inflict a serious military blow to the Japanese strategy. They had proved that the ordinary Tommy could beat the Japanese at jungle tactics. They had raised the spirit of all the Allied troops in Burma. And they had served notice on the enemy that the period of defensive build-up was over. They put the writing of doom on the wall for the Japanese in Burma.

The Japanese Plan
1. To hold Stilwell's Chinese-U.S. forces in the northeast with the Japanese divisions they already had there.
2. To stage an offensive, with two divisions and supporting troops, in Arakan; and to capture Chittagong, India's fifth biggest port and a vital air supply base.
3. To isolate and destroy the British 17th Division at Tiddim and wipe out the forward components of the 14th Army.
4. To push across the mountains in strength, take Imphal, the 14th's main base, and disperse or annihilate the Army.
5. To capture Kohima, and cut the Bengal-Assam railway running along the valley north of it, which formed General Stilwell's principal line of communications, thus isolating from their source of supplies not only the Allied troops already operating in North East Burma but also the Chinese divisions in Yunnan.

In other words, the Japanese ultimate objective was nothing less than the invasion of India. They had enough army in Burma to commit thirty thousand veteran troops to the Arakan operation and eighty thousand more to the main Tiddim-Imphal-Kohima operations.

The British 17th Division, fighting their way north from Tiddim with magnificent tenacity, inflicted heavy casualties on the enemy. Imphal was encircled, almost surrounded for two-and-one-half months. But two entire divisions were flown in to reinforce the defense and with steady air supply, its defenders held the Japs at bay. Komima was completely surrounded for eighteen days and none of those who fought in the "box"—the Royal West Kents, some base troops, the sick and wounded from the hospital—would thank the historian who minimized the critical character of their predicament. The garrison, fighting day and night under terrific pressure, had this great satisfaction: they realized that if the Japanese had simply bypassed the embattled town they could have done in forty-eight hours what its capture was a mere preliminary to—they could have cut the railroad. But the Japanese in their methodical plan to take Kohima first ignored the final objective until it could check off the preparatory one.

The Japanese never took Kohima, although they set twenty thousand men to the job. They never got into Imphal. Their losses mounted, their supplies dwindled and the monsoon approached. It was at this point that the Commander of the Japanese 15th Army ordered his crack 33rd Division, recently reinforced, to carry out a last desperate assault on Imphal. The division was wiped out.

The 14th Army swept the now exhausted enemy southwards. And in the area of Palel-Tamu-Uhkrul there was consummated such a killing of Japanese as had not been known in history. Of the eighty thousand picked troops who had started out so bravely, and on so skillful a plan, to invade India, over fifty thousand were counted corpses. The remainder, riddled with disease and wounds, emaciated with hunger, attempted to escape southwards in disorganized parties, abandoning their heavy equipment, a prey to revengeful Burmese hillmen and with small chance of ever fighting again.

The 14th Army alone had suffered forty thousand casualties. But when General Slim reached Kalewa, he had beaten the Japanese 15th Army. After this harrowing period in the India/Burma campaign there was still no end to the Japanese trying to hold on wherever they could to snipe at the British.

Picking Flowers

Yes, the nightmare of the "box" was over. I worked on my ambulance in the morning and then cleaned up and went for a walk to pick flowers and let my thoughts stray. I walked down little lanes with flowers on both sides and some trees in blossom. I picked some wild red roses and some white ones. Then I found water hyacinth and lilies. I was standing looking at them when a little Indian boy came by and guessed what I wanted because he waded in the water and picked some for me. Before I got back I had quite a large corsage in my hat. I surely enjoyed the walk because it took me back to more pleasant days back home.

When I was in Seattle living with my friends Lewis and Chet, I would bring home a bouquet of daffodils when they were available, and Lewis would shout loud and long about my wasting money on flowers. I believed that flowers brought a softer touch to an apartment, like women bring to a place. For some reason, women always seemed to be able to make an apartment or house so much more bright and cheery.

We counted noses again. The colonel invited us up to his quarters, a hole in the ground with canvas over it, for a drink as a gesture of friendship and thanks for the work we had done. These British officers could produce the most astounding things. I'd gotten over being dumbfounded by the appearance of luxuries in the most unexpected places.

When we got together to play cards and talk, I was labeled a lot of things because I wore sideburns and a moustache. I was compared to a Mexican cattle rustler in a Wild West movie. I had sworn off gambling but got into another game which resulted in my writing enough IOUs to cover a whole month's pay (about $20). As I put my last chip in the pot I got lucky and won it all back.

On Good Friday, April 7, I rose to greet a dreary, dismal morning. This didn't stop me from working on my ambulance. I wallowed underneath it and finally got the oil filter off after barking some knuckles and no little bit of swearing. After that I had to flush out the engine and then change oil in the transmission. After finishing my lunch ration, I had to dig a hole four feet deep and put a tent over the hole and that is going to be where seven of us sleep. The seven are Charlie Horton, "Mitch" Smith, Bill Brown, Robert Wilson, Sam White, DeWitt Morrill, and I. When I was finished, my hands were blistered, I was sunburned, and my back felt as though it was going to break. I filled so many sandbags yesterday that I saw them in my sleep. After the completion of our quarters, we had a party sharing a bottle of rum, which appeared from nowhere and was enough for one drink apiece. We relaxed sprawling on the sandbags at the entrance, enjoying the beautiful night lighted by the near full moon. Tomorrow we have to dig individual slit trenches. God, what a life! And my contract didn't say anything about this!

We have had bad news. Mail has all but ceased coming. Packages are definitely out of the question now. But after the mail can come through again, it will come by the dozens. I can't face not getting letters from Georgie. Her last letter insisted that even though I say I can't sing, I could learn. Maybe she can teach me to sing one day.

[Letter to Georgie]

Returned from a Catholic service, which had to suffice for a non-denominational one. I really feel let down right now. Maybe later I will find a way to settle all this in my mind. I have always heard that Catholics could confess their sins and then be absolved. Does that mean that they can be absolved of killing in war? I have never had a formal religious upbringing so all I know about it is what I hear other people say. This war doesn't seem to me to go hand-in-hand with religion. Evidently, when war is declared and men have to go into battle to kill, there must be some way to relieve the killer of guilt. But it is difficult for me to see a religious leader sanction war by blessing those who are going into battle to do the killing.

It is near full moon. I always think intensely of you when there is a full moon. I think that I will try to stick to a decision I have made—that is to try to do the big things in my life to coincide with the full moon. I think I'm a moon lover. When you look at the full moon, remember that I am here also looking at that same full moon and dreaming of us.

Charlie Horton and I went to the bazaar where we traded with the Indians and Manipurians. We had done nothing for nearly a week since our supplies were only coming in by air and the road was in Jap hands at Kohima. Had some fudge that Horton made from materials scrounged during the retreat from Moreh. The flies were terrible since thousands of us were living in a well-defended box which provided a breeding ground for dysentery, typhoid, cholera and malaria.

[Letter to Georgie]

I received your letter from one month ago. It took so long to get here that I began wondering if the next letter would announce that you were engaged to someone else. That has happened to others out here. It really knocks the pins out from under the fellows, especially when they get the letters in conditions like we are suffering. Several of us have discussed this and have decided that the girls that have been left behind think that by waiting they are taking a chance on not getting married. Consequently, they jump at the first chance they have because they fear we won't come back at all. We are also aware that in the U.S. there are now more women than there are men. These women think, "The war is going to take, for good, many men. Why pass up a chance to marry now."

Please don't ever write a letter telling me that. Just don't tell me. Let me come back and find out for myself or just stop writing letters completely. OK?

[Letter from Georgie]

Dear Norman: You said not to write you if I wasn't going to wait for you. I say that the men who are losing their girls to other men back home haven't chosen the right ones. A girl would wait for the right man.

Horton and I had a feast on popcorn that we popped in the back of my ambulance over a primus stove. Then we played chess. While I was waiting to make my next chess move I had time to ponder over my leave, which I hope to take in Naini Tal. It is six thousand feet in altitude with tigers, fishing, and boating at the foothills of the Himalayas overlooking Nepal. After the chess game and crawling into my bed, I dreamt about the Japs shooting at us.

We went to see a captain in the British Army who invited us to go out riding with him. I foolishly accepted his invitation not knowing that he delighted in taking out softies on a grueling cross-country ride. Horton and I each had a beautiful horse. We spent more than two hours riding over rice paddy fields. My horse, a beige buckskin, bounced me until I thought my teeth would fall out. We must have covered twelve miles. I literally fell off my horse at the end I was so exhausted, feeling like a man of sixty. We carried some petrol for our ambulances and afterwards went with Don Hill in his pawnee lorry (water truck) to the water point and helped him hand pump 220 gallons of water. Lots more exercise than I had had in a long time.

We were just camp followers, never knowing when we would move on. Morrill and I had gone to an out-of-the-way place far from Sectional Headquarters. We had been talking with a Muslim who said he would go to the U.S.A. after the war to study electrical engineering. We answered an endless amount of questions.

We went from "anything goes" to rigid rules when the top brass was around. Our beloved major read us the riot act from the Bennett Committee rules. It seems we could be fined up to a month's allowance (about $20) and given twenty-eight days field punishment and then sent home if the rules were broken. The field punishment was marching most of the day with full pack with hard work thrown in between times. During this lecture, Bob Wilson was looking at a world atlas and dreaming about going to Africa, South America, and England. I told him I would be content to see Russia, Rio de Janeiro, and Mexico. The more I talked about places to go on leave, the more I found myself changing my mind.

First I wanted to be in Naini Tal, then to Darjeeling where the tea is grown, then in Srinegar where it is beautiful and cool, then to the beach at Puri, and then I wanted to go to Muree, also up in the hill country. Interrupting this daydreaming was a "dog fight," a mustang and a zero. Neither could get the other and soon they disappeared.

Morrill had a chat with the colonel and there was definitely something exciting in store for us very soon. He and I were attached to the 410, who hoped to be on the banks of the Irrawaddi by June 1st, and we were to have gotten jeeps to go on patrols with them.

The Gurkha

The Gurkha is a Nepalese mercenary hired by the British. They are wonderful fighters who don't appear to know the meaning of fear. When one gets an arm or a leg shot off, he chalks it up to being a poor soldier or carelessness. When he gets a fever or dysentery, however, he becomes a pitiable sight, not understanding why he should be sick.

Whenever a Jap is captured, a guard has to be put on to keep the Gurkhas away. They kill every Jap they can find. I just heard that if the Japs capture anyone with a kukri (knife) that the Gurkha carries on them they make them sterile for the rest of their lives right on the spot. Who knows if this is true?

Standing by pit holding a Japanese prisoner.
Photo by "Moon" Miller

The term Gurkha comes from the name of a ruling family that conquered Nepal in the late 1800s. They provide most of the country's professional soldiers. Other groups in Nepal are Newars and Sherpas. The Newars ruled part of Nepal before the Gurkha conquest. Most of the craftspeople and government workers are Newars, because the Gurkhas prefer to earn their living as soldiers with the British and Indian army service providing them with a steady income and retirement.

Close Call Near Palel

By April 22, 1944, we were at Palel. I went over to the Sapam airstrip, which was just across the road from our camp, and bummed a ride to Chittagong with some Americans in a C-46, who were flying supplies into the Imphal area. It was a great thrill, being my third time up, and I was all eyes. We stopped at a field on the way, which is supposed to be the biggest in India, one and a half miles long. The Japs had attacked the field just before we got there, and a Beau fighter was smoking, completely burned up after a Zero had strafed it. Bombs were also dropped but failed to hit any more planes. From there we went right on to Chittagong. I had the best dinner I had had for three months in their mess. A sergeant arranged for me to buy a carton of cigarettes, then the navigator on our ship gave me another.

After waiting three and a half hours for the British to load the plane with twenty-six barrels of aviation gas, we took off. It is easy to blame the British for never getting things done on time. The war stopped for the British at tea time and on Sundays. Actually we probably should have been thankful for that.

When we got to the Tallyho airstrip, just three miles south of Imphal, the pilot circled the field and was going to come in against the wind when he got a red flare from the tower and then they told him on the radio to come in the other way. As the field was quite short, he didn't get down in time to make a proper landing. When he did get three wheels on the ground his brakes failed, and we just kept on going.

I was watching out the window when the navigator told me to grab hold of something because we were going to crash. I grabbed onto one of the straps holding the cargo in place as we hit going about ninety miles an hour. We all piled out in about five seconds flat. The pilot shouted for us to run like hell and we did just that.

The first thing I thought of, on getting out of the plane, was my cigarettes, but the pilot wouldn't let me go back because of the petrol we were carrying. When we finally turned to look back, the plane exploded and burned. I didn't miss my cigarettes or the felt Gurkha hat. I was thinking how lucky I was to get out of that crash without even a scratch. Once again, I felt that someone was watching over me and I hoped that my luck would continue. "Georgie, are you saying your prayers for me or something?" was my first thought after the danger had passed. After my close call I realized that staying on the ground had its advantages after all, although I must admit that looking down at the rice paddies stretching out into the foothills of the distant mountains was truly wonderful.

One afternoon I went with Sam White and Bill Brown to a little stream to bathe. We stopped at a bazaar and bought three large cucumbers. I paid two annas apiece for them. Before the war they were two annas a dozen. As I had no sodium permanganate to wash them in I had to peel them. What a boost of morale to have raw cucumber for dessert after a lunch of bully beef. Later I went back for more cucumbers and also bought apricots and Tokay grapes.

I began to wonder how the lives of the people would change after the war. Depending upon the service people and selling produce at elevated prices would not last.

I returned to Sectional Headquarters where I began to have symptoms of dysentery and had to take iodine (three doses). If that hadn't done the trick, then I would have been in the hospital for about six weeks and then have a month's sick leave. At the time, in the midst of battle, I almost welcomed a thirty-day timeout. But it was not to be.

[Letter to Georgie]

You might as well send all my mail ordinary postage because when it gets to New York it all goes airmail anyway. Regular mail is going up to four cents.

If you keep sending me that sweet-smelling soap I won't have any trouble getting the best looking belle around here. Just a joke, my love! Yes, I saw the same full moon that you saw. I look forward to its coming as I look forward to your letters. They are a tonic, like sassafras in the spring! I wanted to send your mother a Mother's Day card because I liked your mom from the first time I saw her in her flower garden. I knew it was your mother standing there long before I could see the house number when I made my first trip down to Chehalis to see you. Your mother must have felt something for me if she told you I reminded her of your father when he was young. I wish I could bring your Mom a huge poinsettia tree from Western India. They are as large as lilac bushes.

Frank Dignam, George Brannan, and Francis "Mitch" Smith were pretty badly hurt when they went for a plane ride with some Yanks who were ferrying supplies for the 14th Army from Chittagong to Imphal, getting in two trips a day. On the way back to Chittagong, they got over Lolyghat and three Zeros attacked their DC-3. As they were unarmed they were at the mercy of the Jap 20 mm. They dove to thirty feet, shearing off a wing on a tree. George got shrapnel through the neck and chest. Dignam was thrown from the back of the plane to the pilot's compartment bulkhead. His legs were shot up. Smith was hit in the nose and cheek by shrapnel. They said George had a fifty-fifty chance of recovering but he didn't pull through.

There was no memorial service for George Brannan, so I thought of something that I could have said at his service. When we were ordered to destroy most everything so the Japs would not find anything of value when we had to retreat, we saved some kegs of rum. A Gurkha was ordered to guard the things that were saved. George went over and pretended to be an officer and handed the Gurkha a list and went over and picked up about ten gallons of rum, which lasted us for weeks.

Colonel Dougherty had been apprehensive all of one day, so he stayed in his slit trench. We had been expecting an attack for the last four days, but all we experienced was the usual air raid two or three times a day. Our ack-ack (anti-aircraft guns) seemed to keep the Japanese from laying their "eggs" (bombs) every time. We guessed that if we were going to be attacked it would be on the Emperor's birthday so Imphal would be given to him as a present.

April 30, 1944, found us anticipating this attack but I, strangely enough, was about to experience a wonderful May Day. There had been shelling all around us from our own firepower. I was once more thinking back to pleasant memories of my childhood. When I was six years of age, I put May Baskets on doorknobs and then ran and hid. On this May Day here in the battle arena I found a gardenia bush. I put two or three gardenias in the buttonhole on my baggy, blue denim coveralls so I could smell them during the movie *Slightly Dangerous* with Lana (sweater girl) Turner and Robert Young. The movie had been set up in a big canvas box made out of bamboo and tarps.

Later we sat up by the Headquarters' tent and watched the sunset. It was like a Technicolor film of a sunset, only we had box seats and didn't have to pay the 85 cents for a movie. It changed colors for a full twenty minutes with different cloud formations every few minutes. While the sun was setting, we could see about one-fourth of the moon. Call me a prevaricator, but I say the moon was actually an aquamarine blue. I have seen red, yellow, and orange harvest moons and white moons in the wintertime, but never a blue moon—a real blue-colored moon, not the blue moon that happens when there are two full moons in one month.

I was now sitting in my ambulance with the fragrance of gardenias surrounding me as I read an Easter letter from Georgie. What a dull world it would have been without flowers and thinking of Georgie.

Vicious Injury

I saw a soldier who had nearly been beheaded by a Japanese officer wielding a sword. The blow ranged from the base of his skull to his shoulders. The whole nape of his neck was peeled back like you would peel an orange. His shoulder had a gash about two inches deep and eight inches long. He had lain in the jungle for five days because he was considered to be dead. I held the light for the major while he scraped the maggots out of the gaping wound and Colonel Daugherty sewed it up. Maggots actually helped to clean out his wound. They said he was going to be all right! Just as I thought I was getting used to things like this, a fellow came in without any jaw. He actually healed very well and probably was a candidate for reconstructive surgery when he got back home.

Searles, Hendryx, Cosgrove, Morrill, Clark, and I drove high up to 42 Field Ambulance Transfer Station for casualties. There seemed to be a breeze blowing, so we looked forward to it being cool enough to sleep. Although there were no Japanese in this area, they might have appeared at any time. After a welcome quiet we went up to the Advanced Dressing Station. One of our patrols ambushed some Japs with forty mules and captured three of the Japs.

Our artillery had been blasting the Japs, and I had to suffer the stench of burning bodies, which almost made me sick. I took a short walk away from it all to pick some orchids. Just as soon as Hendryx and Clark got back we saw six heavy bombers hit a strong Jap position on a hill about five miles away. After they had bombed it for about ten minutes, they came back and strafed it. There were about eight hundred Japs in that position, suffering casualties.

[Letter from Georgie]

(Georgie had censored her own letter, because she said it was too revealing. One half of a page was actually cut off. It upset me for her to keep something from me like that after arousing my curiosity. Guess she didn't realize how frustrating this would be.)

Dear Norman: I have been listening to "One Man's Family" on the radio here in the dining room where I can see out into the yard. We have two trees growing together like a big bouquet. It is beautiful.

Today we went to the local airfield where a Boeing Flying Fortress had landed. Hundreds of people gathered around it. I climbed up on the makeshift platform to view inside the cabin and into the place where the side gunner's and the tail gunner's station is. The tail gunner has a special little door, which he can use to bail out of. Then we saw the bomb doors and could look up into the place from which the bombs are dropped.

Mother just let out a hearty laugh from downstairs when she heard Bob Burns say, "Once when my gal and I were in the courtin' stage, I gave the little brother 35 cents not to peek when I came to call. Afterwards the little brother gave me back a quarter on account of how the whole thing was very dull."

Here I sit reading *Rebecca* as I wait around for casualties. What a strange mix of war events, letters from Georgie, reading whatever is at hand, and picking flowers.

[From My Diary]

Last night was an eerie night. The enemy opened up on us at about dusk and landed a few mortars pretty near. Then our heavies opened up on them. It started to pour rain with lightning bursting like fireworks in the sky. Our guns fired most of the night and about 4 a.m. we were told to go up to Dead Mule Gulch to pick up casualties. Hendryx, Paul Clark and I put our ambulances in four-wheel drive and left. Clark, and Hendryx stayed back and I went forward and helped bring the wounded down. It was very tiring, hard work in the mud. Our feet kept slipping out from under us.

We got 18 wounded down, ten of them stretcher cases, and we are going to go back and get the six that were killed. I went right up to the most forward position and looked out over the hill where the battle took place. We weren't over 400 feet from a Jap bunker. I picked up a Jap bayonet, which I'm going to try to keep. Twice as many Japs were killed. I saw them lying in grotesque shapes. The smell of decaying bodies was nauseating since they had been lying there for several days.

The Tommies that were sent in were Devons, all from the same local area in England. They were green as grass, mostly just young kids, but had been shoved right up in the most forward position. One poor guy had lost all control of his bowels. He smelled something terrible. I saw eight buried in a common grave. The Japs have just lobbed over a couple that landed too close for comfort. Then we opened up on them and they haven't as yet sent any more over. I can hear a lot of small arms fire now. Now our mortars and machine guns have opened up. I think I'll not even plan to sleep tonight.

Paul Clark left the Advanced Dressing Station with a load of patients just before I got to bed one night. He was gone about an hour and then came back and said he couldn't find the right road to the Main Dressing Station. He had been driving over the road for three months, but, nevertheless, I finally had to get in and show him the way in the bright moonlight. I wondered if he had just wanted company while he was driving in the full light of the moon in view of the enemy nearby.

The D Company had been cut off and there were an estimated 110 casualties. The Jap tanks were dominating and we had no tanks. One Tommy told me that the Yanks would have used eight-inch guns instead of five-inch and would have had tanks here, also.

Joseph Desloge, Jr. mentioned this same disparity between the Tommies and the GIs in his book *Passport to Manhood*. He said that the Tommies had little dental care, had to rely on bully beef, and did not have the modern rifles that the GIs had. There was even disparity in pay. He agreed that this caused a good deal of animosity when the troops were in the same battle zone. Toward the end of the war, the GI bonuses were sent home rather than given out to the fellows overseas. This way they wouldn't be seen spending so much money on leave.

Our men had moved in for an attack and we had six Hurricanes strafing the Japs. What a noise! Our artillery and mortars were then laying a barrage for the ground forces. The air was just a whir of shells whining and whistling overhead. I sure hated that sound, especially when the whine was coming at me. You could hear it, but you never knew whether it was going to spare you until it landed and you were still alive.

The attack failed. The Japs had been sending over mortar fire regularly, but Gurkha reinforcements were reported to be coming up soon. It had been my job to keep the ambulances running, but all one afternoon I had been helping the Medical Officer dress the wounded. Blood! Blood! and more Blood! Before I got the last load away from the Regimental Aid Post, mortars were landing too close for comfort. A Company withdrew about three times and then went in again. One Tommy said it was organized chaos.

At last the Gurkhas came up to reinforce the Devons about 4 p.m. Our artillery had been shelling all day. Twelve Vengeance dive-bombers let loose on the Japs. D Company was reported to be holding out after all. We were supposed to attack that night with the support of three Grant tanks.

By May 10, 1944, Hendryx, Clark, and I left at darkness for the Advanced Dressing Station and were shelled. Some observation post must have spotted us. Had just gotten to sleep when we were called to carry over fifty Gurkha casualties. I took eleven the first load, nine on the second load, four of whom were lying down as they had either head wounds or severe body wounds. D Company, which was at one time given up for lost, broke through bringing their casualties with them, forty-five in all. I carried three of them and one smelled rotten as he had been lying out untended for a long time.

Up the next day at 3 a.m. hauling casualties. I brought back about forty myself. D. Elberfeld, Gray and Swenson brought back about the same. The monsoon was breaking with winds of hurricane force driving the rain like bullets. My ambulance was shaking, but I was still living a charmed life. In my diary I wrote:

> I made four trips this morning with the Japs mortaring the road and was missed every time!"

> More blood and broken bodies: arms gone, legs gone, buttocks blown off, faces gone. I really don't know how I stood it. I lost my appetite. I think my ambulance could almost be called a "meat wagon." And I didn't sleep very much either. I had two hours one night and three hours the next night.

[Letter to Georgie]

> I have not been picking flowers for quite a few days or in other words enjoying the beauty of life. Other things of more urgent importance have had to be done. You can imagine what these things are.

> I must tell you a story. I went to a certain place with the medical officer and we piled the rear end of the ambulance full of stretchers, medical supplies, blankets, picks, shovels, guns, and God knows what else and started out to a Headquarters that neither he nor I knew where to find. We also had five stretcher-bearers and a chaplain with us. We finally found the place we were to unload. The MO got out and said he was going to stay and was sending me and the ambulance and some of the meds back to HQ. He then proceeded to get into the ambulance and started checking what he had brought along.

> "Picks, shovels. Yes---yes---yes, we have two of each. Just what I thought we had and perfectly all right. We have shell dressings. Are you sure we have shell dressings corporal? What? What? Yes, yes, that's right." He then grabbed my mosquito net, which I had in a corner tucked away and said, "Yes, I must have my mosquito net. I need my net and I must take it along."

> Then the corporal said, "I think that's the driver's net, sir." "Is it? That's right. That's right. Certainly it must be. I had a net here, I'm sure I did. Didn't I have a net here? Yes, yes, here it is and I must take it with me. I will need it tonight."

> I almost split holding back my laughter but for all he said and for all you would think about his ability being nil as a doctor, you are entirely wrong. He is very competent and a good MO. But he also takes his revolver and scratches his head with it!

On May 12, 1944, some relief at last. I had dinner with the Medical Officer for the Gurkhas. He told me that the Gurkha wasn't the fighter he was credited to be. He was good. There was no question about it, but some Indian regiments were just as good as the Gurkha, if not better, but they did not receive credit when credit was due. Reason: They were Indian.

I remember one occasion when an Indian company composed of Dogras and Punjabs ambushed and killed a hundred Japs. Their commanding officer (British) gave them credit for only sixty. The British had been in the position of master over the Indians for so long that war didn't change this relationship.

The Bengals

The Bengals had not, previous to the war, been admitted into the Army because they harbored most of the opposition against the British. Bengal was given colleges for the purpose of educating leaders, but when these students finished schooling, they would not be accepted in jobs for which they were qualified. This made it difficult for educated people who adhered to the caste system. They could not take a job below their social and educational status. Being idle, they read everything they could get their hands on including Marx and Engels. That probably accounts for the political activism of the Bengalese.

Once more I was out of my "meat wagon" and having some down time. I learned that a tiger skin cost 200 rupees. That was a little more than I wanted to spend, so bringing one home was just a pipe dream. Here we were far from a market and yet we were discussing the cost of trophies we could bring back from India.

We were interrupted by dive-bombing. It was a thrill to see the planes peel off from formation in a vertical dive and see the bombs come out and then the planes shoot straight up again to safety. So far I had not had the chance to see the destruction. It must have been something terrific. I had a funny feeling after seeing this violent attack. It brought me back again to crawling along at a slow pace so as not to jar and shake the wounded and yet have hell all around. I didn't know how to explain it, but when I was in the thick of it all, I just gritted my teeth and thought of the pain my patients were suffering and drove on.

Recently, three of us went to take casualties to the dressing station. I was the first one away with my empty ambulance, Clark was next, followed by Hendryx. I hadn't gone three hundred yards when I heard a loud explosion and saw the flash in my rear vision mirror. Up to that time I had been going quite slowly because of the rough road and because I couldn't see the road very well. That explosion and flash were all I needed. For the next one-half mile I flew low, hitting the high spots, and not all of them. Clark and Hendryx were in back of me, and I was almost sure one of them had "had it." I stopped when I figured I was out of range of the mortars and waited. They finally caught up unscathed. There were three shells, one for each ambulance, but they all missed. Shirley Hendryx was blinded temporarily by one and had sore eyes for a day but that was all. A Jap observation post must have spotted us as we left and told his mortars to open up.

I can't keep from thinking about George Brannan. He was a swell guy. Had he lived, one side would have been paralyzed because of the severe hemorrhage he had suffered. One part of his brain went dead because of lack of blood. It was so difficult to realize that fellows that we had been close to were now gone.

On May 13, 1944, I was still out in the field at the Advanced Dressing Station at Shinam. The positions off the road leading up to the fighting were Gurkha Hill, Gibraltar, Malta where the Regimental Aid Post (RAP) was located, Scraggy Hill, Crete, and then the Nippon S.

I made a trip to the post from Shinam bringing my load back to the Main Dressing Station where I stayed after having been replaced by H. Swensson. The casualties had been pouring in steadily. The Japs seemed to be determined to take Shinam at all costs. The Gurkha 4th and 10th reinforcements had been coming up for two days. The battle was still raging for Scraggy Hill.

Heard that Frank Dignam, who was now in Calcutta, wasn't a bit well. His wounds wouldn't heal and he had malaria, losing thirty pounds. He was soon to be sent back home. So were Kneupfer and Clay, who were totally scared after visiting a ward where some Tommies had lost arms and legs and were complaining of pain in the toes and fingers that they didn't have. I began to feel the war coming closer to me when my friends were being injured and leveled by illness, both physical and emotional.

On Mother's Day I didn't do any work except to disinfect the back end of my ambulance. With time out to rest, I read most of the day and later had a drink of rum with Harry Searles. The Japs were reorganizing for another attack, so it was one of those quiet periods when you just waited. The clouds completely engulfed all our positions, which were all on high peaks. The next day was hectic as the 20th Division moved out and the 23rd moved in.

On May 18, 1944, I had two runs out of the Medical Dressing Station and helped a medical officer dress the wounded as they came in and then brought a load back with me.

The second run, which I hoped never to repeat, was to pick up two British Other Ranks. The Japs made a direct hit on them with their artillery. I helped pick up the body parts. The only comparison in civilian life would be cleaning up after a devastating airplane crash.

Another time I bandaged a soldier's hand that had the thumb and forefinger gone. The fellow was crying pitifully and bemoaning his loss in his own language, but I knew what he meant nevertheless.

Fifteen or more Jap planes went over just before dinner. Our ack-ack kept them up at quite an altitude. They didn't drop any bombs on us but they had us plenty scared. I paid a Tommie 20 chips for a .38 Colt today. Even though we have not been given arms for protection, I felt I needed it.

Don Bragg came up today. I was glad to see him. Our heavy artillery, which is only about a thousand feet from us, opened up about 2 a.m. Four or five guns would fire at once and again every three or four minutes. The concussion would make my ambulance quiver like a leaf. Jap shells were whistling over our heads in a vain attempt to silence our guns. From two o'clock on I slept off and on with horrible dreams and nightmares.

I was being replaced, so I moved out on the plain to our Sectional Headquarters at Palel for an indefinite time. Our camp had two sleeping bashas and one large basha for our mess hall, office, and reading and writing room. I was able to sleep a little better in between the nightly whistling of shells. It was the waiting while they were whistling that was mental torture.

On May 21, 1944, I rode down to the hospital with Robert Wilson and got there just in time to take a seventy-eight-mile round trip down there myself. Had a drink of "zoo," which Paul Clark bought at the village. It was made of rice and really wasn't so bad. I had been busy transporting medical cases, but Joe Ainsworth and I had the chance to stop at a bazaar to buy a lot of potatoes the size of eggs, tomatoes the size of cherries, and some cucumbers for our mess. One woman gave me a snowy white lotus blossom, which now I favor over the gardenia. It smells like fresh apples or fresh ripe cantaloupe. On the way back, I picked a pomegranate, rather green and small, from a bush alongside the road.

Talk of Re-Enlistment

Major King and Major Ives came to visit us and we are talking over re-enlistment, draft deferments, and the like. We had three choices:

1. Re-enlist here in this theatre for six months at a time at $50 a month.

2. Sign over or transfer to the Middle East directly from here for a period of one year.

3. Go home and stay for a while and take the chance of having our draft boards release us for the Field Service. Then if we got back into the AFS we would sign up for eighteen months at $20 a month for the first twelve months and $50 for the remaining six months.

Anyone reading this could guess what the best choice would be. Eventually I succumbed to the pressure to re-enlist knowing that Georgie would be very unhappy, but, after all, she had hinted in a letter that I probably wouldn't want to return until the war was over.

Made a run to Shinam. Heard that the Japs took our position called Malta and then the one called Gibraltar. In an attempt to regain our losses, we put in several attacks. Although successful they were very costly. The Japanese kept up the attack on Bishenpur from the south and west. Frequently they shifted the point of attack or slipped around behind a defended point in an effort to cut it off. The attack developed into what General Slim called "the most prolonged and desperate fighting of the whole campaign." We were told not to sleep without our clothes on.

Don Bragg was under arrest. He wouldn't obey orders in an emergency so is being court-martialed. The sore point is that other fellows have done the same thing that Bragg has and nothing was done about it. I don't think anything is going to be done about Bragg either, but in wartime anyone who does not obey orders in an emergency situation must be dealt with.

The Madman from the Village

A fellow who called himself Uncle, the madman from the village, paid us a visit this morning. He was director of a field YMCA. It was a spectacle indeed to see him coming up the hill to our basha in his blue denim coveralls with puttees on and a crazy looking beige tam with a red tassel and a piece of plaid pinned on the side of it. He also had a large bamboo cane and was swinging it like Lord Whipplebottom. When he approached, he said, "Hello, this is the madman from the village coming to pay you a little friendly visit. Hope you have a kind word for me this morning."

He demanded ten minutes to make a little speech on Anglo-American relations. Knowing how boring this would be, we begrudgingly sat down to listen. He walked up and down waving his cane and making a hullabaloo about nothing before he finally took his silly looking tam off, tipped it, and bade us a pleasant good morning.

He was British and educated in the U.S. and said he owed us a lot for teaching him the meaning of liberty. He sang us two little songs before he left. In spite of it all, he did help morale.

By May 24, 1944, over in Bishnupur the Japs were catching it. We heard big guns going off all night lasting through the day as well. I was not feeling very well, but things perked up when we were invited to eat with the lieutenant colonel in mixed company, some British and some Indians. Usually, we drew our own rations for meals unless we went to Headquarters to eat.

Sam White loaned me some paper so I could write home. Sam had six children: two by his first wife, none by his second wife, two who arrived with his third wife, and she had two more after they were married. This is the first time I had ever heard of a family like this. He told me that all six of the kids, the oldest being sixteen, were just like blood brothers and sisters. He made a joke, saying laughingly, "Sometimes I say to my wife, my kids and your kids are fighting with our kids."

On May 29 I made a run to Imphal with medical cases after an air raid earlier that morning. Heard a dog fight in the clouds but could not see them. The boys were all saying, "When my year is over, I'm signing up again, like hell I am." Cosgrove's ambulance was blown up by a mine, but luckily it didn't hurt him much. We had lost about eighteen of fifty-three fellows so far—either death or illness. Statistics were beginning to point up the dangers we faced. As battlefront fatigue and increased heat zeroed in upon us, more jungle diseases took their toll.

My little interpreter met me on the way to the bazaar dressed only in a loincloth. I was surprised because I had been accustomed to seeing him in western clothes. He wanted me to come down to his basha with him and wait until he put on his shorts, shirt, and shoes. He led me half a mile through little paths and finally we came to his basha. He brought me a grass mat to sit on. I sat down on the porch and waited. Their bashas are always raised about two feet off the level of the ground. This is accomplished by building up the foundation with packed dirt.

I sat there and was the object of curiosity of his brothers and sisters. There seemed to be dozens of them. The kids were all naked. He changed clothes right in front of everyone and then his sister brought him some coconut oil for his hair. We proceeded to the bazaar when he had finished dressing. It really was interesting. I think he just wanted to show me off to all the neighbor children.

At the bazaar I was astounded when I saw an Indian woman walking along with a huge pot of water on her head and a baby in one arm and something else in the other hand. I had finally become an expert at bargaining. I bargained hard to get tiny eggs for about 9 cents apiece and wondered how far that would go in feeding an Indian family.

I paid 2 rupees for two pounds of tiny onions to flavor up our bully beef. They were in a little basket, so I took the basket and started walking away. Soon the woman who sold me the onions was running after me to retrieve her basket. I had a boy who could speak a few words of English tell her that I would return the basket the next day and gave the woman cigarettes. She was then well pleased.

I then found eight more pounds of onions. The woman wanted six chips for them, but finally she went down to four. I traded cigarettes and 2 rupees for cucumbers. It started to rain, so I hurried back to the cucumber-selling woman and got under her umbrella-like affair made of a bamboo frame and bamboo bark. The young woman tied one of my hairs onto a small, orange, sweet-smelling jungle flower. It hung down over my forehead. We got many stares and remarks that I couldn't understand. After buying bananas I went on my way.

When I returned from the bazaar, I had the book *Droll Stories* by de Balzac waiting for me, so for awhile I could lose myself in fiction.

By the first of June I got seven letters from Georgie that led me to believe that she loved me but was just too obstinate and stubborn to say so. I was trying to figure out how to communicate by letter when I had to wait so long for answers to my questions. Even though I had sent her a ring several months before and told her, "Consider yourself engaged," she wrote that she had no intention of becoming engaged—at least for the duration of the war. That was the second time she had written this but the content of her letters gave me hope that she would wait for me.

Back home even Georgie's second graders were curious about their teacher's "boyfriend." She said she was cornered after school one day by three of the second grade children she chose to stay after school and help. Lorelee said, "Miss Bright, when are you going to tell us about your boyfriend? You must have a boyfriend." Then Jane came back with, "Miss Bright is engaged to a soldier, at least she must be, all the lady teachers I know are engaged to soldiers." After saying "No," Georgie asked whom they would pick out for her. Jane said, "Oh, a Marine. You're the Marine type, Miss Bright." Then Georgie said she changed the subject.

Georgie had certainly pinpointed the song that fit us. She couldn't remember all the words, but what she did remember, made this OUR SONG, full moon and all:

I'll be seeing you,
In all the old familiar places
That this heart of mine embraces
All day through.

The song ended with:

I'll find you in the morning sun
And when the night is through
I'll be looking at the moon
But I'll be seeing you.

I hadn't been up to par for a few days. I had a few vertebrae out of place, and my neck and back had been quite stiff. I had Jack Barrett "jump" on my back and it felt better, well enough to help Jack give my ambulance an overhaul.

By June 6th we had heard that the second front had begun. We were so far removed from the European theatre that there were only rumors that floated our way. We had a guessing pool about the start and Mac Wright won 150 chips. I had cut ten heads of hair for one chip apiece so you could see that 150 chips would be a nice win. We also heard that the British and Americans were in Rome.

On June 7, 1944, I made two runs. When I got back, Nat Beeber had returned from his trip to the city. Most of the fellows were down on him because he overstayed his leave. He was selling three Hershey bars from a package from home for five chips each ($1.55). When the shells were falling thick and fast, we got a big laugh watching him with his possessions in his slit trench praying like a man who was going to be hanged. He was also worried that if we had to walk out and leave our ambulance that he wouldn't be able to bring all his kit since it would take two men to carry it. Funny how we were all scared in the battle zone and didn't like to see someone breaking up, reminding us of our own fear.

Our mail brought magazines, six *Saturday Evening Posts,* and about six *Nations.* I'm still reading the *Droll Stories.* We had been getting very good news from all the major battlefronts. The big Russian bear was going to town. The Italian front was going steady too. I didn't think we were doing so well in France, but we were making up for it in the Pacific. Beeber and the lieutenant colonel thought the Germans would fold up in four months and Japan by the end of this year. I was not quite so optimistic.

Artist Joe Ainsworth, John Wilhelm, Robinson, and I went to the bazaar. On the way we saw a small native girl walking on the shoulder of the road get hit by a truck. I thought surely we would have to pick her up with a stretcher, but she jumped up and ran off into the jungle to her home. We flagged the truck driver down and took his name and unit number to turn into his unit officer and let him go. It seems that she had a necklace of gold and silver that was worth about 30 rupees and this Indian driver had tried to steal it from her. He will probably be court-martialed.

Then we took our first aid kit and set out to look for the girl to see just how badly she was hurt. We finally found her, and she came to us to let us look her over for cuts and scratches. After dabbing iodine here and there, we put on a few plaster bandages, then we started back to our ambulance. She tagged along at our heels trying to tell us something. Finally, we got to an Indian officer who acted as interpreter. He told us that she wanted to repay us for our kindness with some cauna (food). We told him to tell her that it wasn't necessary, but she wasn't to be persuaded. He told us that if we didn't accept her offer, she would be offended. So she took me by the hand, looked up at me with her big brown eyes, and led me off with the other guys following. Robbie said it surely looked funny. I was so tall (six feet four and a half inches) alongside of her. She gave us all bananas and mangoes. She wasn't the least bit timid and bashful and self-conscious like most girls of her age. She looked about ten or eleven with a very pockmarked round face with bangs cut very high on her forehead and the rest of her hair hanging about her shoulders. We thanked her and went on our way.

First Anniversary

I was thinking of Georgie. I had no idea I would carry on a correspondence relationship for a year with someone who could keep my morale so high during the trying times I have spent away from home. I never expected that she would mean so much to me or that I would be thinking of the night we met at the Trianon Ballroom. I took her home quite late, and it was slightly overcast but the moon was visible, scudding through the clouds. I wrote to Georgie:

> Something happened to me that night. Yes, I still feel it. I thought the same thing happened to you, too, but you said that things like that just didn't happen in Seattle. Are you not convinced now that things like that can and do happen? That is the question I wish to make clear. Am I to get an answer to it or is it to remain another one of those deep dark mysteries? I'll get you to tell me somehow when I see you. See you!

We always ended our letters with "See you." It had become our promise to each other.

I was in charge of several ambulances to serve with the 20th Division. Wilhelm, Beeber, Rob Robinson, Albert Hill, William Cosgrove, and I moved up on the Ukhrul Road and were at the front again. The Japs were only two miles away. Our guns were giving them a bad time, and I jumped every time I heard one because I hadn't been around them for quite a while.

Now I was once more out of danger. My life was a teeter-totter; sometimes experiencing the deafening sounds of battle and sometimes back at Headquarters where we could find some semblance of relaxation. Our New York office had worked a deal with the U.S. Army so that we could get the same things that the doughboy got in the canteen or PX. Now we could get fruit juice and lots more.

Every time I was at the bazaar the young woman who sheltered me in the rain wanted to give me a flower or some of her sweetmeats. She made puffed rice balls with sugar cane syrup. I hated to refuse and yet when I ate them I feared I would get dysentery.

I was going to be shifted to another place where I would be in the thick of things. I would again go back to sleeping on the stretcher and you can imagine my long legs fitting onto a stretcher for sleeping. I thought, "Give me a good old charpoy (a rectangular frame on legs with a woven rope center). It is comfortable when you have enough blankets under you."

On the way, we stopped at a new bazaar and the prices were high. So I used the British issue cigarettes, which aren't fit to smoke, in bartering. I got cucumbers, pineapples, five large ears of corn, and mangoes. The mango meat was a golden yellow-orange, similar to a ripe cantaloupe. They were sweet, juicy, and had a tang that didn't compare to any other fruit.

FOOT CARE IN THE JUNGLE

I have found a remedy for athlete's foot. I must keep it on hand when I am in the jungle. Melt phenol, measure 3 cubic centimeters into a mortar, add 3 grains of camphor, rub the mass until liquid. Put up in a bottle. Two or three applications per day for a week will cure the worst case of athlete's foot. Mark bottle poison and not to be taken internally. To be applied only on dry skin.

Bill Cosgrove, Rob Robinson, Don Hill, Nathaniel Beeber, and I were at the Advanced Dressing Station, which was fifteen miles from Imphal. It was pretty quiet but the Japs had shelled right where we were parked. Allen Clark, Bennett, Lutman, and Fritzsche were driving jeeps from the regimental aid post to the Advanced Dressing Station, a most dangerous job because they were exposed to snipers near the battlefront.

I was awakened in the night to bring three British Other Ranks down to the Main Dressing Station. The rains had reduced the road to mud, making it all but impassable. My boots got so heavy with this sticky stuff that I could hardly lift them. It wasn't as bad as what happened to one of our fellows, who slipped over an embankment and would have gone on for another couple of hundred feet but was stopped by barbed wire which happened to be full of booby traps. He was lucky that he was discovered and pulled out safely after being thrown a rope. I didn't slip down any bank but four mortars landed behind me as I was coming out. On the attack yesterday we did not gain our objective as the Japs were too well dug in. We suffered more than a hundred casualties. It was impossible to drive without lights but I had to. To add to this night of misery, I was bitten by mosquitoes even though I tried to avoid it.

Malted Milk Really?

I received a package from Georgie labeled Thompson's Malted Milk. I did not open it right away as I was on my way to a hospital with a load of casualties and met Robinson who gave me my letters. I didn't get supper there, but I was looking forward to getting back for some malted milk. When I got back I got my cup and spoon and the can of Thompson's and climbed in the ambulance to mix myself a drink. I tore the tape off the can, my mouth watering in anticipation, but when I removed the lid I found a mass of paper. I pulled out enough packing to choke a cow not realizing it was ink inside the packing and not malted milk. The surprise came with a shock. I was really let down, but very glad to get the ink. I learned that Georgie wasn't trying to make a "Superman" out of me after all! I smoked a cigarette, brushed my teeth, and turned in to think about Georgie's letters.

By June 15, 1944, I was busy all day carrying back casualties from the Advanced Dressing Station. It rained steadily so I had to go in the four-wheel drive. This weather reminded me of bad weather when I was young and I would have to stay in the house. I used to sing a little song with my sister, "Rain, rain, go away. Come again some other day." I remember when my sister and I pressed our noses against the steamy window and wished that we could be outside. The window was steamed up because Mom was washing clothes in an open washtub and we were lonesome because our other brothers and sisters were all in school.

[From My Diary]

Here it is June 16th. Sometimes I compare myself to an imaginary man in a huge whirlpool who is almost sure to be drowned and destroyed and is grasping for the faintest straw in the hope of saving himself from a horrible death. Instead of a whirlpool of water, substitute a turbulent and tumultuous world, a crazy world, and you have put me in the proper place.

For eight years I have been tossed around like a straw in a wind, never knowing what life would have in store for me from day to day. Now, as I look back, I can see that I was like this man in the maelstrom. I was looking and groping for something that I could hang onto, a purpose in life. I hope I'm not taking too big a step or taking too much for granted when I say that I have found that which would help me, if not make me, lead a more purposeful life. I'm referring to Georgie. That is one of the reasons I'm feeling so good tonight.

Peril at Night

It was late at night and I was in my ambulance in a very forward position when all of a sudden four shells came over, one landing quite near. I almost jumped out of my stretcher, entangled in my net like a captured tiger. But I got hold of myself and remained calm, wondering where the next one would land. Suddenly out of the pitch darkness, rain, and mud came a "somebody" to the back of my ambulance. It could easily enough have been a Jap as their code of arms says attack in the rain, in last light of night, first light of dawn, and in the most adverse conditions. First, he asked me, in broken English, if I wanted a cigarette. I accepted suspiciously and procured a match, which I had to get out of my net. I lit up first, shielding the match extremely well and gave him a light from mine. I was becoming more wary all the time.

We talked about the shells landing, where they were landing, and if any were killed or wounded. I found out that the shell had landed very close to his tent and that his slit trench was up on the hill. He, in his hurry to get into a trench, fell down the hill and slipped in the mud onto the road where my ambulance was parked. He had skinned his nose and cut his toe, but I didn't know this at the time. I finally told him to run along; I wanted to sleep. I still had no idea who he was and I was becoming uneasy because I could not see him and dared not turn on a light. He then said he was afraid to go up to his tent as everyone in the area was standing to (at the ready) and he was afraid of getting shot. He finally said he wanted to stay in my ambulance till morning. I exploded. I said to him that he might be a Jap or a traitor. This he denied. I have a pistol now so I got it out and said, "Feel this." I then told him it was a gun and that I would have no qualms about shooting him if I had the slightest provocation. I didn't sleep much. I gave him one of my blankets, which he got all muddy. Just at first light a few more shells came our way. I looked him over in the light and found he was a Viceroy's Commissioned Officer in the Indian unit of the British Army.

Three days after my rest at Imphal I parked my ambulance in a new place and found a completely new flower on a bush right outside. It was white, about the size of a carnation, and smelled like one but it had very delicate petals resembling white crepe paper crinkled on the edges. This just proved that you could find beauty anywhere, even in the most despoiled places. It was time to rest once more. I now had time to read *So Little Time* by Marquand.

A couple of days later, I went up to Wykhong (Main Dressing Station, 55 Field Ambulance) with a convoy to check out the road I would be driving. The Advanced Dressing Station was only eleven miles away, but it took us eight hours in four-wheel-drive Dodges to get there. The road was across a rice paddy, so we were wading mud and water and digging ourselves out every hundred yards. After arriving at midnight, I slept in one of the wards where the medical officer was kind enough to find a net for me. It was a nice gesture, but the net was full of holes. My return trip took only six hours but I realized that it would be impossible to take patients down that road.

Colonel Daugherty (our British Medical Officer) said that we really were beating the Japs. I heard that there were only eleven miles more of the Dimapur Road held by them, and it should soon be cleared. The colonel's orderly was a very intelligent Indian whom the colonel praised as the most obedient servant he had ever had. The fellow worked from 6 a.m. to 10 p.m. every day without exception. It was no wonder that he turned up at sick parade with a pain in his chest.

The crickets and frogs and insects were filling the air with a steady, never-ending noise. The lightning bugs were flitting here and there, piercing the darkness with their brightness. Wonderful! Perhaps the Asian philosophy is getting to me after all—the feeling of being one with all the creatures in the universe. Soon Beeber and I were going forward where the British 80th Brigade was in contact with the Japs. We completed our trip after dark and once our headlights picked up a Naga woman lifting her skirts to urinate alongside the road. In this area, many were fleeing from the battle zone without benefit of any privacy or safety.

Casualties were going to be evacuated by elephant to the river and then Baars, Feddeman, and I would become gondoliers.

INDIAN ELEPHANTS

A colonel who has lived in India half his life told me about Indian elephants. He said he doesn't start working them until they are about seventeen or eighteen years of age. They are still growing at age twenty-one and reach their prime in strength at forty or thereabouts. They can be worked up until they are about fifty-five or sixty. They are not worked in the hot season but only when the rains start. Hunting is done from the back of an elephant.

Before this difficult duty was to begin, there was a break in the routine provided by a Manipur festival. The floats, about fourteen feet high, were decorated with colored cloth with paintings of the gods Shiva, Brahma, and Vishnu. All this was mounted on wooden wheels. In the center, on a throne, was a god bedecked in finery and imitation jewels. The women were dressed in their best saris and the men in snow-white lhoungis (a wraparound garment) with paintings on their foreheads and across their upper chests. Some even had paintings on their shoulder muscles. The middle-sized children were pulling the conveyance along, with drums beating and big and little brass plates banging together. Bells were jingling and Indians were singing. Every once in a while they would stop to burn incense and accept gifts for the god, mostly pineapple, cucumbers, and mangoes.

Just across the road from us was someone we called Dorothy Lamour. Every day she had been there in her fuchsia pink lhoungi selling betel nuts and Indian cigarettes. Not that I needed either one.

At last I left the 59 Medical Dressing Station with Beeber and an English lieutenant. We were each in command of a boat with two Indians to take care of the Johnson Seahorse motors. We didn't make Wykong by dark. The lieutenant broke down and then Beeber and I continued. I broke two of the shear pins that hold the propeller on and only had one for replacement, and Beeber ran out of fuel. I limped with one motor and met Beeber. We were two miles from Wykong by walking and three miles by river so we asked some villagers for help to take us. It was a tough march through rice paddy fields and ankle-deep mud. We didn't know whether we would be turned over to the Japs on the way or not.

RICE PADDIES

I have always hated the look of rice paddy fields when I knew I had to walk across them on the little dikes, over and over again. The dike is about one foot high to keep the water on the rice while it is growing. The Indians plow the paddies by scratching the ground with the most primitive of tools.

Having more time to contemplate, I noticed that these little plots of ground are very irregular in size and shape. They have an effect upon the eye as one looking at a patchwork quilt, no two pieces alike, especially beautiful when looking down on them from above so you can view several square miles all at once.

We stumbled our way through the pitch darkness and finally came upon the river. We were now just across the river from the Advanced Dressing Station where we were planning to stay for the night. By shouting, we finally roused some sentries, and then it was only a matter of a few minutes before they sent a boat across the river to us. We had some hot tea and went to bed in a basha (hut).

Beeber got up early and took the two guides back to get the boats. I was waiting for him to continue on up the river. We had to be at Checkpoint 25 by noon the next day to get the casualties. We knew we were in Jap country, and I didn't feel so good riding in a boat that only made about a mile an hour through the dense jungle. That evening I wrote to Georgie about the cuckoos and blue doves and the abundance of insect life there. Always something new to discover in this rich environment when we could let down and rest enough to notice.

By June 26 we were at 42 Field Ambulance, 55 Main Dressing Station with Colonel Daugherty. We made it to the next checkpoint and were greeted royally by Captain Webster of the Sikhs. They were supplied by parachute and had been getting another brigade's rations so we ate like kings. They told about having to be cautious when the rations were being dropped, as one time a large cache struck an ambulance and dented it pretty badly. Imagine what it would have done if a fellow were in direct line of the drop. Since the parachutes couldn't be used again, I was able to bring one back with me. On the boat trip through the last ten miles of beautiful country, I didn't enjoy it quite as much as I would have if I had known there were no Japs for fifty miles. We weren't fired on once. Stopped to give the motors a rest at a Kaki village. The kids were all naked and the women half dressed. The men wore loincloths. One little boy had on a beautiful necklace of turquoise beads. I wanted to barter for it but couldn't take the time.

Both motors broke down, and I had to float and paddle for more than ten miles. Arrived after seven o'clock. Everyone was talking about getting to Mandalay in six weeks. Just the word Mandalay is like the carrot at the end of a stick for so many in this jungle area. Personally I had given up on getting to Mandalay long ago.

Now suffering from diarrhea, I missed going on another trip. On June 26 I spent two days at our Headquarters in Palel getting my rods and bearings tightened. Saw the most beautiful Manipur woman I had ever seen. To look at her just made my heart jump. I wrote this in my diary, not in a letter to Georgie!

Even with the sound of artillery fire, our Imphal Headquarters seemed like a dead place. Only four new replacements had arrived, and just about everyone in the first section had gone home. Bill Brown suddenly got a pain in his side and couldn't drive. This was nothing new. Maybe he thought the same about me when I missed a trip because I was ill.

Just heard that before we broke the siege we were using our last bit of reserve supplies. We had been on quarter rations for over two months. Had the Japs been able to hold the road another six weeks, we would have been starving or would have had to start walking. It was much more serious than most of us thought, and the danger wasn't completely over yet.

Baars quit our little boat party. He was having difficulty making it when the going got tough. Watching so many in our ranks become ill or wounded or suffering death from their wounds took its toll on the ones who were left. I often wondered how long I could hold out.

NAGA ENTERTAINERS

Today I took a walk through the village to a place where I heard music. Upon investigation I found four Nagas from a tribe of hill people who grew rice on little terraces up in the mountain region. One blind fellow was beating the drums. A woman was playing a small organ with air pumped by one hand. The third was a small boy clanging little cymbals together, and the fourth was a dancer, a charming little girl of about eleven who was considered the best dancer in the valley. She had a little round piece of gold in the middle of each of her two front teeth. Her singing did not match her dancing ability as her voice cracked when she tried to reach the high notes.

It was a strange scene to a Westerner being initiated into Eastern culture. I gave them a rupee to show my appreciation.

The second time I took Fred with me the little dancer did a sword dance that was quite wonderful. We shelled out more money. Then I found that I wasn't the talent scout I thought myself to be. A medical officer in our unit told us that the entertainers were hired by many officers' messes in the area and were paid over 1 lakh (100 rupees) and received many tips.

Just before dark I heard a clanging of bells and went out to find evidence of the last festival of the season. People came carrying an idol in a chair. They set it down and lit some wax sticks that resembled candles and started singing and beating their drums, clanging their bells and clashing their cymbals. Then a deep, shiny brass plate full of fruits and vegetables was placed in front of the idol and the singing continued, now getting faster and faster.

Suddenly the music stopped, and all the kids under sixteen made a rush for the offering, grabbing whatever they could. This was done three times. Then a delectable looking young thing came over to me and with her finger put a red mark in the middle of my forehead. She left for a moment and came back with a garland of peas (large garden variety) and put it around my neck. I was very much surprised and pleased with it all, although I knew nothing of what it meant. While in my state of bewilderment, a Hindu who spoke English told me that I would be blessed with a long, happy, and fruitful life. I left the scene feeling extremely elated, not so much because of the paint on my forehead or the garland of peas round my neck, but because of the coy glances that had been cast my way by that beautiful young thing.

Just before dinner a colonel visited us from another field ambulance station. He was Irish and from the south while our colonel was from the north. The padre of our division, a true-blue Scotsman, soon joined us. The conversation then got around to who had received the most decorations—Irish, Scotch, or English. The Irish fellow said that they had more distinguished service medals than either the English or Scotch. Our Quartermaster, Lieutenant Teanby, who was English, piped up and claimed the most. No wonder we have wars. If those on the same side of a war can't stop arguing amongst themselves, how can peace ever be achieved?

After I returned to my ambulance to write in my diary, I began to hear rain lightly falling. My ambulance was not only protection from rain, but had I been out walking I would have been challenged every few feet to give the password. If I couldn't answer very quickly, I might have been in deep trouble. Once again my ambulance became a haven which the British Tommies of lower rank could not enjoy unless they were wounded or ill.

I spent a full day wandering through villages and thumbing my way to each one looking for bargains. I first had an offer of fifty eggs for 7 seers (between 3 and 7 pounds) of salt, which was impossible to get. Then I was offered a chicken for 3 seers. At one stop I watched the women and young girls making cloth from the raw cotton to the finished product. I realized that I was very thirsty, but I didn't dare drink the water without boiling it, so I offered cigarettes to anyone who would boil water for me.

On July 4 Feddeman and I spent the day bargaining and found four chickens and thirty-eight eggs for 48 rupees. I spent a half-month's pay and so did he, but it was worth it to enjoy an egg omelet for an entree and fried chicken. Later, we had a wonderful party with Colonel Daugherty and staff—played poker and won 5 rupees—but the underbelly of all this fun was that Japs were reported just six miles from here.

REVERIE

Letters from my love are coupled with another beautiful moonrise. The fellows that have seen the Mediterranean said the sky looked like Mediterranean blue. Everything is bathed in that soft mellow light that my love and I know so well. The night is so nice that I feel a thrill creep over me when I think that I am so fortunate. I had a good dinner. I am well. I am happy. Who could ask for more?

At the same time, I was in a quandary, wondering if anything could come of my dreams. I love Georgie more than anyone I have ever met. She says she loves me and yet I wonder if this love will remain when she sees me again. A subject like this would drive a guy crazy if he let it. I'll just use Scarlet O'Hara's philosophy in Gone with the Wind and say, "I'll think about that tomorrow." Seems like I'm always running away from something.

Georgie's letters have changed a lot since we started writing. Her June 18th letter greeted me as DEAREST, the first time she has used such an endearing salutation. Am I getting an answer to the questions I have been asking about her feelings for me? She seems much warmer and much more revealing of the real person she is underneath the stubbornness, independence, and loquaciousness. I feel as though I am really getting to know her. My love said in her letter that life was not long enough to do all the things she wanted to do. Sometimes I feel that way but when you have seen a country that is so much lower in living standards than ours, it makes me want to get back to the dear old USA and just settle down and enjoy each day. Would I go home after my year or stay on? After these unbearably hot nights, I wake up drained and wish that I was back home with frost on the ground.

Bad news. One of our boys, who came over before I did, was standing on the platform ready to get on a train, which would take him to his port of embarkation, when his heart failed him and he died. I had known him just long enough to give him a few haircuts, that is all. A guy never knows when his number is up over here. Life is one great gamble from start to finish.

Chasing the Enemy

By July 10 we had started our move forward chasing the Jap back up Ukhrul Road. We already had Ukhrul and were working a pincers movement. Came up to 22 milestone, formerly a village called Litan. Evacuated about 150 casualties, but I just about slipped over the khud twice on the last trip as it was raining making the road slick. I finally got to Main Dressing Station 42 at midnight. The smell of the dead was almost intolerable, since half hadn't been buried as yet. Our water tasted like mule's smell for several days. I caught some rainwater in a four-gallon tin and now had potable water again.

Now, filling in time waiting, feeling like a vulture waiting to pick up the wounded. A soldier who was moving up with his company came by my ambulance and said, "Yank, get that meat wagon of yours ready!"

Found a Jap hand grenade this morning. I thought I might like to keep it for a souvenir so I brought it back and showed it to some sappers and miners (British soldiers who are in charge of disarming unexploded artillery shells) and asked them if they could fix it so it wouldn't be lethal. One look and they said, "Get rid of it."

Saw seven Jap prisoners being guarded until they could be moved. They were a pitiful-looking bunch and probably hadn't eaten much for a while and could barely walk. I couldn't help feeling sorry for them. Seems like I was always feeling sorry for somebody.

On July 10 about sixty casualties came in. I took the first load down and got back just before midnight, falling onto my cot and was able to sleep through most of the night's artillery firing. The stench was gradually disappearing as most of the bodies were now buried or limed. The Royal English were forty-eight hours behind schedule on the bridge they were putting across the river so they could bring back casualties. Supplies were so piled up you would think it was a beachhead.

We were in a beautiful spot with high hills close to a river, which reminded me of the Washington coast, except that the jungle had so many different shades of green. The Sikh Medical Officer was educating me about his beliefs. He did not eat beef because he believed cattle are to be used for transport and plowing. Sikhs could eat pork, goat, and mutton. He didn't always observe his beliefs when we were issued rations that included beef with a variety of vegetables, called MV. Our captain happened to come upon Kessar Singh one day just bolting down MV and asked, "How come?" Singh replied, "This is all right. It is mutton and vegetables." His eyes twinkled, and you could see the faint trace of a smile underneath the heavy beard.

A miserable night after a long, tiresome trip lasting until daybreak. I didn't think I would be able to finish the run I was so tired, so tired that I didn't put up my mosquito net. As I fell into my stretcher-cot, I hoped that the atabrine I had been taking would protect me from malaria. Loud explosions shook my ambulance. "Moon" Miller said every one of them turned him over while he was sleeping in his stretcher.

During the first six months of 1944 there were 237,000 hospitalized disease and fever cases in the 14th Army alone (85 percent of its combat strength). We had evacuated nearly two hundred who had been in the jungle for six weeks without clean clothes and not much to eat but bully and biscuits. After we had driven about thirty-two miles of very rough road, we were kept waiting at the hospital for three hours, even with stretcher cases that had been on the road since 5 a.m. I exploded and finally got my patients unloaded.

It was difficult to keep calm sometimes after the stress of a long ambulance run, especially when seeing what I saw last night—a Jap who had had a bayonet run up his rectum, coming out alongside his penis. He had a five in one hundred chance of living.

By July 18, I was in Palel to get my "hack" fixed and was back at Litan for the night. Came back from Litan and went back to Palel to Headquarters. Went up to Ukhrul by jeep on a God-awful road. Could hardly navigate even with four chains. Got back to Litan again at 5 p.m. bringing a load. The casualties were always "browned off" (disgusted) with their army when in this predicament.

War is so full of extremes. Letters from home. Shocking sights of wounded soldiers. Moonlight. Enemy attacks with shells falling close by. A beautiful green parachute dropping supplies. A canteen being stolen. Now there was a poker game going on as others were arguing or carrying on conversations on numerous topics, to say nothing of Robinson's and Eberfeldt's singing. They were always making up parodies, especially to the tune "Inky Dinky Parlez Vous.

Stopped at the bazaar and even got a pineapple on credit! As I drove back, a rainbow appeared and I chased it. I drove along for miles, and the end seemed to stay just the same distance from me. If I'd caught up with it, maybe I would have found that pot of gold I fantasized when I chased a rainbow in South Dakota. The thought of finding gold was a real delight for a six-year-old living in hard times and eating a breakfast of grease, flour, and water gravy over bread.

Colonel Daugherty was to be posted in a peacetime station in India very soon and invited me down for a farewell party. Getting ready for a party with a colonel and other officers reminded me that we had been getting rather lax out here, away from civilization, living in our greasy coveralls. Now I had to be as "pukka" (dressed impeccably) as any English gentleman. Previously, if anyone even shined their boots, they got a ribbing for being too proper.

There were eighteen of us. I sat across from a lieutenant colonel. A major was on either side of me, a full colonel across from me. The Assistant Director of Medical Services was there as well as the Deputy Assistant Director of Medical Services and captains by the half dozens. I felt a little out of place being the only one without rank, but not after three rum punches that Lt. Norm Fenn and I fixed.

PUNCH CONCOCTION

1½ gals.of rum
2 quarts (4 cans) grapefruit juice
1 can crushed pineapple
1 bottle of lime cordial
1 bottle of lemon squash
Cinnamon
Juice from a can of pears
Juice from a can of sour cherries
Sugar and water

We served it in glasses with a finger of fresh pineapple, a sour cherry, and a quarter of pear. There was also whiskey, beer, and gin.

After a good dinner we sang songs (not me, but all the others) until 2 a.m. Each person around the table had a turn at a solo (skipping me each time round). This was one time when I really wished I had known how to sing. The party ended just in time to save us from observing a lieutenant colonel upchucking his dinner, which would have been very embarrassing for him I am sure.

Eberfeldt and Spallone were "stir-happy" and were raising hell. After they calmed down everything fell back into a routine again. They were now playing hopscotch. Too long in India or too long in the AFS. Is this what I was to be reduced to in time?

[Letter to Georgie]

You asked me what I thought about your buying a fur coat. I figure it is an all around good investment since it can be worn for casual wear as well as for dress occasions. The soft wooly fur makes you want to cuddle in it, right? I think it will be an ego boost. I will be looking at a glamour girl when I get home.

Sam Goldwyn, the movie producer, always gave his actors and actresses the real McCoy when he was doing a scene for a picture. If the script called for jewels, he gave them real jewels. If it called for a fur coat, he gave them a real fur coat. And yet my Mom always said that clothes don't make the person. But I think they can make the person feel good!

We got lots of rumors about the German people revolting and a shakeup in the Japanese government. I realized that I wouldn't be able to set all these rumors straight until I was out of the battle zone. At this moment I was watching the sun peeping through the clouds lighting up a beautiful valley with the rice growing tall. It varied in color, some light green and some dark green, in contrast to the hills, which were covered with dense, almost black, greenery. Regardless of the war, this was beautiful country.

There had been much land left unplanted because of the war. As rice was the staple of life, you know what that meant when there was no harvest to look forward to. Areas where rice paddies usually looked luxuriously green were now uneven with weeds, symbols of hard times to come.

On July 24, 1944, I picked up four battle casualties. Half way down to the hospital I stopped and tried to relieve my patients in any way that I could. One was cold although he was covered with blankets and was feverish. The blankets were coarse and held little warmth. One fellow asked for another blanket, and I put my own around his wet battle dress and then covered him with the coarser one. Before I helped take his stretcher out he said in a wavering voice, "May God bless you for your kindness." It made a lump come into my throat, and I could not find an answer.

We started the push down the Tamu road. Many casualties. The push continued with the support of the artillery. We had taken about thirty-five miles of the road. Wilson, Beeber, McWright, and I were now waiting for a load, but nothing happened.

On relief away from duty I saw a movie, the first one in months, out under the sky. Upon getting back to Headquarters, I had a pile of letters, three from my love including the words to several songs. After reading them, I played Offenbach's *"Gaite Parisienne,"* which a fellow who had been on leave in Calcutta had brought back for us. A wonderful day.

Fred Feddeman and I took a walk over against a hill and did a little target shooting at tin cans. He only had twenty rounds so didn't have enough practice to lose his habit of flinching when pulling the trigger. This was the first time I had fired a gun since I shot a Tommy gun last October.

A Special Tea

[From My Diary]

Took a load of "sitters" today, most just sick cases and trench foot from going around with wet feet in this jungle climate. On the way, I saw a mule company coming back for a rest after a month in the jungle. They had walked at least 25 miles and were still walking into darkness. Some were being pulled along as they held on to their mules' tails. My heart went out to these foot soldiers. Their lot was the toughest of any in the army.

I stopped at General Headquarters for lunch and Tim Krusi, head of the AFS mess, wanted me to stay for tea. We were to be honored by the presence of a general who came in later and was greeted by clean-shaven faces and clean clothes. Krusi had planned an elaborate tea for the occasion but the general didn't stay, so all the red salmon, cucumber, deviled egg and bacon sandwiches were just for us. We also had some grated cheese sandwiches and some cinnamon toast all served on nice clean green banana leaves to cover up our tin plates. The cinnamon was bought in the stick from the bazaar and then ground between rocks.

"Cookie" Krusi was known throughout the AFS since he wrote a letter to Mother India who answered his mail directed to the Question Box, a column in the *American Indian* magazine. Everyone identified with his letter, which inquired about how to make bully beef taste better. When we had to eat it two or three times a day, it was one of the things that got bad-mouthed. The answer was: Try the following recipe for Gurkha-Goo that has found favor with the Gurkhas.

Use one can of bully beef.
Take three rocks—to keep the rats away.
Take a hundred cans of beets.
Mix with a hundred cans of cheese.

Add a sack of onions.
Season with ten bottles of chutney.
Cover with a wet blanket.
Eat when starved.
You'd never guess it was made with bully beef!

Funny how little inconveniences can be upsetting in this horrendous war. I could overlook the rutty roads, the heat, and the insects but I lost my pen, after carrying it almost two years, and had to write with a pencil for a while. I bought another from Kelly. It scratched but was much better than the pencil. Now I was back in my routine of writing in my diary and complaining about the bully beef.

Section One and Two were merging as so many of each section had gone home. Many others were going on leave. I thought of the months that had passed out of Georgie's and my life and hoped that we could make it up after this part of my life was over. I was now talking to my love in my own mind.

"There is a nice moon out tonight. Should we go for a walk along the beach? It will be nice and cool and when we have cooled sufficiently we can go back in and dance some more. We could even go paddling in a canoe and watch the phosphorus the paddles kick up. Yes, we will do such things. We will catch up on lost time. You pick out the lake and we will go there some June or July at full moon time. We can always find something to fit the weather. Then when it is stormy and cold we will sit in front of the fireplace and play our favorite records."

Last night Ainsworth and I got happy on beer. We sat in the moonlight and talked. His home was on Telegraph Hill in San Francisco where most of the painters and writers hung out. He said he was a direct descendent of the man who carried the message to Garcia in the Spanish-American War. He said that his middle name, Rowan, attested to that. That got me curious and after the war I looked up information about Ainsworth's ancestor, who was Lt. Andrew S. Rowan of the U.S. Army. He carried a message to Calixto Garcia, who was a Cuban lawyer and revolutionary general who commanded a Cuban Army against Spain in the revolt of 1885 to 1898, which preceded the Spanish-American War. (The message asked what aid the United States should send.)

Smitty came back from leave in Calcutta with a cold and diarrhea and a tattoo! He told the tattoo artist to copy his St. Christopher's medal the same size onto his upper arm but it turned out the size of a teacup. Was he mad! My theory was that anyone getting a tattoo did so in an inebriated state.

Time to Meet the Commander

By August 5 we had all moved back to Headquarters at Imphal where we had electric lights. Our bashas, the mess hall, and bar (Cafe El Malaria) were comfortable.

Another section had replaced us up the road so we could have a rest. Seven months had been quite a long duty. Spallone and I played a few games of Ping-Pong but he couldn't quite cope with my backhand drive that foxed him.

CAFÉ EL MALARIA*

The Café, under the management of Latham, has turned out to be an excellent job. Without doubt it is the only bar within several hundred miles. It caters chiefly to the AFS, but outsiders are allowed to come in. It takes up the entire building that used to be the office—50 by 16 feet, constructed of . . . mud walls and thatch roof supported by poles. One of the inside walls and the floor are covered with bamboo matting. The three remaining walls are divided into three layers of panels. The top two rows are painted yellow, and on them are drawn the insignia of various nightclubs: the Stork Club, the Panther Room, the Glass Hat, and the Brown Derby are represented. The four windows and the door are covered with green curtains. Throughout the room, are a number of small tables each encircled by chairs. At one end stands the Gramophone on a table covered with a large assortment of records. At the other end of the room is the bar, a very pukka, homemade job with foot-rail and all, constructed chiefly by Whiteside. Latham presides as bartender. . . .

*From *History of the American Field Service: 1920-1955*

Robinson and I went for a long walk and met an English-speaking native who told us about his life. We asked him how he thought the country would be affected when the military pulled out. He said the standard of living would be higher than it was before they came. I wondered about this as so many were living off what they made serving the military. The British kept saying they were going to allow India/Burma self-government after the war. At least that was something to look forward to. The Indians who opposed the British weren't so optimistic about a British win. The Japanese were using the Indian yearning for independence as a way to seduce some of them to serve the Japanese cause.

I had time to notice the flag we put up a couple of weeks ago. The weather was so hot and muggy that it was just hanging like it would never wave its stars-and-stripes again. We had a break in our day when we noticed three jeep loads of Gurkhas coming down the road toward us. The jeep in the middle carried an officer and his aides. It was Lord Wavell, Field Marshall, who in 1941 became commander in chief of all British forces in India. Rarely did we meet those in command, so this was a welcome visit.

When he got to AFS driver Alex Roach, our major told him that Alex was deaf. Wavell raised his voice a little and said, "What was your hard of hearing caused from?" Alex replied, "Michigan." All of us stifled a laugh. Alex came from Michigan all right, but that wasn't the answer to the question Lord Wavell had asked him.

It was Sunday. I was awakened by a small civilian boy we hired bringing in the regular chota harzi, which is the before-breakfast snack. When served in Indian hotels it consists of tea, toast, and fresh fruit. Ours was only tea and small semi-sweet crackers.

Robinson and I went to the bazaar, but prices were high so I spent the rest of the day cutting hair since I was the only one who offered to be the barber. Then off to the local cinema which opened again after several months. We saw Lana Turner and Clark Gable in *Somewhere I'll Find You*—lots of Turner but threadbare plot, which was cut so much that it was difficult to follow.

Although I was here to rest, I did some duties when requested. I made a run to Dimapur to take Japanese and Japanese-influenced Indians to be interned there.

[Letter to Georgie]

Moore tuned in on a radio broadcast and we heard Jerome Kern's "The Way You Look Tonight." I immediately thought of you and the way you look in your picture. I'm still wondering why I haven't worn out your picture by looking at you so much! Having a dekko (look) at your picture whenever I want is very comforting. It will be wonderful when I can see you as you are, in the flesh. What a happy day to look forward to.

It was such a beautiful night last night that I couldn't help thinking of you and wishing you were with me walking along in the soft moonlight and jasmine-scented air. Words are inadequate to express the yearning I felt. I think the world could have ended right then if you had been with me and I wouldn't have cared much.

As I write this letter, my heart is heavy and brimming over with things I want to say to you. I don't know where to begin really. I'll start off first by saying that I love you more than anything else in the world. I need you just as much as you need me, if not more. Please say that you will forgive me and that you love me enough to wait a little while longer, please. Please.

I have been told that I will be leaving for Italy as soon as I can get a ship. I am so sorry that I have to stand you up this Christmas but if you love me like I love you, and I think you do love me a lot, time will not mean much to either of us. I know that I would not be happy back in civilian life with a war going on and me not doing my part. I would really feel like a slacker if I came home now. Please say that you will forgive me and that you will wait a little while longer. I love you so much. I almost cry when I think how much this letter will hurt you. I promise on my life that I will come back when the war in Italy is over and if it is not over in a year, I'm coming home anyway. Please don't cry. Consider yourself engaged.

Back to Calcutta

While I was still at Imphal, I drove 132 miles over rough and crooked road taking five Jap officers to Dimapur. On the way back, I picked up a coolie who had been hit by a truck and left to die. He was barely alive when I got him to a hospital. This was my last drive in India. In mid-August I caught the train to Pandu, then rode across the Bramaputra River on the ferry and took another train. Slept on the floor of a third class coach all night. Got in Parbatapur at 6 a.m. where I changed trains to a broad gauge. Our railcar compartment smelled like a pigsty, as there is human excrement all over the floor.

When I got settled, a scruffy, dirty, ragged boy came up and started singing. Sure enough it was "Pistol Packin' Mama." The veins stood out on his scrawny neck as he squeaked out the song. I was considering giving him a few annas when he broke out in "Oh, Johnny." When he finished, I gave him four annas. I figured a kid who could sing two songs I didn't even know the words to deserved "bhakshee." All we could hear when he stopped singing was the cry of "Bhakshee," the cry of India.

At last we were in Calcutta where I headed to the American Express Office after lunch in order to send flowers to Georgie for her birthday. I was told it would take six weeks. I made up my mind to send them anyway. Four of us had a suite of rooms in the Grand Hotel with a bearer to shine our shoes, make our beds, and bring us tea; a dhobi (clothes washer); a wet sweeper; a dry sweeper; and another bearer that served us drinks in our suite. Our bearer lay outside our door waiting to serve us. It certainly beat living out of my ambulance.

Every time I stepped out of the hotel, shoeshine boys swamped me. They tagged along repeating, "Sahib, Sahib, shoeshine, Sahib" until I hollered jao (go) in a gruff voice. Today one had a variation, saying, "Shoe shine, Sahib. No-God damn good, no God damn pay."

We had music with our lunch and dinner, which we could have in the winter garden if we wanted. The dining room was huge. When you entered you could view a sea of waiters (bearers) in white uniforms with different colored head turbans and arm bands. Some served only liquors, others did nothing but reset tables, others took plates away, and still others kept water glasses full.

There was a band for dancing, but the respectable kinds of girls were scarce. The music in the Princess Room was wafting out to me, beckoning me. I watched the soldiers dancing, but the type of girls they were dancing with were not quite the type of girls that appealed to me. I thought of my love and visualized her being the belle of the ball, dancing with me. And once again I was worrying over breaking my promise and going to Italy instead of heading home.

I went to the swimming club with Frank Mayfield and Fred Feddeman. We had a good time rubbing elbows with the higher social strata. There was a large hemisphere with a round board platform on top covered with canvas. The whole thing floated on top of the water like a cork. A bunch of guys and gals would get on it and start it going around in circles, tipping all ways trying to make someone lose balance and fall into the water. I fell off frequently until I learned the fast footwork to maintain the proper equilibrium to stay on top.

Had dinner with Ruppert, Spallone, and Elberfeld at a special table where the bearer was very attentive to us.

SAMPLE MENU

1 Consomme Doria
2 Crème d'Orge
3 Escalopes de Beckti Egyptienne
4 Poulet Saute Valencienne
5 Primeurs des Indes
6 Glace Crème Maltaise
7 Friandises
8 Mocca

We talked about those who were going on to Italy—Don Hill who was already studying the language, Ruppert who had been to Italy before, and Spallone who spoke it a little, so I wouldn't have much difficulty picking it up. We heard there had been a new landing in France. Maybe Germany and Italy would fall before the year was up.

The orchestra was knocking itself out playing "My Devotion" followed by "Tiger Rag." I don't think anybody could realize how nice it was to get back to civilization unless they had been out in the war zone roughing it for six months or more. Even though we were not in danger any longer, the heat was still with us. My bearer just brought me a tall glass of lemonade with lots of ice, since I learned that liquor doesn't mix with hot weather.

I was reading letters from my love and thinking when I answered them that it would be months before I would get answers back. I probably wouldn't know if I had been forgiven for staying longer until my mail caught up with me in Italy. W. T. Smith was leaving on a merchant ship soon, so I gave him the ivory that a little Burmese had given me, so that he could mail it to Georgie when he arrived in the U.S. I looked at a lot of silk today, but didn't feel the quality was up to standard. The merchants are clever and will get the better of you if you aren't wary.

There are beggars everywhere. They do everything to get sympathy so they can be assured of getting "bhakshee," but most of the time their everyday plight would invoke sympathy in anyone. Once I threw some banana skins out the window of the train and saw a child pick them up and bolt them down instantly. Also I saw a woman who could barely crawl picking up grains of rice, two or three at a time, between the ties on the railroad siding. It reminded me of picking up coal along the railroad tracks in Yakima when I was a kid. Finally, the woman moved her legs that were nothing but skin-covered bones. I admit that I had become hardened to such sights over the past few months. I couldn't help them all so I couldn't worry over it all the time.

THE BLACK HOLE OF CALCUTTA

Went on a Red Cross tour where we stopped at the site of the original Black Hole. It was covered with marble and had an iron fence around it with a plaque telling the horrendous story of the capture of the English fort in Calcutta on June 20, 1756, by the troops of Surajah Dowlah, the Nawab of Bengal. They thrust 146 prisoners into a room fourteen feet ten inches wide and eighteen feet long for one night. The room had two small windows and the night was intensely hot. Only twenty-three prisoners survived.

Another visit was to a mosque that the Mohammedans (now called Muslims) had built. We had to take off our shoes before we stepped from the sidewalk onto the white marble and on up many flights of stairs to the top of one of the two towers. This afforded us a perfect view of the whole city. At 6 a.m. and 6 p.m. a man in each tower called the Muslims to worship while praying to Allah facing their holy city of Mecca.

Next was a visit to the Jains Temple, which is Hindu. While the Mosque was plain but beautiful, the Jains Temple was in varied colors with hundreds of spires all brightly colored. There were sparkling chandeliers of cut crystal and gold and silver leaf. The main dome was stained glass, with figures of men and horses. The god had a huge three-fourths-inch diamond between the eyes. A flame burning in a small glass case had been burning for nearly a hundred years and was giving off no smoke. The Hindus believe that if it does give off smoke, the temple will be destroyed.

CREMATIONS

A visit to Calcutta would not be complete without visiting the burning ghats. The bodies are brought to this holy place and for a fee they are burned and tended by men who make this their life work. There were places to burn about eighteen bodies at one time. We saw the body of an old woman lying on a charpoy with flowers all around her and covering her. There was no weeping. It is said that relatives put rice into the mouth of the dead one to sustain the person on the journey. After they turned to ashes, the ashes were thrown into the river, which carried them to paradise or hell.

Even before we arrived we saw from afar huge piles of wood (mango) used for the cremation of bodies. The price for cremation with this cheap wood is 10 rupees. The wealthy Hindus are burned with sandalwood, which has a pleasing odor. Otherwise the smell is quite unpleasant. Little beggar outcasts are there straining and washing the ashes in hopes of finding some gold or silver.

The British have stopped the women from watching their husbands burning on the funeral pyre. It seemed that when the bodies were burned they sometimes sat up due to muscular contraction and the women took this as a signal that their husbands were calling them to throw themselves into the fire. The British now make the body burners break the joints so the body will not twist out of shape.

Bob Grey, of the Boston Greys, came back this morning with a hammer and sickle with a clenched fist under it tattooed on his left forearm. He isn't a Communist, and he didn't seem the least bit inebriated. No one could understand this. Later Grey sat cursing himself for getting that tattoo. He said that his mother would go wild when she saw it. Of course he could have it taken off, but it would be very painful and might leave a scar.

[From My Diary]

I am pretty low today, confined to my room with the GIs (gastro-intestinal disorder). Our bearer just came in and said goodnight. The poor bearer has a hard time because Mayfield is always breaking glasses and bottles on the marble floor and lying on everyone's bed but his own, messing them up for the bearer to straighten out again.

Am now in Serampore Hospital, 20 miles from Calcutta on the banks of the Hoogly River. My first and second tests were negative and if my next one is also negative I will be discharged. I am taking tablets for my illness and feel better if I drink enough water. I had to be left behind when everyone was ordered to Italy, so I want to catch up with the other fellows as soon as I can.

While lying here in the hospital bed I have taken a vow that I will be faithful to Georgie. I belong to only one person and that is Georgie. Hospital time gives me the opportunity to think about things like this, to read (am now reading Strange Interlude by Lillian Smith which I can hardly put down) and to lie back without worrying about driving over the bank in my ambulance or being the target of Jap attack. I can muse about anything I feel like.

Now I can even walk down by the river to watch the little sampans float by on their way to fishing. I again have taken time to smell the flowers! I found two new kinds. One is white in the shape of a five-pointed star with a tiny yellow center. It has no fragrance but is pretty. The other one is varicolored and about the same size only it looks something like a honeysuckle. It grows on a tree that has leaves something like a black locust. I picked one of the long stems of leaves and started plucking them off like I used to do sunflowers. "She loves me. She loves me not. She loves me. She loves me not. She loves me." It ended up the way I wanted it to. Do you think I would gamble and try two out of three? Not on your life!

My love said in her letter that I must be a person who is easily hurt. I admit it. Much of the time I can be hurt but never show it outwardly. I have a tendency just to draw back into my shell and wait for my chance to blow up.

I heard that in the Central Burma campaign Merrill's Marauders (U.S. Special Forces) not only captured the air base at Mythinya, but also captured the town itself. The Chinese were supposed to come and relieve them immediately and take the credit for it but through friction between Chinese and American forces, they didn't show up in time and the Japs retook it. I hear that Romania has seen which way the pendulum is swinging and finally switched to our side. Bulgaria, the same.

The breakfast we had this morning was something! A slice of black looking bread with weevils in it, two pieces of salty bacon three fourths raw, a spoonful of Welsh rarebit which was nauseating. To wash it down we had a cup of watery tea with little, very little, milk and sugar. I learned to consider the weevils as extra protein!

While I am waiting for mail again, I am reminiscing about Yakima. It is very beautiful in the Yakima Valley when everything is ripe and ready for harvest. The trees each seem to have a different color. The pear trees range in color from light yellow to a deep violet. The leaves on the peach trees are equally colorful. Mom wrote me from Yakima about her peaches, plums, and blackberries. Melons were ripe and the grape arbor was loaded, filling the whole back yard with their fragrance.

At last, Captain Craven came bringing me mail and two books. I was now reading *Between Tears and Laughter* by Lin Yutang. On the radio I just heard "I'll Get By" sung by Frank Lund on Abe Lyman's program "Waltz Time."

From the time I began moving closer to Calcutta and then ending up in the hospital, the Franco-American Seventh Army (supported by British airborne troops, RAF, Allied flyers, and by British, American, and French warships) landed on the Mediterranean French Coast. The Seventh drove north to join up with the U.S. armies driving east. The French forces threw the Germans out of one city after another in the path of their advance. While the British and Canadians were sweeping across the north of France, the American Third Army converged on Paris. On August 19 an insurrection arose in Paris pushing the Germans out of the city. Six days later General Leclerc, leading a French tank force, entered the capital. American forces followed, and General de Gaulle arrived amidst great acclaim and rejoicing. By August 27, 1944, German resistance inside Paris was ended.

At Kalyan, thirty miles east of Calcutta, I saw the medical officer, but he would not discharge me until September 5. As soon as he left, though, I packed up and left through the back gate, hiring a rickshaw to get away from the place as quickly as possible. I hitched a ride to Calcutta in a jeep and took a room in the Grand Hotel. I called up Craven and told him I was out and asked him when he could get me a ride to Bombay. We had to pay "bhakshee" to an Indian ticket agent, but we got the seat the next afternoon. Lieutenant Fernley and I came to Bombay first class with a dining car and a berth for overnight.

Since I left the hospital, where I felt starved, I have made up for it. In Bombay, we had lunch at the Parisienne, a sidewalk café, looking out over the sea. I then caught the train back to Kalyan to catch the rest of the guys (Hamilton, Clark, Spallone, Elberfeld, Feddeman, and Ruppert) who are going to Italy.

The transit camp being built at Kalyan plans to take care of nearly a hundred thousand troops. I saw the devastation left after the Jap bombardment in Bombay in April. Blocks and blocks of the city were completely leveled. Wartime India is taking its toll. Mayfield flew home. Baskin is sick. Gilliam is in Calcutta, sick with jaundice. Bennett from The Dalles is working his way home on a transport. Chet Long has BT malaria and won't be going with us either. Spallone had a relapse, but I think he will be okay in a day or so.

I am awaiting orders to move but have no clean clothes. The regular dhobi has refused to work because a British officer cussed him out when he brought back his clothes late. I decided to wash my own clothes. An Indian saw me and offered to do them. He couldn't stand to see me lower myself in the presence of other Indians or see me do a menial job that is usually done by the dhobi.

Feddeman, Clark, Hamilton, Spallone, and I got permission to go to the city yesterday. We immediately got a taxi and went to the Taj Mahal Hotel to meet our officer and hopefully pick up money and letters. Fred and I went one way and Paul C. went another way, the way to find liquor. He once wrote a little piece about it.

SOLILOQUY

When I am tight
I sometimes fight.
I seldom read.
I never write.
More often I just
Sit and think,
And pour myself
Another drink.

Fred bought an alligator skin purse for $50. I got some little trinkets for my nieces and a piece of silk for my love. It was seven yards of forty-five-inch gold sari material embroidered with silver metallic thread. We ate at the Taj where we luxuriated in air-conditioning while we ate the best hamburger I have had in India.

LUNCHEON MENU
September 7, 1944

We could have one each of ABC, or two of A and one of C

A. Oxford Brawn and Salad or Hot or Cold Consommé
B. Fried Fish and Lemon, Fried Potatoes and Vegetable
    Grilled Hamburg Steak, Mixed Vegetable and Fried Onion
    Bombay Curry and Rice
C. Chocolate and Vanilla Ice, Cheese and Biscuits, Coffee

Our train stopped at every little place for the thirty-three-mile trip back to camp. Had news that we would have to wait longer to leave. No getting letters or mailing the ones I had already written. I waited a full two months for letters from Georgie when I first came over, so I guessed I could wait again.

We saw the movie *Buckskin Frontier* with Richard Dix and Jane Wyatt. It cost one rupee and on the ticket it said no refunds for any reason whatsoever, even though I thought it was Hollywood at its worst.

Tonight we were invited by the captain in the Royal Engineers who is building this camp, to dinner and to the club. They treated us like kings since we were the first U.S. service people who had visited the club. They had invited three sisters (nurses) to the mess. One was a major. Then on to the club where there were about fifteen western women and about forty-five men. Since I had committed myself to Georgie it was frustrating to be in this social situation without her to complete the picture. I found myself dreaming of my love dancing with me in a big ballroom back home. When the music stopped after each dance, I was brought back to the reality of not being home and not going home very soon.

On Shipboard

After a last fling in Bombay on September 13, Paul Clark, Richard Hamilton, and I went aboard ship and were soon comfortably settled in second-class cabins. From our porthole I could look west at the round domes of many buildings etched against a varicolored sunset.

At last on the sea I felt free. The jungle always gave me a feeling that I was being crushed. I couldn't seem to get enough oxygen from that hot, humid air. That night, I got a terrible chill and shivered under three blankets while the temperature outside was 90 degrees F. I took five grains of quinine and ten grains of atabrine. The chill that I had turned out to be malaria. I was admitted to the ship's hospital with a fever of 103 degrees.

Had thirty grains of quinine in short order and was to get thirty more that same day. It affected my spleen, which was enlarged and caused severe pain. I would have given up my place in Heaven (if I have one) to be able to eat just one piece of fruit. Instead they brought me two pieces of dry cheese and three pieces of hard tack plus a cup of tea with the merest trace of cream and sugar.

A week later I came down with jaundice and was so yellow that an Indian officer took me for an Afghan. I was so sick, but did manage to keep down a dish of oatmeal. They brought in a fellow with pneumonia who spent the night coughing up his life. They buried him that same day.

POSH

I have just learned what POSH stands for. When many English citizens were serving in India (before air-conditioning), they would go out to India on the port side of the ship, which was cooler. Then when they traveled from India to England they requested the starboard side, which was cooler. Hence POSH, port side out, starboard home.

After reading the book *The Lost Weekend* I thought I'd stop drinking altogether. The character in that book not only lost one weekend but many during his life. I had lost a year of my life myself serving overseas. I was trying to think of what became of this year. Was my wanderlust like an addiction? Would I lose many more "weekends" away from my love?

We reached Aden, one of the hottest places on earth, on September 21. There were quite a few ships in port and even one Italian submarine. Aden sits on a huge rock with its skyline of many buildings. I only saw it through a porthole as no one was allowed ashore. I wouldn't have been allowed ashore anyway as ill as I was.

Left Aden at sundown after discharging some soldiers and sailors and taking on some Royal Air Force and British Other Ranks. Slept on deck because of the heat and no breeze whatsoever. The deck felt very hard even with a hair mattress under me because I was so skinny that I had no padding at all. This malaria, jaundice, and heat took their toll. It was five more days and five more nights before we reached the Mediterranean, where we had to put on warm clothes. Going through the Red Sea we passed islands that were scorched rocks rising out of the sea looking like the landscape of Hell.

On board were about 125 Italians going home on leave after being on the cruiser *Eritrea*, which is in Ceylon working for the Allies. One of the fellows brought me canned milk and taught me a little Italian.

At noon I discovered the loss of my wallet, which had everything that I owned in it, except my passport. I had 470 rupees and a $10 bill, which I was saving for a rainy day. My picture of Georgie with the lucky penny was gone. In all my travels I had never had a wallet stolen before. I am such a tall man that not many people will tackle me. But this was someone creeping up when I was asleep and in the ship's hospital no less.

We got into Suez at 3 p.m. on September 27. I was shuttled about several times because I had lost my papers. Finally, they put me in an officers' ward in a British hospital eight miles out of Cairo where I learned I would be in bed for at least six weeks. The other fellows going on to Italy took up a collection for me before they left so I am not completely flat on my heels. The nurse came in and changed the curtains on my bed stand and said she was going to make a worthwhile husband out of me for some girl. I wondered if that would be possible.

[Letter to Georgie]

Please do not tell my sister about my being in the hospital or she will tell my Mom and I don't want her to know. She worries so much. Since my brother and I have gone overseas, she has aged something terrible. I can tell you that I am in Egypt where the climate is pleasant.

Am now hearing on the radio "I'll Get By as Long as I Have You." That is the way I feel but I don't really have you, Georgie. Now they are playing "The Isle of Capri." That song takes me back to the spring of '32 when we got our first radio in Yakima.

With the help of one of the "up" patients I went out on the balcony just as the big full moon was rising. I could hear the hymn singing from across a narrow street. Those twenty minutes spent on the balcony without the MO's orders was breaking a law in the army, but after all, you know what the full moon does to me.

Here is my day.

5:30 a.m. tea,
6 a.m. temperature taken and I wash and shave,
7:30 a.m. breakfast and bed made.
9:15 a.m. tea again,
10 a.m. doctor comes around,
12 noon lunch and nap,
3 p.m. tea and cakes,
4 p.m. bed remade,
6 p.m. dinner,
9:30 p.m. Ovaltine,
10 p.m. lights out.
Between times is reading, napping or writing letters.

Now I was confined, spending my time looking forward to meals such as onions, cucumbers, and tomatoes plus a leg of boiled chicken for lunch. I relied on one of the "up" patients to bring me colored pencils on his trip into the city so I could make my own Christmas cards. Getting acquainted with the other patients involved a disagreement with Rusty concerning whether there will be World War III someday. Smitty seemed to be interesting and well-versed in French, Italian, and Arabic with a smattering of Greek, but a loner since his wife deserted him some eight years ago. He told me a story about a soldier who hadn't written his wife in many months. He was told he had to write a letter a week from then on, a command. Was this autobiographical? Probably.

Boredom was relieved by a visit from the flower man who sold me a dozen roses, which I have begun associating with Georgie. A radio station is playing "The Dance of the Flowers" from Tchaikovsky's *Nutcracker Suite*.

I am getting lessons in the geography of the area from Smitty and Rusty, who have been in Jerusalem several times. They say that the old city is about thirty feet higher than it was in Biblical times. When it was destroyed by invaders, the new buildings were built over the ruins. Smitty told me that the women in this area tear their hair out at funerals when some relative dies. A law was passed prohibiting it, so the women now go to funerals with bunches of loose hair attached to their scalps and they pull that out only to pick it up afterwards so they can use it again!

[Letter to Georgie]

I purposely let Friday the 13th pass by without writing. I am not superstitious but just careful! I was thinking this afternoon just after lunch how I would like to hear the wind singing through pine trees, or to hear a stream as it gurgles its way over a rocky bed. How much I would like to be lying on my back on a hill looking up through the tall pine trees as the wind sways them gently back and forth, catching fleeting glimpses of the stars. Then I would like to see a fine rain falling, a drizzle or a mizzle. I would like to walk through a flower garden with plenty of fruit trees and a vegetable garden as well. I would like to feel the warmth of a bright fire on a bitter cold day and I would like to hear rain pattering on a roof and I would like to be trudging through the rain with you by my side, just walking through a foggy darkness. Just give me these plain things and a generous helping of my love and I'm sure the biting of the wanderlust bug would have no effect whatsoever.

A Year of Duty

I had reserved this date, October 16, as my going home date, but now if the war lasts another year it will be another October 16 before I get home. Rusty left today, and I have had no one to talk with but a psychopathic case who came in uninvited, pulled up a chair alongside my bed, and started in on me.

I had been thinking about my Mom who expected me to be home for Christmas. She was as disappointed as Georgie because she canned my favorite fruit for me and was planning a Christmas dinner of my favorite dishes. Being the "baby" of the family my mom was always concerned about me. Now I remembered that Georgie and I had something in common. She is also the "baby" of her family, the last of eleven.

By October 21, I walked over to the club, then on down to a canteen to pick up some razor blades. As a result I was so tired that I had black spots in front of my eyes. Our new Medical Officer, just out of training in England, was going over me with a fine-toothed comb, resulting in evidence of a malaria relapse and also anemia so I am on quinine again. Besides my head buzzing with side effects, I had a letter from Headquarters stating that my next year doesn't start until I get out of here. Oh, well, another full moon is coming up.

The weeks of my recuperation were filled with taking Sister Fraser to a movie and going out to lunch at Groppis Tea Garden in Cairo. Captain Smith, who spoke Arabic, was a great help as the waiters don't speak English. We spent two hours walking through the bazaar and saw the Blue Mosque. I almost got a stiff neck following the pedestrian traffic on the sidewalk! I hadn't seen so many European "skirts" (as I called females then) since our docking in Tasmania. There were French, Syrians, Greeks, and Italians.

Stopped in at the famous Sheppards Hotel for lemonade as I still didn't trust myself on alcohol. Took a taxi across the Nile out to the pyramids and then had tea at Mena House. It was here in Cairo where two of the "Big Three," Roosevelt and Churchill, met with Chiang Kai-shek for a conference on November 22-27, 1943, discussing plans for a British-U.S.-Chinese operation in northern Burma.

I had always wondered about the great pyramids, which served as royal tombs. The Egyptians believed life after death depended upon the preservation of the body. They developed embalming and placed valuables and objects of daily life in tombs for use in the afterlife. I was fortunate to be able to visit The Great Pyramid built during 2600 B.C. It is estimated that the Great Pyramid contains 2,300,000 blocks of stone, averaging two and a half tons each. When I look at anything this monumental, I empathize with the slave labor it took to complete the task with forty men needed to move each block into place. Imagine a hundred thousand slaves working over a period of twenty years to complete a structure whose base is large enough to cover more than eight football fields and whose height is as tall as a forty-story skyscraper—and all for the glory of Pharoah Khuyfu.

As I came back from this exciting place with such historical significance, I began to wonder how I could convince Georgie to wait for me. I found this piece to express my concern. Guess I want my cake and I want to eat it too, as Georgie sometimes says.

WAIT FOR ME
by Konstantin Simonov

Wait for me, I will come back, only wait and wait.
Wait though rain clouds looming black make you desolate.
Wait though winter snowstorms whirl.
Wait though summer's hot.
Wait though no one else will wait and the past forgot.
Wait though from the distant front not one letter comes.
Wait for me, I will come back.
Pay no heed to those who'll so glibly tell you that it is in vain to wait,
Though my mother and sons think that I am gone,
Though my friends abandon hope and back there at home rise and
*   toast my memory.*
Wrapped in silence painted,
Wait.
And when they drink their toasts, leave your glass undrained.
Wait for me, I will come back though from death's own jaws.
Let the friends who did not wait think it chance no more.
They will never understand, those who did not wait,
How it was your waiting that saved me in the war
And the reason I've come through.
We shall know, we two,
Simply this: You waited as no one else could do.

Armistice Day, November 11, 1944, was just another day. Arrived at the British Convalescent Depot 2, El Balla, on the banks of the Suez Canal. They wanted to keep me a month, but I hitched a ride down to Deversoir (American Air Base) and had a talk with the adjutant and he said he could get me on a plane to Paine Field in Cairo. If I had waited any longer it might have taken me a month or six weeks to leave for Italy.

In this camp there were Poles, Greeks, Yugoslavs, Italians, Canadians, Australians, South Africans, and one lone U.S. fellow, me. I only stayed overnight and then went down to one of the bases which was about sixty miles away and made arrangements for the trip to my Headquarters in Italy.

I ran into a British captain who was liaison officer at this American Air Base. He was being sent home to England to try and hush up the scandal of two thousand babies whose fathers are American Negroes and whose mothers are English "girls." There didn't seem to be any scandal because white soldiers were making English "girls" pregnant.

PART FOUR:
AFTERMATH IN ITALY

Naples

On November 15, 1944, I arrived at Headquarters in Naples. I was picked up at the airport and dropped off at our convalescent depot where we lived in a large, high, drafty, cold, and dimly lit villa that belonged at one time to a Fascist. The first two nights I was bedded down in the tower and caught a terrific cold. I had to climb seventy-eight steps of a winding staircase to get up there. No decent heat, light, or plumbing though we did have a piano, radio, and bar, plus scads of late books and magazines. And let me not forget the excellent food cooked by an ex-chef of one of the best hotels in Naples. So there were compensations.

Now that I was at Headquarters, I had forty-one letters from my love. All these letters answered a lot of previously unanswered questions. Georgie forgave me for not coming home at Christmas as I promised I would. It didn't seem possible that I had someone who was really in love with me and who would wait for me. When I wrote letters to my love, she called them K rations. She wrote me a poem she composed:

Glancing rays thru gloomy raindrip
Hunted tune midst songs amaze
Finding you alone so tender
Clear and glazed now my repose.

Amid such yearning there I stretch
And far along you sit and wonder
Is it you then makes me fonder?
For I will not tell it all.

'Tis you then doubled wonder
You who charmingly persists.
If I wanted could I muster
All that stubbornly resists?

I didn't always understand poetry but I did get the message that I was so persistent that she couldn't resist me. She might even be growing fonder!

[Letter to Georgie]

I am sending you some things: a Sudanese leather handbag, a set of 18 hand-laced leather coasters of three sizes, 7 yards of embroidered silk, and a piece of brocade from India, and a nice pair of shoes I found in a Cairo shop. They are Swiss made and I don't know why I bought them but you can probably set them on your fireplace mantle. You could wear them if you stretched them a little. You are going to be really surprised to receive these beautiful rust-colored, high topped-leather shoes with button closures. (They were toddler shoes. Georgie was beginning to get a taste of my Missouri wit. Or was this a hint that we might need them someday for our children?)

Just to get an idea of prices here, men's shoes on the civilian market were 4,000 to 5,000 lire and women's shoes were about 1,750 to 2,250 lire. Prices were rising all the time. There were still black markets that could not be squelched. I sold my mosquito boots for 600 lire to Peter Young. It was a good thing that he bought them because two hours later his billfold was stolen. (A lire was approximately a penny in U.S. currency as I remember.)

I was now out and about. I attended my first opera ever, *La Traviata*, in the opera house built more than a hundred years ago and sat just above the Emperor's box.

Thanksgiving dinner was a feast of turkey, cranberry sauce, celery, dressing, pumpkin pie, and ice cream. On Thanksgiving Day, I could always find plenty to be thankful for. This year I had so much—my life after a year of war, my love after standing her up, receiving her swell letters and her waiting for me another year, and my health—what is left of it.

I just heard about someone not so fortunate, Richard Hamilton, whom I was with two months ago. He ran over a land mine and is now in the hospital, paralyzed, but I learned later that he recovered except for losing the sight of one eye. He later received a Purple Heart from the U.S. Government. Then I heard from India that we lost Ralph E. Boaz and William T. Orth in a plane crash on October 23, 1944. They volunteered to assist the crew of a U.S. DC-3 that was to drop supplies to a unit stationed in the hills northeast of Tiddim. In dropping the supplies, the last bundle failed to clear the tail and the plane could not gain altitude and it crashed.

Getting word of all these AFS drivers made me feel very low. Letters from Georgie lifted my spirits. Georgie and I had a little joke between us—she sent me a paper doll and the words to the song "Paper Doll" beginning with, "I want a paper doll that I can call my own." I pondered over the idea of having a paper doll of my own. It certainly would have had its advantages. Just think how nice it would be. She couldn't get mad at me. She couldn't talk back. I couldn't disappoint her for not coming home when I said I would!

She wouldn't feel bad when and if she got bad news. I told Georgie that she might be sorry for sending me the paper doll. She might lose me altogether!

My thoughts were interrupted by a brewing argument here at our Headquarters in Naples. It focused on the discrimination that exists in the states and what could be done to make our government the ideal of all nations. So far we had agreed that one way would be to have a more liberal form of education and to improve social conditions. Big job, eh? I could never resist such heated debates. After such discussions we then resumed our down-to-earth duties.

George Collins and I had been working on a battery-charging gas motor. We planned on tearing it down so we could set the magnet points and clean the carburetor and do a few more minor adjustments. As no instruction book came with it, we could not figure out how to get the flywheel off. We didn't have the necessary tools anyway, so we had to just clean the carburetor and spark plug (a one-cylinder motor). We got it all together again and started it up only to have it burn out its main bearing. Well, that fixed us. We cannot charge batteries now so that is one less thing for us to do. I really didn't have to work because I was on "con" (convalescence) leave but sitting around gets tiresome.

With time on my hands, I had been giving Peter Young driving lessons. He was from a rich family in Connecticut, but never had a chance to learn to drive before coming overseas. I tried to be patient with him, but when he got into a tough situation such as approaching a busy intersection he got so excited that he forgot what to do. Luckily he came through without an accident.

We went out to the medical center to a GI show put on by a ballet troupe. Just as I had begun to appreciate this program, the GIs whistled and howled like an audience in a cheap burlesque show back home. It was embarrassing for the performers I am sure. Between the numbers, they had a pianist who played serious music, which was not geared to providing relief from battle fatigue. Consequently, a large part of the audience talked all the time and many just got up and walked out. Sitting in our Headquarters playing records turned out to be more recreational for me.

The next day, I put on my new ankle-length brown shoes and some nice-looking gaiters and went for a long walk. I felt very self-conscious for wearing such well-made shoes when so many poor people going by were wearing tatters of shoes or no shoes at all. Many would stop and admire my beautiful new shoes to my embarrassment.

Just got a letter announcing that I was a new uncle to my brother Shirley's boy, Gary. Shirley was in the Philippines. Later I learned that he had been hit in the back with a sniper's bullet and was eligible for a disability pension after he got home. My mother received a two-star pin for two sons serving in World War II.

I had seen the doctor who said that my blood test wasn't up to normal as yet so I must go in again tomorrow. Got the results of an Icterus Index test. They injected some of my blood into a guinea pig and the pig developed jaundice, which means I had not recovered. I now had two more kinds of pills to take.

At our kitchen there was a barefooted lady with four barefooted kids who usually came about twice a week for food. The oldest child, about five, was a little scantily clad girl who knew a few words of English. I gave her a chocolate bar one day and she was overjoyed. I felt so sorry for this woman and her children, walking barefooted over cobblestones in December.

Shirley Kunkel served in the Philippines.

Back in Service Again

Yes, here it was early December and I was still convalescing, but by December 8, 1944, I was back in service again and assigned a three-fourths-ton Dodge ambulance. Latham and several others were waiting for a ship to France. Peter Stewart was on his way to take a commission with the Indian Army. This was the fellow who told me in Burma that if he got back he would never leave home again unless his town pub dried up!

I was again with the Headquarters' staff and being served good food and enjoying pleasant discussion. But the Ack Ack Club (Allied Officers Club) was thoroughly disgusting. Many of the men had found women who would act as their prostitutes, and they treated them very shabbily. What an example of what the victor does to the vanquished. But in our way, we were all gaining from our status as winners in battle. As we moved into the Italian countryside, we were deferred to and served well. From our position, we could rate the women who pleased us and feel superior.

By December 10, I was in Monte San Vito where our Dodge broke down. We spent the night in a farmhouse. To keep warm, we were put in with their four cows and two calves, which had been hidden from the Germans earlier. The farmer offered us straight wine, but poured his own drink using about two spoonfuls of wine in a glass diluted with water.

We danced to Gramophone music along a narrow edge next to the manure trough! I was afraid that I was going to slip sometime and find my foot in the manure. The Jerry had just sent a few planes over. I think they were planes with bombs because we were near Bologna. Always that fear in the back of our minds, even while trying to forget.

I went to Headquarters at Forli and then came back to C Platoon Headquarters. It was very common to see a city or small town or a village built on a hill with a wall around it, reminiscent of the days when the barbarians were plundering everywhere. Wondered if we ought to call these modern victors "plunderers" as well.

One morning recently we stopped at a farmhouse and asked if we could use their fire to cook our breakfast. The daughter brought out three eggs and fried them over the fire-place fire. Eggs are almost impossible to buy. They gave us wine and some walnuts and I, in return, gave them some chewing gum and gave the old man some pipe tobacco. "Mama" was going to make us a choice Italian dish similar to our chicken and noodles, but we had to go on.

The next farmhouse we reached was not meant to be our destination. Our car stopped, and we had to tear the fuel system apart to clean it out. The people took us in and fed us with our rations with some of theirs thrown in. Later, we all went to the stable to keep warm. The lower floor of the house was divided into stable, kitchen, chicken house, pigsty, and storeroom. They lived in the upper rooms, which were warmer since the animals were down below. They only had fire for cooking, not for heating.

About midnight I opened a package I had received from my sister. Luckily, there were many small things that made nice gifts such as a pack of cards, a comb, candy, and gum, which I gave away. It was so much fun to give things away, especially to people who needed it and appreciated it.

We spread out the straw we had been sitting on, unrolled our beds, and had a good sleep. They awakened us at 8 a.m. and gave us some more eggs and wine. We were awaiting a call back into service so we could just enjoy ourselves for the time being.

I began to think of India and the hot, steamy climate. Now that I am out of the hot climate, I think I like heat and mud better than cold and mud. When we were in a hot climate, we could wash our clothes and get them dry in a day. Here we had to let the mud dry and then shake it or brush it off. The grass is always greener.

[Telegram to Georgie]   LOVING WISHES FOR CHRISTMAS
AND NEW YEAR.
YOU ARE MORE THAN EVER IN MY
THOUGHTS AT THIS TIME.
ALL MY LOVE DEAREST

I got into a strange mood after receiving Georgie's last letter. I began to think what I would do if I couldn't bring all Georgie's letters back home with me. I overheard someone who had just come back from leave say that customs would not let you bring any correspondence back to the states that had been written to you. They impounded it and sent it to you in a year or two. I hoped that rumor wasn't true.

[Letter to Georgie]

You're still the only one I find creeping into my thoughts throughout the day, darling. I'm always wishing you were with me when I pass through beautiful little villages or see a nice landscape scene. Beautiful sunsets and big round moons I always want to share with you. Guess there is time to do that when I return.

December 14 and we were sitting waiting for an order to move. There was no place to keep warm and no fuel to burn. The U.S. rations were taken away the day after I came. We had thirty new Dodge ambulances, but the guys were tearing them to pieces by racing the motors when they were stone cold. Our villa had bomb craters all around it, and the building itself was pretty well shot up from our strafing. Rimini was flattened. There were hardly twenty buildings in the whole city that had all four walls standing.

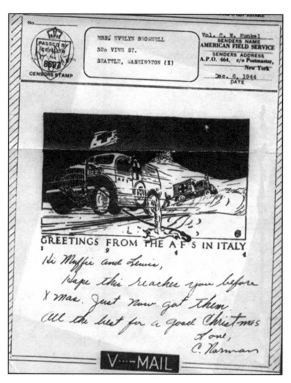

Fred Feddeman got a big "green banana" in a letter. He had been tossed over by his girl, who wrote that she was getting married, so he is now in the process of getting drunk. He and Dick Elberfeld are tight as ticks on Italian gin. My mind was at ease because I had already been assured by Georgie that if a "girl" had found the right fellow, she would wait.

We had moved to a new billet, smaller than the last one, but much more comfortable. "Maggie" (an old ambulance we used to generate electricity) was producing light again and we had a diesel stove that made enough smoke to be a foundry. We still had our piano, and John Meeker was beating out songs for everyone to sing.

We moved the beds that were downstairs and scraped off some of the mud so we could have a dance. The students we invited were mostly girls and fellows who had attended the university and were considered the elite here. Our dance music was provided by an accordion played by the different invited guests and one improvised some drumsticks and beat out time on some chair seats. Everything went along well until we announced "sandwiches and coffee" and then what a rush for the food. They ate every one of the sandwiches and grabbed handfuls of sugar and ate it like they had never tasted sugar before.

As soon as they had filled their bellies, they wanted to leave. They had only been with us about one and a half hours. We had invited some farm girls also and they stayed on. The mail ambulance came in and added excitement to the occasion. I got four packages. I waited until morning to open them. It was like waiting until Christmas Eve is over to get your presents. What a spread. I got filberts, handkerchiefs, and a nice fruitcake.

I went to a nearby town and got a pair of rubber boots at the officer's shop. Now I could step outside the villa knowing I was not going to get my feet wet and muddy up to my ankles. While there I visited a tenth century Guidara Castle and saw their torture chambers. Whenever the feudal lord wanted to get rid of someone he ordered the person to be taken to an archway and shoved through. The victim fell one hundred feet down a hole with sharp projectiles sticking out of the walls. There was a torture pit where they chopped off fingers and hands or put out both eyes at once with red-hot irons. A Canadian who has done much research on the history of the family gave lectures, which brought out the intrigue and immorality that existed within the walls.

THE FALL OF FAENZA

According to *History of the AFS*, it was on December 17 that Faenza fell and the enemy retreated a short distance to prepared positions and stayed there. There was little action throughout the winter. To relieve the boredom small groups went on leave to Florence or Rome. There was always scrounging for wood or anything that could be converted to heating the quarters. The stoves were discarded oil drums and could burn wood, coal, or diesel oil. When they exploded, which was not infrequently, soot spread with a roar over everything within range. A week after Faenza fell it was reported that not a loose stick of wood was left in the town. The wrecked railroad between Forli and Faenza was stripped of broken ties, and boxcars were reduced to their steel skeletons. Shortly after the advance halted for the winter, the army had to issue an order putting all trees in rear areas out of bounds and making the felling of any tree subject to the same harsh penalties as for looting.

On December 19, after driving forty miles to Ancona, we took a nice hot bath in a real tub in the bathhouse for officers. Like Rimini, most of the town was flattened. What devastation! We had billets waiting for us in Riccioni, which was at least twenty-five miles closer to the front. Our grand piano was sent to our new quarters. Of our two piano players, Tom Barbour played nothing but the best in the classical field, while Meeker played popular songs.

(Recently, Barbour told me that he was faking it when he played there in Italy. He needed music when he played, and he didn't have any music. He would just horse around and pretend he was singing and playing opera. I would say that he faked it quite well!)

We were at our new home now. The place was a summer resort hotel with about two hundred rooms. It must have been quite nice, at one time, but there were even fewer windows in this place than in our old villa. Practically all the wood had been torn out and burned. As a result, I had no door, but I had solved the problem by putting a blanket over the opening. The wind blew in from the Adriatic Sea with a vengeance so what the former inhabitants gained by burning the doors and window frames, we lost by feeling the cold. We could very well play the roles of the actors, in the opera *La Boheme,* who debated whether they would burn their creative writing and paintings to save two starving artists from the cold.

One night I had a strange dream. I felt something crawling on me, but couldn't waken enough to tell whether it was a dream or reality. As a matter of fact it was both. Just as it was getting daylight, I awakened enough to realize the crawling sensation was actually a mouse that was sharing my blankets. I began grabbing and finally squashed it underneath my blankets. One squeak and it squeaked no more. Afterwards I was sorry I had killed it, because I could have let it go if I had not been so suddenly awakened in fright.

It was one of those blue-gray days, nice and comfortable, in Pappy's ambulance with the heater on. Pappy was really George Hursey, a Texan who had spent the better part of his life in California serving as a motorcycle patrol officer. I went with him to the artist shop, as he wanted to get a portrait painted from his wife's photograph. It should be good, as the artist had pictures on exhibit in Rome. While there, I bought some San Marino stamps for my nephew from a philatelist who shared the shop with the portrait artist.

Christmas 1944

Here it was, Christmas Eve on the Adriatic Sea. We could see the breakers coming in and hear them roaring all the time. It even looked like Christmas as it had snowed all day the day before. On the way here we bought turkey for a dollar a pound to be ready for this special holiday event.

Our Christmas tree was beginning to show some color with those red berries I had picked and strung on it. We had been making round balls out of Christmas wrapping paper that looked like real glass decorations if you stood about fifteen feet away! If the mail truck had come in, our tree would really have been surrounded. No matter how much we tried, each of us missed a mother, wife, or special someone who could have really put the finishing touches on this celebration.

Christmas nostalgia was expressed in many ways. Some got blue and others just got drunk. I bought a bottle of sherry and passed it around, but I couldn't drink any because my doctor's orders were no alcohol for four months.

The local Italians (whom we called Ities, pronounced with a long "I") tried to keep us entertained and even helped cut up the scarce wood that we scrounged. We were invited to a concert and were all enjoying ourselves until one of our gang started shouting "thank you" in Russian at the end of every performance. He had been drinking before we went and had slipped a bottle into the concert hall. Finally, just as the orchestra was playing "Silent Night," he passed out, and we had to drag him out with the whole audience staring. I threw him over my shoulder and carried him down to the ambulance and tossed him on the stretcher and locked the ambulance and went back for the rest of the concert. He was out cold for twelve hours.

The day after Christmas, Ted Chapman, George Collins, Tom Barbour, Bob Blair, Mort Wright, Art Ecclestone, and I went on a sightseeing tour to Ravenna. We had a wonderful guide in Collins, as he had been a professor in Italian art at Columbia University. Saw Dante's tomb and Theodoric's tomb, the top of which was a piece of stone thirty-three meters in diameter and weighed three hundred tons. It was put up in the fourth century. The Byzantine mosaic art was really beautiful. These were some of the few historic sights left standing. Most of the churches were badly damaged by English and Canadian shells.

I began to feel ill. My liver was hurting and I was retching after dinner. Jaundice no doubt was trying to lay me up again. Christmas away from home and I was sick to boot! Spent much of one day with Fred Feddeman taking all the wheels off his ambulance. They had to be repacked with grease.

There was no war going on here since the Germans had retreated. While the Germans were here, the young women were kept hidden as rape was prevalent. It was no wonder that the three peasant girls who invited us to a dancer were accompanied by chaperones as they were respectable girls. The dance started at 2 p.m. and lasted until the wee hours of the morning. Rosina was taller than the other two and with a nice personality as well. Maria was a little older and much neater in her personal appearance. Anfina was a stout girl of about twenty with a pleasant personality, but she had danced with so many girls in the leading position that instead of her dancing with me, I was dancing with her. As a matter of fact, all three were the same in that respect. I would get them started and then just keep out of their way. We danced and danced until 4 a.m., stopping now and then to go to a nearby house for small Italian sweet biscuits and vino.

REVERIE

For days now, I have been thinking of the song "This Love of Mine." Funny how tunes stick in your head. Even though I couldn't sing on pitch, I could hear wonderful tunes in my mind. They always say that music soothes the savage breast. Too bad we didn't just play wonderful tunes during a battle. Then both sides would stop killing.

Every morning a woman, looking worn and old but probably not more than fifty, came after our garbage with a wheelbarrow. She must have had pigs to feed because I didn't think she would have eaten the stuff, although a lot of it would be edible and the person wouldn't have to be starving to eat it, just hungry. At any rate, when she came one morning I watched her as she brought the garbage from the kitchen. She was bare handed, and her hands were the color of raw meat from the cold. After she had carried out the garbage, I noticed she had a small bucket with live coals in it to warm her hands. As she moved down the street, I could see her stop every one hundred feet or so to warm her hands.

One of the women who did our laundry came in this morning to bring back the clean clothes. She did one fellow's laundry and returned it to him, but on the list he made out he called an underwear top a pullover. To her, a pullover was a sweater. When she did the laundry she couldn't account for the pullover. She thought that we thought she had stolen it, and we just couldn't make her understand that everything was all right. At one time she was actually crying in her attempts to tell us that it (the sweater) wasn't in the bundle of dirty clothes when she got it. She will not do his laundry any more.

Another woman who worked for us had a grandchild one month old. The baby's mother was sick because of improper food causing her to have "niente lata" (no milk). Before we came the child was being fed on sugar and water, but now we saw that she got enough canned milk for the baby.

Most of the time we were not aware of what went on outside our billets. We heard rumors that the Italian prisoners of war who worked in one of the big airfields were kept in line by the U.S. soldiers who told them if their work wasn't up to standard they would be sent back to the British. That was the most severe punishment they could dish out. When I was at Bergen-Belsen, the scare for Nazi prisoners was to be sent back to the Russians.

New Year's Eve 1944

We were invited to a New Year's dance in Albereto. I met a student from Bologna who had left her house and family when the Germans occupied the city. She wanted to know about her home and plied me with all kinds of questions. Then she started to cry and said she was sure her casa would be destroyed. I tried to explain why the allies bombed Italian cities, but in her emotional state over the possible loss of her own home, she was in no mood for the "big picture."

I also met a schoolteacher, Tina Monti, just twenty-two, whose house had been completely destroyed. She was now living in this small village with some distant relatives. She wanted my name and address and said that she would write to me after giving me three pictures of herself. It had been rumored that many Italian girls were looking for U.S. fellows to marry, mainly for a passport away from this war-torn country. That seemed logical. If my country and home had been wrecked, I might want to go to some new place and get a new start as well.

The civilians were at the mercy of the war. The Jerry (the Germans) came along and took over a village or city and fortified it after making the civilians move out. We came along and bombed and shelled the Jerry so that he had to leave. Then we took over what was left, and the Jerry shelled and bombed us until we had pushed him back out of range. Then the civilians come back to what was left of their homes, usually nothing but a pile of rubble. Their vineyards had been cut down and used for fuel. The wood beams of what were their houses had been burned and their land sown with mines which were liable to go off at any time. They couldn't rebuild their homes because they couldn't replace the timbers. They couldn't get new bricks or cement and most of their food was gone. A deplorable situation.

The small village had an epidemic of typhoid, and I took some hard-to-come-by serum for inoculations to the Italian doctor. As he spoke English, I used this time to learn some Italian.

To prepare for the long evening hours, Russ McKinnon and I devised a little stove by cutting a petrol drum in half and then, after lighting the fire, plugged up the cracks around our window to keep in more heat. Our candles were difficult to come by and each one only lasted about two hours. It was during these long evenings that I wondered if my love was dating and going to dances. She never talked about that.

A LETTER FROM AN OLD PAL

I had a long letter from my old bachelor pal and boyhood chum Chet Dutcher, who was not in the service because he suffered from a heart condition stemming from the rheumatic fever he had as a child. He says he is getting all ready to go steelhead fishing. He made himself a pole and had the nerve to ask me if I would like to go fishing with him. I wrote back and told him to pick me up at 6 a.m. any day he decided to go!

Our work here was evacuating patients from a general hospital, routine work and only for a short time. One guy in the platoon, Robert Nemecek, was tall and heavily built with coarse features. He carried himself like a brute of a man, one whom you would expect would speak with a deep, bass voice. Actually, his voice was high pitched, quite a surprise when he began to talk.

Recently, against regulations, I gave two Italian women a ride in my ambulance. In the back I had my raincoat lying on the seat with a tin of fifty British cigarettes in the pocket. After letting them off and getting back to the billet, my cigarettes were gone. It made me mad to think a person would steal from me when I was saving them a twelve-mile walk in the mud. So much for breaking the rules.

When I was in Italy, I attributed everything that the Italians did to their belief in Catholicism. I had no roots in this religion and so blamed it for anything that went wrong in Italy. It was easy to express biases when one was suddenly thrown into a culture that was foreign to me in language and religion.

Back on Duty Again

I had just heard that most of our runs would probably be at night after we were called back into duty. Not a pleasant thought. By January 23, 1945, we were back in the thick of things. One day, on a big advance, traffic was lined up for a long way on the road with my AFS ambulance somewhere near the middle. Things were held up for a long time, and finally a soldier came alongside one ambulance and started making conversation. When the conversation started to lag, the soldier on the outside, in an attempt to bring the conversation back said, "I see you have no stretchers or blankets in your ambulance." The AFS character in the ambulance, being aware of the red band on his hat, said, "Listen, Bobbie, you take care of your traffic, and I'll take care of this ambulance." The brigadier general slowly walked away! You might not see the humor in this right away. You see, the

British MPs did a lot of traffic directing, and they wore a garrison cap with a red band around it. Brigadier generals also wore a garrison cap with a red band around it. This was one brigadier that learned how an MP can be treated sometimes.

The last few days had been beautiful but rather cold. All the trees that hadn't been chopped down for fuel were hanging heavy with fresh snow. We had been debating about the good points and bad points of going to Florence for a few days leave. If we had gone right away, there would have been more souvenirs to buy, but all the gardens would have been frozen. By waiting until spring, the gardens would then be beautiful and they would have some of the statues ready for the public to see.

On the way back from getting rations, Russ McKinnon was driving our ton-and-a-half truck and he tried to stop and couldn't. We smacked into the tail end of the guy in front of us, the guy behind us hit us, the guy behind him hit him, and he hit us a second time. We had to go about five or six miles for rations, and we counted eight trucks that had skidded alongside the road. Three were turned over.

I took my gloves that needed sewing to the daughter of the woman who is caretaker of the hotel we live in. She was like most Italians who wanted to go to the U.S.A. as soon as the war was "finito." They seemed to think that Italy was finished and would never rise again to any prominence in the world. If you could have seen what was left of Italy you would have understood.

The daughter, who was thirty-one, had never been married, but she said after the war she would marry and raise a family. It made me sad. So many girls in Italy would never get married. It was the same in all the other countries that were in war, which would have such deep and lasting effects upon the people. Our war generation was in urgent need to marry and raise a new crop of children who would probably fight the next inevitable war. It was not a pleasant thing to look forward to. But the hatred and vengeance left after a war lies in waiting, to erupt again.

I went to the theatre one evening and offered myself to a hypnotist as a subject for demonstration. I saw other guys hypnotized but he couldn't put me under. I tried to be receptive to his commands but my body wouldn't react. He told one guy he would not feel pain in his hands. To prove it he took a pin and stuck him a number of times and the guy didn't move. Then he poured cold water over his hands and told him it was hot. He reacted instantly as it if were hot.

LETTERS

Received letters from my love dated December 25, 26, and 27. Seemed she got some perfume for Christmas called Jade. I wrote and asked her if it challenged her like

Tabu and if she could meet that challenge. She said she was going to be an aunt for the fourteenth time! I was to be an uncle for the twelfth time since my youngest sister Josephine (Jopey) was pregnant. She had been ordered to bed for rest as this was a difficult pregnancy. My sister Diane said Georgie visited her. She said that Georgie had more energy than any person she had ever seen. I wrote Georgie and asked her where she got it all, and if she would send me some!

At last I had two pictures of my love replacing the picture I lost when my wallet was stolen. They now provided a distraction so that I couldn't concentrate on writing. Georgie hadn't changed. She was still just as beautiful as ever.

One of her letters included this query, "How could you tell me about all the beautiful women you are meeting?" I learned that Georgie could become jealous. I apologized, but with such a lag in communication the hurt lingers longer.

Heard a good story last night about a fellow who went in to see the Medical Officer with a minor complaint and decided to play a joke on him. When the Medical Officer asked his name, he said in one big long breath, "I am from HM Forces. That big AFS ambulance sitting out in front is mine, and I'm going down to Naples and load it up with Coca Cola and chocolate bars and bring them up and pass them out to all my friends in this company." The Medical Officer scratched his head and turned around and had two armed guards subdue him as they do bomb-happy cases. Before he could explain, he was evacuated about three hundred miles south, with a dozen or more mental cases. He was there five days before anyone in our outfit knew about it.

[From My Diary]

The Italians are singing the song "Lilli Marlene" that the Germans introduced. When I heard that song I remembered the German pictures on the walls of our first billet here in Italy. One of the fellows, fluent in Italian, translated the words of the song and they fit with the pictures the Germans had painted on the walls of the villa. The last verse is a poignant reminder of Georgie waiting for me back home:

> *Resting in a billet just behind the line,*
> *Even tho' we're parted*
> *Your lips are close to mine.*
> *You wait where that lantern softly gleams,*
> *Your sweet face seems,*
> *To haunt my dreams,*
> *My Lilli of the lamplight,*
> *My own Lilli Marlene.*

I still have a cold and am using all the handkerchiefs Georgie sent me. I can stand up to anything but washing handkerchiefs, so luckily the laundry woman does them after I soak several of them each day.

I was listening to "Serenade for Strings" by Tchaikovsky, which I really enjoy. Fortunately we had access to the radio in an ambulance that was not on duty.

From the clearly audible night noises, the sounds of war, I would say that there would probably be more than enough work tomorrow for everyone. But for now, I am watching the fire die down, as the fuel is almost gone. I wonder if love dies out for lack of nourishment. Are words written on the page in letters enough to keep love alive? When my love gets these unanswerable questions I wonder what she will think.

I hated burning any more wood so I was off to bed to keep warm. Every time I chopped up a door or a window from a bombed or otherwise wrecked building I realized the labor and expense that was required to get that wood to Italy and in that particular form. I thought that burning wood that could be used again was about as bad as burning a grape vineyard for firewood but we had to keep warm.

By February 12 we were moving into the occupation phase of the war, a turnabout for the Italians who had surrendered. The Allied Military Government was now in charge. The extracurricular jobs consisted of civilian welfare work. W. G. Congdon was assigned with his ambulance in Faenza in early January. Although it was a front-line town, only two miles from the enemy positions, it had a civilian refugee population of more than eight thousand. The Army didn't want civilians that close to the front, but there was no other place for them to go. Congdon's work at first was to gather the sick scattered through the area and bring them into Faenza, then either to unite them with their families or to evacuate them to rear areas. I was serving there, along with some Irish and English, picking up the sick and wounded and taking them to their homes or the hospital. I had moved down to the Governor's house where the U.S. major was, along with other occupation officers. None of them spoke Italian, so they each had a good-looking gal as translator. Need I say more?

The AMG could requisition anything they wanted from the civilians that the Germans hadn't already taken. So here I was driving out to a big wine distillery to pick up some vermouth for our mess. The Padroni, the civilian head of government, gave the AMG the wine for personal favors, such as a pass and the use of a military truck, for example.

Jerry was sending over rockets every night. One landed so close that I thought the glass in the window frames would fall out. After it hit I could hear a nearby building falling down.

A Father Finds His Lost Child

Our Red Cross was most beneficial here because the Security Section hauled the friends and relatives of sick and wounded civilians in our ambulances without special passes. I went to Forli, Ravenna, and Bagnacavallo carrying patients. I took a man, whose wife had been killed to Bagnacavallo to look for his little girl, lost in the shuffle. At the start of the day he was very unhappy and resigned to never seeing her again, but at 2 p.m. he was tearful with joy when we found her. I felt like I was doing more when I helped civilians than when I was carrying wounded soldiers. Working with the military I felt as if I was a pawn in the hands of the Army. When I carried a soldier off the battlefield, I was actually helping men to live and kill more men. Knowing that the big three—the Nazis, Japanese, and the Italians— had to be stopped did not make a killing war any more palatable. It was certainly a Catch-22 situation.

An Italian is reunited with his daughter.

[Letter to Georgie]

This marks the second year of holidays we have celebrated separately, my love. We have missed two Thanksgivings, two Christmases, and two birthdays.

I remember when I used to ride on a train and wish that the daylight would last longer as I enjoyed watching the scenes pass by outside the window. Now I feel that it would be much better to be blind, if I knew I was going to have to keep on seeing what I see now every day. Everyone seems to have lost all sense of proportion as far as moral values are concerned. Can't people see that if they put materialistic values above moral values they have defeated themselves? Hitler ended as a defeated dictator, but in a sense he won the war because he succeeded in destroying in many of us our ability to tell right from wrong during wartime and in the chaos and disorganization after the war.

I have been feeling ill lately and worried that my malaria might be coming back. When I feel down I begin thinking. When I look around and see destruction and moral decay I feel that what I am doing is of little consequence. It hurts me when people ignore the brutality and unfairness of military personnel in Italy. The military say, "That's all right, he is just a damned Itie." Everyone has gone crazy. Could I be the one who is crazy? Maybe I am wrong and everyone else is right. Sometimes I wonder if life is worth this kind of struggle. You would think that with what I see every day I would become callous to the pitiful sights, but I feel each one.

I really appreciate the letters and packages from home. Evelyn Brownell has told me that I have a standing order for a big cherry pie with a huge dinner built around it when I get back. We are telling all our correspondents to write V-Mail from now on as the *Stars and Stripes* advised us that airmail letters will now go by ship because there aren't enough planes to carry them all.

The billet we lived in was owned by a count. He had been forced to move into one room of it since we took the rest. This was our first billet that was actually warm and comfortable. I was caught in the U.S. military government, which was able to confiscate anything from the Italians, from wine to their supply of coal, and all for our own use according to Captain Fitzgerald, an Irish officer. We heard that an American major was taking the best pottery and ceramics in Faenza and packing them in boxes in preparation for sending them home. I had to look the other way because we were helping the Italian people by our presence even when some took personal advantage of it all.

I heard that the Germans, before they left, contaminated most of the prostitutes of Naples with venereal disease. The medical officers said it was a very bad type of syphilis. There wasn't much a medical officer could do when a soldier was fed up with the battlefront and had drunk himself into oblivion and then stupidly exposed himself to sex so readily available in this poor, vanquished country. To help our own forces, the prostitutes were rounded up and incarcerated on the third floor of the local hotel and kept there so the occupational forces would not contract venereal diseases. Every time we would walk past the building, they would hang out the windows shouting and catcalling. What else did they have to do while they were being fed and housed without their usual profession to keep them busy?

I was signed into Brennan's old ambulance, which was in pretty poor shape, so I cleaned it up to make it more presentable. He had backed into something and the rear door was pretty well shot. One of the interpreters for the commanding officer of the Allied Military Government said she knew where there was a cache of Marsala wine, which had been hidden from the Germans in a barnyard closer to the front. The commanding officer "laid on" our ambulance, and the interpreter went with three of us to find it. After we dug it up and brought it back, the military government staff had good wine to drink for a long time.

The Jerry dropped a few more in the night but not one landed near. The sounds of war continued.

Rehabilitation

The February holidays that we observe back home were spent here in picking up medical supplies and clothing from the British Red Cross to help the destitute people who were living like rats packed into every habitable house. I heard that the Reds staged a revolution here two months ago that was quickly squelched by the military. Since so many homes had been destroyed, there were about four families living in the same space that one formerly occupied. Our American Major Palloti went to Rome on leave. A young British captain, about twenty-four, took over as governor of the city. The town's thieves refused to steal tires for the British Captain's "Cinie" car, because they would rather sell them for $200 each on the black market.

Bill Congdon hired a pianist and a violinist to play for us each afternoon from 5 to 6 p.m. Life with the AMG was the best I had lived since leaving the U.S. Another proof that the Yank seems to be better served than the British soldier.

Had a chat with Evelyn Antonelli, who had dinner with us. She was born in the U.S. and was here with her mother studying music when the war trapped them and she couldn't go back home. Her father was still in San Francisco, so they were returning to the U.S. as soon as possible.

My next adventure was to drive to a place near Brisighellia to see an old woman, who had not walked for twenty years. She wanted to be brought down to Faenza where some of her relatives were. I had to park and walk one kilometer to the house through mud. She wanted to be moved out along with all of the "roba" (furnishings). It couldn't be done. Actually, she was better off right there than she would have been in Faenza, which was so crowded. The Poles had taken over the house and moved her and her two sisters and a small child into one room of the house.

There were quite a few Poles killed during this campaign when they were attached with the U.S. military. They made a graveyard and buried their dead. The remaining Poles dug up shrubbery anywhere they could find it and planted it around the gravesite. This didn't go over well with the Italians who came and took all the shrubs away.

After leaving there, I went through Brisighellia up a steep mountain road to get a man who had both legs amputated and took him to his brother who was a priest. The move was more than twelve miles over the worst kind of roads.

A girl came into the office one morning wanting to get her mother and father up from Caesna. They were sick. I investigated the house she was living in to see if it was large enough to accommodate two more and found it was, and also found that she had beds for them if they did come. I didn't know if we would let her parents come back because there were so many people in Faenza living in cellars. We considered taking these people out of these places and making the other people of the town share what they had with them.

At midnight I had just returned from a party the British town major gave us. Captain Fitzgerald was to leave the next day for Florence to work at a refugee camp. Everyone got drunk but me. Why? Because I had diarrhea again along with a headache and a fever.

The next day I was called upon to go out in the country and dig up two bodies and put them into caskets and bring them into town for a decent burial. I had three gravediggers that did all the work, but I had to see that it was done properly. While they were digging, I went to a nearby farmhouse and talked with the occupants. There I found twin girls, six years of age, both paralyzed from the hips down from birth. It was a pitiful sight because their legs were completely frozen in the hip sockets. How sad for them.

My opportunity to escape the horrible sights and terrible odors being exposed by the gravediggers was not the relief I had hoped for. When I got back, the loosely constructed coffins had leaked. It was horrible! The bodies were in a bad state of decomposition and as a result my ambulance was flooded with the fluid that ran out of the bodies. I almost got sick. When I got back I had to completely disinfect my ambulance.

In the afternoon, I took a young girl to Forli for an emergency appendectomy. After all this, I was looking forward to dinner. Eddera, Olga, Lola, and Emma ate with us. Eddera told me that about 10 percent of the people of Italy owned their own farms. She said that the farmers of Italy were taxed very little and that the "cittadini" (townspeople)—industrial workers, shopkeepers, tradespeople—were the most heavily taxed. Lola told us that two hundred people were recently hanged in Imola by the Germans. This report was just the tip of the iceberg of what the Germans did in their takeover.

In an information bulletin prepared by Ilya Ehrenburg and released by the Embassy of the USSR in June 1944, there were quotes from the diary of the Secretary of the Secret Field Police in the German armed forces. It exemplifies what Soviet civilians had to go through at the hands of the Nazis. The diary reported on February 26, 1943, that five fellows, of about seventeen, were caught north of Budyennovka and were beaten. He writes:

> I broke the handle of the lash into little bits. Two of us beat at a time, however they wouldn't confess anything. Two Red Army men were brought to me. They were flogged. I'm finishing off the shoemaker from Budyennovka, who thought he could allow himself some offensive remarks about our army. Corporal Voigt has shot the shoemaker. He's been thrown into the common grave.

The diary continued with details of the German secretary's physical complaints all the way from diarrhea, depression, and constipation and his fear of retaliation and the Russian air force coming over. As so many Nazis said after the war, "I had to do what I did. I had to obey orders."

That night the war was cracking again. Much artillery fire, both incoming and outgoing, plus machine gun fire and grenade explosions from the front, which was just two miles away. The next morning, I went out in Santa Lucia commune to get two patients and was stopped by a frantic man whose child was horribly burnt while playing with cordite, a powder used in artillery shells. I didn't give the child any hope of recovering.

By February 27 I had left the Allied Military Government for the New Zealand Casualty Clearance Station in Forli where we were with the 5 Corps to relieve the New Zealand forces who were going out for a rest. We were with the 8th Indian Division and the 56th and 78th British.

Here we were invited to a party at the house owned by Count and Countess Cazzini. Among those present were Captain Fitzgerald; Captain Campbell, who was acting Chief Allied Officer of the city; Captain Jones, Bill Congdon; the Polish town major; the British town major; Lieutenant Chan Keller; Art Ecclestone; Evans; Gunther; and Edwards. There were at least sixteen "girls" there. Punch was served plus sandwiches, cakes, and coffee with gin and whisky to keep us going.

Three Polish lesser officers, who had not been invited, came up after hearing the music, and Bill Congdon had not the heart to turn them away so they stayed a while. I had been dancing with Dorina Goldoni, who was one of the best dancers there. Then the Poles took over. I caught a glance of Dorina's distraught face and decided to ask for the next dance. I learned from her that the Poles had completely destroyed her house and her beauty shop to get rubble to build a road. Again, civilians took the brunt of soldiers who were carrying out orders. The Chief of Royal Engineers had been turning people out of what he considered to be uninhabitable houses and then ordering the Polish soldiers to tear down the houses for road-building materials. The American major, who was town governor, was trying to stop it.

In Bed Again

By March 6 I was in the hospital at Senigallia, Italy, diagnosed with amoebic dysentery, and scheduled to stay at least a month in a ward with twenty-four Kiwis (New Zealanders). After a whole day with nothing to eat, I was evacuated further back to Bari #1 New Zealand General Hospital.

On St. Patrick's Day, Feddeman and Elberfeld came to bring me some mail and money and to raise my spirits, a truly appreciated visit. Hearing from everyone gave me hope that I would soon be back with my unit.

REVERIE

I now had time to think about my usual belief that war is senseless. I wondered how the average soldier felt when he came into a hospital wounded after having killed twenty Jerries. Everyone was pampering him because he had killed so many men. Was he not a murderer? And yet, he was praised and pampered and nourished back to health so he could return and kill more men! Being with the nonviolent ambulance service, it was difficult for me to justify the role of the actual wartime killer. And yet, here I was serving the ones who chose to kill during wartime.

The sulfa pills I took were toxic. They made me feel like I was living outside of my own body. I had a terrible headache along with indigestion, and my eyes were out of focus. I was actually afraid to go to sleep. Then, when I finally got to sleep, the nurse would wake me to give me more pills.

Daydreaming was my favorite pastime. I built air castles then tore them down, saying to myself that it could not happen to me and that I was meant to be a bachelor—but where did it get me? Nowhere! Seeing Georgie again seemed to be the only thing that would clear up matters. Between letters I daydreamed of Georgie being here to dance a Viennese waltz or to go out to a nice French restaurant with me.

Rumors were flying about what was next for our AFS. Working with UNRRA (United Nations Relief and Rehabilitation Administration) in China was mentioned. It was announced that the entire Company was to be reviewed by General Sir Richard L. McCreery, GOC 8th Army. This was to be the last week with the British Eighth Army.

Representative Claire Booth Luce visited Company Headquarters at Forlimpopoli on March 18, 1945. She inspected the ambulances and admired the neo-Venetian castle we used as headquarters and said some very complimentary things about the Field Service. George Rock's take on her visit was, "When Mrs. Luce waved good-bye, everyone agreed that world relations would be vastly improved if more statesmen were blondes dressed in blue slacks and jackets who floated gracefully in an aura of Chanel. . . ." I found this out later as this happened while I was holed up taking my sulfa pills in the hospital.

I also missed the big review on the twenty-first, when for the first time everyone was dressed in regulation uniform—battle dress, gaiters, boots, and caps. George Rock's history stated:

> For once the circus got together in parade without Indian moccasins, cowboy or Russian boots, blue overalls, corduroy breeches, Yank field jackets, turtle-neck sweaters, red fezzes, or green tennis hats. It looked like a military outfit and acted like one. . .
>
> In his address to the Company, General McCreery said that the Eighth Army had tried hard to keep 567 Company in its command, but that higher powers had insisted that it be detached and removed to another theatre of war. This, he said, should be taken as a high compliment to our service during the past years of the war in Africa and Italy.

All the AFS Ambulance Drivers in 567 Company were requested to strip off any identification relating to that company and the British Army. Some were sent home, others were sent on to Burma/India or carried on other duties regarding repatriation.

[Telegram to Georgie]

HEALTH IMPROVING.
ALL MY LOVE DEAREST.
MY THOUGHTS ARE WITH YOU.

Yes, my health was improving, but since I was sentenced to three weeks flat on my back, I was allowed to do nothing for myself. I had six more days before they would let me feed, wash, or shave myself. My friend Jeff, an ambulatory patient from New Zealand, offered to write letters for me. Since he was a historian writing the history of the war, he was in a position to share many interesting details. He wrote in one of my letters that I could not only give him the Yank point of view, but that I could enlighten him about the women in my country. I don't know where he got the impression that I knew all about women.

Franklin Delano Roosevelt Dies

I was shocked by the death of our dear President Franklin Delano Roosevelt. My first thoughts were that twelve years and more in such a stressful position as president during recession and also wartime would kill anyone. It doesn't seem possible that anyone else could fulfill his place as the leader of our country. We had become accustomed to his face, to his fireside chats, and his attention to the needs of the people whom he helped up out of the depression. I often wondered if his own disability, which was not often seen by the people of this country, helped him to be more empathetic to the plight of those needing help in hard times. It was unfortunate that he had to hide his physical handicap, but in a day when only the finest examples of manhood were picked to lead and command, he was never allowed to be seen in a wheelchair or being helped out of his chair. Though our leader was gone, we knew our job was not yet over. We had to carry on.

Even after having the smell of wartime success in our nostrils, the Germans bombed an ammunition ship and oil tanker down at the docks in Bari. All our windows were blown out, even though we were one and a half miles away and on the opposite side of the building from the dock area. Some of the nurses had gone downtown just to get out for a while, and the oil from the tanker that exploded spread into the air and fell down like rain. Their white uniforms were ruined.

[Letter To Georgie]

I had a dream last night, a terrible dream that I was married and very unhappy. I got to thinking about being an escapist and not wanting to settle down and get married. Then I think that I have to share my life for better or for worse. I will try to face life from now on instead of running away from it. That is easy to say and more difficult to do but I am going to be found trying. All the things that I can see standing in the way of happiness in marriage will disappear into thin air when I see you.

I wish I could see you in your new Easter apparel. You would probably be a "wouzer" or a "bottler" as the Kiwis would say. Those are very complimentary terms even if they don't sound like it.

I was diligently studying Italian, since I had only ten days before being discharged from the hospital. A large percentage of Italian words and English words have the same root. For example, elegante, diligente, assistere, and consistere.

My anticipated visit in Bari, after lying in the hospital for so long, was clouded by the poverty of the people and the big black market thriving with inflation in its wake. This realization and the fact that I wasn't quite ready for all the exercise was enough to make me depressed. That depression wasn't alleviated by the opera I attended that evening. *Tosca* was a tragedy in which the female lead commits suicide after her lover is killed. The setting of the opera was Rome, and it was supposed to be a true story. The prison where Tosca's lover was incarcerated is on the banks of the Tiber River with St. Paul's Cathedral in the background. I planned to see the prison when I got to Rome.

I just read that the people in Germany were going to have a very hard winter. Guess that meant that rationing in the U.S. would continue if we intended to feed these people until they could start producing for themselves. I sure hoped they didn't have to starve because if they did face such a fate, all our efforts toward peace would be shattered. It would be impossible to build good will and peace on an empty stomach.

I had been in Naples four days by May Day, 1945. We had flown here from Bari via Rome, which I saw from a B-15 airplane. I visited Pompeii, an ancient city, which disappeared after the eruption of Mount Vesuvius in 79 A.D. It was built in the form of an oval about two miles around. A great wall with eight gates surrounded the city. In the center of the city was the open forum surrounded by a group of buildings, theaters, the gladiators' court, temples, and several public baths. Pompeii attracted many wealthy Romans who enjoyed the baths and the affluence of the city.

It was almost unbelievable to see houses that were built over two thousand years ago and to walk along the street with stepping stones for crossing when the rains came down from the mountains. They still had a lot of excavation to do.

Little kids were selling brass replicas of the male sex organs. They were calling out, "Cock and zee balls." That cry was reminiscent of the graffiti on the walls of the brothels. There were pictures of the various positions of sexual intercourse. All this was quite foreign to a small town boy like me who didn't realize how open the old cultures were in regard to explicit sex.

By May 3 George Collins, Dave Demarest, and I were sailing from Naples on a Liberty ship. I hated to leave William Washburn, Thorn Young (the guy that kept Headquarters going) and Frank Marler, but we three were serving as guards for our three locked ambulances in the hold of the ship since we couldn't trust anyone whenever we were in a port city.

We sailed smoothly through the blue waters of the Mediterranean, passing Capri (which was easily recognizable because of its unique shape), Iscia, Sardinia, and Corsica. Mount Vesuvius was free of clouds and really beautiful. Passing through the straits between Corsica and Sardinia revealed Corsica's rugged snowy peaks. After we pulled into Marseilles, once a beautiful harbor, we were shocked at the debris lying everywhere. The Jerries had scuttled many ships in an effort to make the port unusable. Within an hour from the time we had our ambulances sitting on the dock, we were on our way to Avignon. Our party now consisted of four since Don Colvin, a little guy from Princeton, joined us. We parked the cars in a park and stayed at the nicest hotel in the city of Avignon. France was beautiful.

PART FIVE:
CELEBRATION, HOLOCAUST, AND HOMECOMING

An Announcement

Just now heard that the war was over as of 2 p.m. I recorded this momentous event in my diary as V-E Day at Last, May 7, 1945. Spent the night in Dijon at the officers' transit hotel (where John Ruskin once stayed) after attending a dance without speaking a word of French. Once again I was bouncing between battle horror and high-class accommodations.

Not until many years after I recorded news of V-E Day in my diary, did I learn what a problem the news agencies had about releasing this story. Radios across the United States were airing the announcement by Germany's new foreign minister, Count Lutz Schwerin von Krosigk that Germany had unconditionally surrendered all its forces—land, sea, and air—to the Allies, at General Eisenhower's Headquarters, Rheims, May 7, 1945.

My family and friends on the West Coast of the United States were not even up yet, but the East Coast heard it immediately. Then there was hesitation in admitting that the Allies had announced this victory. It was rumored that Joe Stalin wanted to wait until the Ukrainian armies had dealt with a small force of Nazis who still remained in Moravia. So the official Allied announcement of V-E Day did not come until May 8, 1945. It was only then that Winston Churchill was heard around the world saying, "We may allow ourselves a brief period of rejoicing, but let us not forget for a moment the toils and efforts that lie ahead. . . Long live the cause of freedom! God save the King."

President Harry Truman celebrated his sixty-first birthday and his first day in the White House announcing this great victory in Europe as he praised the sacrifice and devotion of the Allied armies. "I only wish that Franklin D. Roosevelt could have lived to see this day."

For the British nation it meant no more blackouts, bombings, or the threat of invasion after more than five and a half years. For the Russians it meant that they had defeated the German invasion one more time. For the U.S., it meant getting back to prosperity after years of rationing, expensive war production and, most horrendous, losing so many young people who were sent into battles fought around the globe.

At last the reign of Hitler was over. In twelve years he had conquered twenty-two countries and authorized the deaths of more than thirty-five million people in a war that reduced Europe to rubble. His crumbling body and mind, along with his crumbling empire, reduced him in the end to dispatching orders to units that no longer existed before he took his own life.

Paris on V-E Day

On V-E Day, we stopped at Lyon, a city built along the banks of the river Rhone. The people were milling up and down the streets with apparently nothing to do but feel exhilarated because the war was all over. We stopped at a sidewalk cafe and took in our rations (a can of milk, a can of sugar, and packages of biscuits) to add to what we could afford on the menu. Then we headed for Paris. As our movement orders did not call for Paris, the military authorities would not give us any help in finding a place to stay. We really didn't need a place because Paris just didn't go to bed after V-E Day was announced.

On the way into Paris, we gave a lift to two young French officers in the women's division of the French Army. One was Simone Sclar, who invited us up to her family's apartment when we were ready to sleep that night. We parked in a square in the center of the city. There were so many people that it seemed like Broadway on Saturday night. People were gathered on the Avenue des Champs Elysees by the tens of thousands, marching up and through the Arc de Triomphe where the five flags of the leading nations were flying—the biggest flags I had ever seen. I'm sure you could have wrapped a medium-sized house in one of them.

People were passing through the arch, where the Unknown Soldier lay, in a steady stream from 3 p.m. until midnight. Every few minutes the soldiers of the different nations would give a salute with their guns while big spotlights played on the arch from all angles and rockets of all colors were being shot from the top. There were small parades on all the thoroughfares all night and the beautiful French gals were grabbing us and kissing us as we walked in the streets amongst the crowds. No wonder they call Paris the "City of Love."

The heat and excitement of this momentous occasion made me feel very weak and shaky. Maybe it was also the shock of learning that the pressures of war were no longer with me. It was a feeling like trying to push against a door and then having it suddenly

PARIS IS LIBERATED

ON AUGUST 15, General Patch's Franco-American Seventh Army, supported by British airborne troops, R.A.F. and Allied flyers and covered by British, American and French warships, landed near Toulon on the Mediterranean French coast. The Seventh drove north to join up with the American armies driving east. The French Forces of the Interior threw the Germans out of one city after another in the path of their advance. While the British and Canadians were sweeping across the north of France, the American Third Army converged on Paris. On August 19, the F.F.I. started an insurrection in Paris, pushing the Germans out of the city. Six days later General Leclerc, leading a French tank force, entered the capital. American forces followed, and General de Gaulle (center of picture above) arrived amidst great acclaim and rejoicings. By August 27, 1944, German resistance inside Paris was ended.

* From British Information Pamphlets

open, leaving you without the need to push any longer. I was experiencing the beauty of Paris, the most beautiful city I had ever seen, in a glorious atmosphere of celebration. It was at Simone Sclar's flat that I stayed for a party, drinking toasts to victory with her mother, brother, aunt, and some more friends. The champagne and cognac were flowing.

I spent the next afternoon with George Collins and Don Colvin driving around Paris in my ambulance and the night on the Rue de Montmartre. As we walked along we would hear, "Come on in Yank and drink to victory."

The next day planes flew over the city in the formation of the Cross of Lorraine, and I even saw a black French poodle clipped on his back to reveal this cross! The French really love their dogs! We had begun this day tired from our celebrating, but we had to grease our cars and maintain them for the trip on to Holland where company Headquarters was located.

We finished our work on the ambulances, slept for four hours in the afternoon, and then took an ambulance back to Paris so we could drive around and see the sights. Darkness found us down in the Montmartre night club district. More champagne and sidewalk cafes. Most of the evening we just watched people passing in the street. Even though we were exhausted from our revelry in Paris, we left for Brussels, Belgium at 8 a.m. and arrived 4 p.m. at General Headquarters. There we crashed for fourteen hours of sleep.

Bergen-Belson Concentration Camp

May 12 was quite warm and all the apple blossoms had burst, filling the air with that wonderful fragrance which only apple blossoms can produce. It reminded me of the apple country I had forsaken to become an AFS "character" for two whole years. I hoped I would soon be back in apple country.

When I crossed the border into Germany, my life took a dramatic turn. The country in general appearance was beautiful, but to see where the war had scorched the landscape made me sick inside. I saw whole cities completely destroyed with rubble everywhere and only an occasional partial wall standing against the horizon.

Refugees, walking barefoot, were streaming by the thousands along all the main roads pulling wagons or baby buggies. Some were riding bicycles. Looting was commonplace. Everyone it seemed was taking anything they wanted. It was all too terrible for words. People were no longer human. They were animals and nothing more. Or perhaps people were like little pet dogs that observe the rules only when their owners are present.

Germany had succeeded in perpetrating a war that was dragging the moral standards of the world down into the gutter. I was ready to go home now that I had been in Germany. The sights I had seen I would never be able to forget. God, how terrible it all was. Ready to go home or not, I was to live through yet another week of horror that would stay with me the rest of my life.

When I arrived at Headquarters, I learned that our platoon was working at a concentration camp at Bergen-Belsen. I was appalled at what I was hearing about this place. In addition, the Germans were being treated like dogs. My sensibilities were upset by this retaliation even though I was certainly not a Nazi sympathizer.

On April 26, D Platoon, along with a few members of a reserve section, joined nine British General Hospital in Venray. They, with half the hospital personnel, set off for Bergen-Belsen Concentration Camp, which had been liberated on April 17 by the 15th Scottish Regiment of the British Second Army. Only one day after arrival, most of the cars returned for the rest of the hospital's personnel. They had such a tremendous job of evacuating this camp that they set up tents so that they could stay until the job was done. On May 2 they were joined by members of our C Platoon.

The camp was in a wooded area surrounded by barbed wire and completely away from the outside world. Signs, which had been posted by the Nazis, warned that anyone trespassing would be shot without question. You can be sure that anyone wandering by would not have offered to come inside while the Nazis had it under their control. What George Collins, and I and others who were called to help found at Bergen-Belsen was appalling beyond anything in our imagination.

My first day of arrival in camp, I worked all afternoon in the women's section of the camp. We would take clean stretchers and blankets into the building, help the women strip off their flea-infested clothes, and lift them onto the stretchers and take them to the "human laundry." It was ghastly to see them huddled on the floor in their filthy clothes and blankets. Those who could still talk were pleading in hysterical tones to be taken out of the filthy place.

Most of the poor, tortured creatures had diarrhea, ulcers, and God only knows what else. After many years without any kindness being shown to them, they often did not understand the kindness being offered. Some felt we were just coming to cause them more pain. Some just wanted to be left alone to die.

We would lift them up on stretchers, and they would cry out from pain because they were so emaciated, with their skin pulled tightly over their bones. When we got them to the laundry tent, they were washed in strong soap and disinfectant and given clean clothes,

THE HORROR CAMP AT BELSEN

THE BRITISH ADVANCE overran the concentration camp at Belsen, a scene of staggering horror—thousands of emaciated, rotting human corpses stacked in piles; thousands more lying among the still-living prisoners, who were too weak to move either the corpses or themselves. The place stank of filth and disease. British soldiers forced S.S. men and S.S. women, at point of gun as shown above, to bury the corpses and help care for the starved and diseased survivors. The big job of rescuing the 39,500 helpless victims was organized at top speed. British army nurses, Red Cross and civilian experts rushed to Belsen. The victims were moved to clean quarters, disinfected, clothed and fed with scientific care. Within a few weeks they were beginning to look human again. Members of the British Parliament who visited Buchenwald, scene of similar horrors, ended their report with the words, "The memory of what we saw and heard at Buchenwald will haunt us ineffaceably for many years."

* From British Information Pamphlets

which had a powder similar to DDT sprayed on them, and then we took them to a temporary hospital.

A deathly odor hung over the whole camp. After a short while my olfactory senses were so numbed that I didn't notice the smell of excrement and dead bodies. I was like a

zombie with blinders on, only doing what I had to do to move these pitiful creatures as quickly as possible to permanent hospitals. Their feet were bloated from starvation. Some had suffered with their feet being frozen as early as January. They had lain here until May without any treatment. It was a terrible sight.

Partial view of Bergen-Belsen taken prior to 1945.

My eyes locked on-to the eyes of a skeleton of a woman looking up at me with an intense gaze as if to say, "Take me, take me first." I knew that there was limited room in the ambulance and that I could only take one at a time, but I was able to take her. The next day, the woman who had lain next to her had died. A few days later I looked up the woman whom I had taken to the hospital, and she had also died.

[From My Diary]

Today I came back to HQ but I am going back tomorrow to work again in the camp. Even though it is a duty no one would wish to do, I want to help these people. It does wonders for me to know that I can save the lives of so many even though many also die. After the horror and terrible down side of war, to be of such service to so many people gives me renewed hope for humanity.

The next day I set to work again. Collins, Murphy, and I were now helping wherever we could. We didn't have ambulances, but there seemed to be plenty to do with D Platoon and the British. I had deloused myself three times in one day and I could still feel things crawling on me. Maybe it was my imagination. I heard that the British were playing up the liberation of this camp in their publicity releases. No matter, the camps were finally being emptied and the living brought out to start their lives again.

It was not until the final reunion of the AFS Ambulance Corps Drivers in Baltimore in 2002 that I met two fellows who had also been at Bergen-Belsen. Howard Mayhew shared with me a videotaped interview about his experiences, a story which mirrored my own pain in remembering the horror of this awful place. He said that his own son had never heard his story until he was asked to put it into history by doing the interview. Like me, he

On entering the camp, the massive barbed wire fence
symbolized the cage that victims lived in.

had been told he would go to Germany, after having served in Italy, but he had no idea of what he would be involved in.

He had driven his ambulance just briefly in the Italian campaign and felt rather fortunate that he was not a common soldier, sleeping on the ground in all kinds of circumstances. His Dodge ambulance was considered superior to those of the British. It had four-wheel drive, which could take him up a steep incline of 45 degrees and also navigate snow conditions if necessary. It had at least sixteen blankets for the wounded that we carried off the battlefield, and he could use the blankets for sleeping in the ambulance. I could have used such an ambulance during my driving in India/Burma since mine was a General Motors with only rear-wheel drive. I didn't get a Dodge until getting into Italy and Germany.

Mayhew talked about his brief training of about three hours in handling the ambulance, for example, the double clutch to shift up or down and other basic information. That was about it. There was no map. He was pointed in the direction of the next dressing station and from there on it was easy to follow the only road because of the tracks left by the heavy trucks.

Taking inmates into the human laundry.

As Mayhew drove on the great German autobahn he thought conditions were excellent until he came upon one of the many bridges that had been blown up and had to take an alternate route. Soon his section of about six ambulances, part of a platoon of about thirty ambulances, was ordered to Belsen, which had been an S.S. training camp. He thought all the Germans that he saw going by seemed to be friendly.

A few miles away from the camp he began to smell a terrible odor, which was evidently coming from the concentration camp. After passing through some trees, he approached the women's section. From almost anywhere in the camp one could see the gallows that still had bodies hanging from them. If this was meant to put fear into the hearts of those still living, it was unnecessary. The piles of dead bodies, the piles of shoe soles, the crematoriums, and the emaciated creatures lying on the floor of the buildings housing those still living provided enough fear and hopelessness.

Looking at just one of the graves, each holding approximately 1,000 dead.

The doctors involved in the medical evacuation had decided to liberate the women first. They went through and singled out those who seemed to be more likely candidates for living and marked each one with an "X." Mayhew said he felt that the doctors must have been really upset by this situation in which only selected people could be taken out to hospitals. Their Hippocratic Oath required that they were to save lives, but there simply were not enough personnel or medical supplies to take care of everyone needing help right away. There were literally thousands dying.

Dressed for protection against typhus, AFS Ambulance Drivers carried the living on stretchers.

Most of the people, who still had enough energy to speak, could speak English. Mayhew was about eight years younger than I, but he reacted in a similar fashion—not letting the horror cloud the job to be done. Even if some of the poor creatures lying there were capable of speaking, the job of taking them out to the human laundry and then coming back for more did not leave time for talking. He said that he had to suppress his emotions until he got away from the place. After returning from the war, he buried it deep inside because so many people looked askance if he mentioned what really happened. It was too much for anyone to comprehend.

According to Mayhew, there were four thousand women taken out before those in the men's area were marked for rescue. It was traditional in any disaster to rescue women and children first. Many who had been waiting died in the meantime. Since he had not spoken of all this until this interview and meeting Alice Kern who was a survivor of Bergen-Belsen, he said over and over, "I may have been the one who saved her life." I certainly related to this since I had no closure of my own experience of this horror until I finally met a survivor for the first time. On May 15, 1945, Carl Ziegler wrote an account of Bergen-Belsen Concentration Camp to Stephen Galatti, Director General of AFS. I draw from his account as follows:

> As the lights went up in Europe last week, a group of ambulance drivers worked side by side with drivers of a British light field ambulance unit. They evacuated the starved, diseased, and mad remnants of humanity from filthy stench-ridden huts to quickly improvised hospital wards in Belsen. Before this evacuation, the now called Bergen-Belsen Concentration Camp was little known but now it is one of the most notorious concentration camps in Germany.

> Lt. Red Murray's D platoon and a section of Chan Keller's C platoon arrived at Belsen bringing with them, in two trips halfway across Germany, the personnel and equipment of a British General Hospital. They were installed in the barracks of the Elite SS troops who had guarded the camp and used the area as a training center.

> When the drivers first went into the concentration areas, they saw scores of one-story brick and wooden huts surrounded by double-and triple-barbed-wire enclosures. Thousands of dazed animal-like human figures shrunken to skeleton shapes were wandering through the dead, which were piled four-deep in many places throughout the yards.

> The internees, who had been herded a thousand or more into the huts which at most could have accommodated 300 persons, had had no food during the week prior to the capture of Belsen Camp and little more than turnips and beet roots for the past six months. Starvation plus tuberculosis, dysentery, and typhus were killing hundreds every day, faster than the German guards and prison slaves could bury them. Internees, still able to walk, had tried to carry bodies out of the huts into the streets, but when U.S. and British drivers first went into the huts they found the dead and the living lying together, ten to a bed. In many respects the living were hardly distinguishable from the dead.

> At first the drivers, inoculated freshly against typhus and other infections and dusted against typhus-bearing lice, cut the foul clothing from people to be removed and loaded stretchers and ambulances. Later special medical teams performed this loathsome task while the drivers concentrated on making the nine or ten trips each day from the huts to the human laundry where the sick and withered people were washed and deloused before being removed to the hospital wards.

> Work of evacuating people from the huts continued until all hospital space in the barrack wards was filled. To overcome this bottleneck and to bring relief to the thousands, who still lay helpless and befouled in the stench of the huts, required reinforcement help. AFS drivers, aided by workers of several nationalities in the camp, removed old clothing and bedding from some of the better huts, scrubbed them down and installed wooden bunks to provide additional hospital space in the concentration

areas. This work was still going on under Whit Bell's section of C platoon while Murray's platoon set off on a three-day convoy to bring sorely needed nursing help and medical supplies back to the camp.

When hospital space is available the drivers work from 7 a.m. until there is no more room for patients. Each of the seven to nine times the ambulances go back into the concentration areas each day, they are met with the sights and the stench that can never be forgotten. But they are rewarded with daily reports that fewer people are dying in the huts and that the death rate in the hospital wards is being cut to negligible figures. They still see the high gallows rearing its five dangling cords in the center of the camp. There has been no time to remove that. But they see the barbed wire going down around the huts they have evacuated and watch how the yards are being cleaned of the human debris that littered the whole area when they first went in. They all pass the pile of shoes, twelve feet high and twenty-five feet long, that were taken from the people who died in camp and were buried in communal graves containing up to 2,000 or more nameless bodies. But they see fewer people walking around the camp area or lying dead on the roadsides.

Most of these drivers have seen the violence of war in Africa, Italy, and some in India/Burma and have carried the horribly wounded under shellfire through fields littered with their own and enemy dead. All agree, however, that nothing in their previous experience equals the impact that this work has left on them.

Joe Fogg said, "There is nothing like this in war. What we have seen begs description. No one will believe it. It will sound too outrageous, but everyone ought to know about this.

Bergen Belsen was a concentration camp located near Hanover in northwest Germany, between the villages of Bergen and Belsen. The camp was built in 1940 for French and Belgium prisoners of war. In 1941, the camp housed twenty thousand Russian prisoners and was renamed Stalag 311.

The camp was renamed Bergen-Belsen in 1943 when it was converted into a concentration camp. Jews with foreign pass-

Even after liberation, the gallows was a stark reminder of the terror.

ports were kept there to be exchanged for German nationals imprisoned abroad, although very few exchanges were made. About two hundred Jews were allowed to immigrate to Palestine, and about fifteen hundred Hungarian Jews were allowed to immigrate to Switzerland. Both exchanges took place under the rubric of exchanges for German nationals.

Bergen-Belsen mainly served as a holding camp for the Jewish prisoners. The camp was divided into eight sections, a detention camp, two women's camps, a special camp, neutrals camps, "star" camp (mainly Dutch prisoners who wore a Star of David on their clothing instead of the camp uniform), Hungarian camp and a tent camp. It was designed to hold ten thousand prisoners, however, by the war's end more than sixty thousand prisoners were detained there, due to the large numbers of those evacuated from Auschwitz and other camps from the East. Tens of thousands of prisoners from other camps came to Bergen Belsen after agonizing death marches.

The following statistics help to comprehend the immensity of the situation and the variety of people who were interned there.

BERGEN-BELSEN STATISTICS
Compiled by Whit Bell, C Platoon, 567 Co. AFS

The camp was about two miles southeast of Belsen, which is a tiny German town about 75 miles southeast of Bremen. They found there between 40,000 and 50,000 internees—barely alive. There were about 10,000 unburied corpses in a camp of less than 50 acres.

January	6,000 died
February	10,000 died
March	17,000 died
Between April 1st and 16st	17,000 died.
Between April 17 and May 1st,	another 10,000 died.

During the last 10 days of German control there was no food. Normal daily ration was one liter of turnip soup. The weekly ration was one loaf of black bread.

Camps were segregated in order to separate families. There were 60 percent men, 30 percent women and about 10 percent children. In some barracks where our army might billet about 150 men, the SS troops had put 1,500 inmates. They lived packed in single-story wooden huts about 100 by 30 feet. There were rarely any beds, only straw pallets or plain wooden boards.

Diseases in the camp included dysentery, which was suffered by most everyone, 75 percent with typhus carried by fleas, about 95 percent with tuberculosis and most all suffering starvation. Those who were not starved were block masters and mistresses in command of individual huts who received special favors from German guards.

> It is estimated that there were 20 percent each of Poles, Hungarians, and German Jews. Russians, Czechs, and Yugoslavs made up about 20 percent while another 20 percent were French, Italian, and Greek. Most all were Jewish. Most all had previously been at Auschwitz.

Although the Jews were the major group targeted by the Nazis, there were others, considered inferior to the Aryan perfection lauded by Hitler, who were also incarcerated. Criminals, enemies of the state, and the mentally ill were just some of those suffering torture and finally being killed by the most convenient method available in the camps.

Another AFS driver whom I met in Baltimore was Thomas Hale, a friend of Whit Bell who was able to gather the above statistics as he was one of the first AFS drivers to set foot in the camp. Tom had seen many camp survivors dressed in blue-and-white striped pajamas struggling westward and mixed in with former POWs. He had heard tales of the conditions in these camps, but was totally unprepared for the horror that soon was to confront him. He said in his account of it all:

> Everything you have read or heard about the camps is an understatement. Words simply have not been coined to describe the shock, the horror, and the disbelief that assailed one's senses when standing in the midst of this scene of utter depravity.

The crematory had been operating around the clock. There were cartons of burned human bones to be used for fertilizer. The stench of death and of piles of human excrement was overpowering, and yet the townspeople nearby said they knew nothing of the camp.

The following is an excerpt from Tom's letter sent home during this experience:

> I suppose you all have been reading accounts of the conditions found in the captured concentration and prison camps here in Germany. I presume there have been pictures as well. And I suppose that there still are many people who are trying to "debunk" such stories, regarding them as false or as gross exaggerations. The conditions in those camps are too horrible for exaggeration to be possible. I have seen and talked to and carried in my ambulance many of the poor human beings, who are the living, barely living, examples of what horrors those camps were.
>
> We first saw some of the poor fellows about a week ago when we were parked in a field beside the highway. A long convoy of about 50 trucks began to pass on the road and we wandered over to watch them go by. We soon saw that there was something unusual about the convoy, for every truck was flying a huge French, Belgian, or Dutch flag, some of them obviously made by hand from scraps of cloth. The trucks were crammed with men and a few women, all dressed in utter rags or in filthy, dirty suits that looked like striped pajamas. The convoy stopped and many of the people crawled out to talk to us. They were of almost every nationality in Europe and in the most shocking

condition imaginable. These emaciated freed prisoners were from the notorious concentration camp at Belsen.

This was the camp where huge piles of unburied dead were first found, and it was here that the townspeople were forced to inspect the horror that their own country people had wrought, and then made to don their Sunday clothes and dig graves and clean out the camp. The British driving these trucks were so incensed at the conditions they found that they could hardly talk. They had all seen endless examples of senseless, wanton brutality, the like of which it is hard to imagine. Many of these prisoners were political and had been placed there for daring to speak out against National Socialism. Some had been there since 1939 and 1940 and still others for only a few months. They all told of being forced to do hard labor for 12 hours a day and having to exist year in and year out on clear soup and black bread with occasional rotten potatoes and turnips.

Only a fraction of the original number had lived to see the light of liberation. They were being transported by truck to a big camp on the outskirts of town, where they would be outfitted with new clothes and given proper food and medical care if possible. Every one of them was a case of extreme malnutrition.

As we were talking about these harrowing sights, German civilians were constantly walking by, right beside the convoy. Upon them the ex-internees heaped all the insults and abuse that they could think of and that had been building up inside them for years on end. Don't tell me those Jerries didn't know what the score was; of course they knew who those people in the trucks were and where they were from, but did they show the slightest compassion or pity? No! They merely tried to look indifferent and proceeded on their way.

Then the convoy moved along. That night many of the stronger persons left the camp, which was naturally unguarded, and proceeded to terrorize the town. They walked into people's houses, looted them, and proceeded to the next. About 4 a.m. we were all awakened by a German woman who wandered into our camp looking for help and to escape from the mobs of freedom-wild people. She kept crying out: 'Alles kaput. Alles kaput!' (All is finished.) Apparently, her husband had been killed, her house burned, and everything stolen all in this one night! Although she went from car to car and woke up almost everyone in our detail, she accomplished 'Nichts,' and no one so much as got out of bed.

According to AFS driver Norman Shethar's oral history account:

The camp commandant, Karl Kramer, who was called The Beast of Belsen, was captured there. The only place they could find to put him was in one of about eight big refrigerator rooms, which were not served by electricity at that time. They chained his legs together and tossed him in . . . locked the huge, iron door and put two guards on it. During the night . . .the electricity was activated again and when they found the guy in the morning he was nearly frozen to death. He was taken away then and stories differ as to what has been done with him. The most generally accepted one is that the

Russians, who had lots of old scores to settle with him, have been given full rein. They'll do a good job on him, I think.

Thomas Hale stated in his World War II memoirs that Kramer was found guilty of war crimes at Nuremberg and subsequently hanged, as was his second in command, Irma Greese—an attractive but cruel and sadistic woman S.S. Officer.

The six hundred S.S. and Gestapo guards left behind at the camp were disarmed and put to work digging burial pits and burying the dead without any protection at all. It was known that handling people with typhus might be certain death. They were finally declared to be prisoners of war and an order was issued against this brutality. It was understandable that the liberators might take such action after entering this camp and realizing the terrible plight that the inmates were suffering and had suffered, some for many months, at the hands of the Nazis.

This poor woman seemed strangely more animated than some of the living skeletons.

There were graves where five thousand people were buried in one big heap. Typhus was everywhere and everyone handling the bodies had to take extreme precautions. The average death rate during this period was about six hundred daily.

Before the British stormed the gates, no care was given to the living or the dead. Starvation had precipitated all kinds of behaviors, hoarding the little food they had and agreeing to do jobs in the camp that one would look on with horror if death were not imminent. Toward the end of German control, cannibalism was prevalent. When anyone died, the inmates who could muster the strength simply pushed the body down through a broken place in the floor. In many huts, the dead were mixed in with the living, who didn't have the strength to move. The living could only lie and stare up at those trying to save their lives. There were no latrines in the camp and so human excrement was a common sight. In the center of the camp was a gas chamber and also a crematorium where some survivors said people were thrown in alive.

Shethar described the excruciating task as follows:

Our ambulances held only four stretchers at a time. When we went into the huts, we were faced with up to 750 people lying in several inches of muck, people so thin you wondered how they could be alive. We were only 120 ambulances, and we had tens of thousands of people to move.

Being in a hurry, we couldn't take time to communicate with the people we were trying to save. Besides I certainly did not know what language each of them under-stood. The only way we could operate was to move the next four people we came to. That often meant separating people from their only human connection, a relative or maybe a person from the same town they had lived in or just a person they had lain next to and who was experiencing the same human misery. After a day or two, that didn't matter to us. Despite their cries and obvious terror, we just loaded the next four people onto our stretchers and carried them away. I'm sure that those desperate people thought we were just new guards ready to do them some new kind of injury. To me, these people became objects, not people. We couldn't think of them as human beings, individuals with their own personalities and their own histories, their own rights to be considered and cared for. No. We didn't have the emotional strength or the time to offer them that basic sympathy. We tried to help—we did help—but on our own terms.

In trying to save as many as possible in as little time as possible, the result was often pain and suffering for these poor, starved, and tortured people. Just being moved about was difficult for them to endure. Having to be put through the "human laundry" was more than many could survive since they were so near death. At first, the food that was provided was in too large quantities and too rich for them to cope with. But the end goal was to save their lives. The harm that their Nazi captors had done was for the purpose of eventual death. We had to develop a kind of callousness in order to survive the horror of the camp. Personally, that is what I did. I had to shut off all my senses, other than those needed to concentrate upon each poor soul that I was carrying out, hoping they would live through being moved and treated.

What we had to do in shutting off our emotions might be compared to the wall that the German citizens developed in the face of what many must have known was happening in their midst. They closed their eyes, ears, and minds to what was going on around them, never asking about the neighbors who disappeared, never mentioning the dark, locked trains that rumbled past in the night. They, no doubt, did this for their own survival amidst the madness of a country dominated by Nazi terrorists.

My son later said to me, "People do what they do." Yes, we cannot truly know their reasons or motivations. We would have to walk in their shoes in a world run by a Hitler before we would know how we ourselves would act.

As I witnessed this place which was beyond description in normal terminology, I was shocked at the contrast with the S.S. officers' billeting. Not only did W. J. Bell, Jr. attest to their sumptuous quarters, but Shethar aptly describes the place that housed the S.S. troops:

> Their quarters were grand in scale and contained an enormous ballroom about as big as the whole floor area of a barn back home. There are a half dozen dining rooms and a dozen sumptuous sitting rooms. The kitchen has a layout that puts Princeton's to shame. And as for the chinaware, glassware, and equipment of all kinds, it's unbelievable. Several hundred of everything, with wine, cocktail, and highball glasses of every shape and size. The basement is just a string of wine cellars, one after another.
>
> You get an idea of the kind of life the pigs led when you hear that the bathrooms had vomitoriums in them. They are basins about four feet from the floor or a little less, with large drains, no strainer, and with a handle on each side about shoulder high. The drunken Huns just grabbed the handles, leaned over, and puked, so that they could start all over again while a mile away three hundred people a day were dying of starvation!"

In the midst of this harrowing experience, time was taken to note the Allied victory. Lieutenant Murray represented the U.S. forces at a march past of the anti-aircraft regiment that guarded the camp, taking the salute with a British and a Russian officer. This brief celebration had to suffice, for there was still a lot of work to do.

[From My Diary]

> We evacuated over 500 women, diseased and starving, today. God! How terrible! We took them to a big building where many of those starving and diseased skeletons had to sleep on the floor on straw pallets. It makes me feel so bad because not over 1,000 feet away a British hospital is camped and they have 600 new beds not being used! I only hope that they were being saved for Allied casualties and were not just lying idle. Who knows what decisions have to be made in a crisis such as this—thousands needing attention without the means to serve everyone who needs help. There is a serious shortage of medicine and doctors and nurses. I saw many people die today. Their eyes burned holes in me that I feel are still there. One died on the makeshift latrine. I just about threw up when she was lifted off by some Germans in charge of collecting the dead.
>
> There was a girl of 20 who was so starved and skinny that I refused to lift her out of her 2nd tier flea-ridden nest. I was actually afraid she would come to pieces because there was so little holding her bones together. I got some help to get her on a stretcher.
>
> I met a little Rumanian Jewish girl who spoke four languages and was an opera singer in Bucharest before the Germans interned her. I hear that the women who are in relatively good health are pregnant by the Germans. Many stories were told to explain why some were able to walk out of the camp while most of the others were just skin and bones, lying alongside the dead.

171

I think that if I get out of this place without TB or some other disease I will be very lucky. These people have really gone through hell! Our tent blew down last night and we got soaked. It wasn't funny but Collins, Murphy, and I got a big laugh out of it after we found another place to sleep. We needed the release that this laughter brought. There are still 27,000 in the camp, probably more than half still in the hospitals.

When conditions are this pitiable and awful it is handy to have a scapegoat and I am afraid that I blamed the British because they were the ones in charge. But can you imagine breaking down the gates of the camp and taking the remaining S.S. troops as prisoners, not knowing what conditions you would find there? There was probably no way that any army unit could have anticipated the horror and great medical need. It took all the medical resources in the area to tackle this horrendous job. But even that wasn't enough. Those who were dying needed so much care, and it wasn't always available. For example, those who needed intravenous feedings because their digestive systems had shut down could not all be saved.

Bell recorded that in fourteen days just five of his ambulances had carried 2,245 patients, of whom only twenty-nine were sitting up when evacuated.

ANNE FRANK
Born June 12, 1929   Died March 1945

Anne Frank died here at Bergen-Belsen several weeks before liberation, but I had no idea who she was when I was faced with evacuating all these starved and diseased women. In 1952 her father, Otto H. Frank, copyrighted her diary under the title *Anne Frank: The Diary of a Young Girl.* Eleanor Roosevelt wrote an introduction stating, "This is a remarkable book written by a young girl. It is one of the wisest and most moving commentaries on war and its impact on human beings that I have ever read."

It is impossible to sum up the poignant and intimate expression that was poured out every day by this young girl while she lived in hiding. She searched her own soul for new insights, day after day. Her learning of the attempt on Hitler's life was described without rancor, only praise for those who expressed their disapproval of the war and of Hitler and his part in it all.

[From My Diary]

Collins, Duncan Murphy, and I visited the hospital at least two times a day giving out our cigarettes and chocolate, if we had any, and taking them flowers and books when we could get hold of them. Most of all, though, our visits were for the benefit of the patients' morale. We always created a stir when we came walking through the wards, stopping at patients' beds and giving them a word of cheer in the few words of German we knew.

You can imagine all the nationalities in the hospital, with German being the language that they all understood. Some who had been interned for a long time had almost forgotten their own language. But as their strength began to come back, so did their own special prejudices. The Polish hated the Russians. Italians hated Germans. I became acquainted with patients of all nationalities and tried to treat them all the same, but there was jealousy. I found that the Poles didn't like me to go to the Russians and give them cig-arettes and that the Italians didn't like it when I talked with the Poles—on and on. The bias, if not outright hatred, that had been passed down from generation to generation was still imbedded in the minds of the people we rescued. The torture and suffering that the survivors experienced did not wipe out the bias that they had been carefully taught throughout their childhood. Generations of hatred created by past wars cannot be wiped out just by surviving a Holocaust. If one is carefully taught bias, then one must be care-fully taught to shed such bias.

Torching Bergen-Belsen

[From My Diary]

I returned to Bassum, Germany HQ from Bergen-Belsen today (May 20) with a trip to Hamburg and Bremen. Hamburg has the smell of death everywhere and the city, which no doubt was beautiful at one time, is now a shambles. We found Bremen in the same demolished state. Feel very depressed about it all.

On May 21st, the job at Bergen-Belsen was finished. Farthest from my mind was ever returning to the death camp and its images of emaciated humanity waiting to die, but the very next day I was invited back for the celebration of the burning of the last hut in the concentration camp. So just as I had started the process of burying these images, they rose up again.

As I made this last trip to the camp, visions of the young woman who had died on the makeshift latrine kept pushing everything else from my mind. This one memory, which erupted in the midst of trying to keep the blinders on while removing all these tortured women, was to flare up whenever I tried to talk about Bergen-Belsen. Why was I going back? Then I realized why we were all coming to watch this final event of our participation in the war. It was not only to eliminate the terrible filth and vermin which enveloped the hellhole, but to act as a ritual of cleansing for all of us. As the British flamethrowers shot fire into the hut that had housed such filth and terror, there was a strong odor reminiscent of the camp before it was torched. Thoughts of all the recovering survivors who could live on into the future gave me hope as the last wooden hut was engulfed in flames.

According to George Rock:

It was a formal occasion with speeches and the erection of a commemorative tablet. Two days later a special order from the commanding officer of Light Field Ambulance thanked all who had worked in Bergen-Belsen for achieving the impossible . . . where the majority of internees were suffering from the most virulent diseases known . . .You have had to deal with mass hysteria and political complications requiring the tact of diplomats and the firmness of senior officers . . . By collecting medical equipment from all over Germany you produced a dispensary which has supplied drugs for 13,000 patients a day and has met the demands of excitable medical officers of all races requiring the most exotic drugs in half a dozen different languages. You have without hesitation acted as undertakers . . . a task which the RAMC (Royal Army Medical Corps) can never have been asked to fulfill. Life can never be quite the same again for those who have worked in the concentration camp.

Flame throwers turned the filth-ridden camp into charred rubble
after all inmates had been liberated.

At the moment I did not realize what a toll this experience would extract from me. Only later, many years after my wartime experiences, could I mull over what it all meant. Then, and only then, could I let out the sorrow. Only then could I wonder what happened to all those I rescued from the Holocaust of the camp.

[Telegram To Georgie]

ALL WELL AND SAFE.
MY THOUGHTS ARE WITH YOU.
ALL MY LOVE.

[Letter To Georgie]

It has been an awfully long time since I wrote you a letter. Something has happened to me. Guess I am changing because I can no longer settle down to writing long letters. As a matter of fact, I can't even write short letters anymore. To prove it I have about 20 or more from my family that I have just neglected to answer. I can't settle down to serious letter writing.

[As I read this letter in preparation for writing this book, I understood the shock that I was feeling after my Bergen-Belsen experience. I am sure that it influenced my homecoming and my reluctance to settle into civilian life after returning from this wartime Holocaust.]

Wildeshausen, Germany

In late May, I arrived at this German officer's TB hospital to replace Graney, who was hauling some ammo when it blew up in his ambulance. The sides and top were bulged out like a bun. Several were deaf from the explosion. Pete Burr and I had the only two ambulances. There were five Canadians overseeing the place, which was located in the middle of a large wooded area. The hospital was staffed by German doctors and nurses. We had to do a certain amount of fraternizing with them, but it was frowned upon and so it had to be done very openly. The sisters (German nurses) worked from 6 a.m. to 9:30 p.m. every day and the whole place was run with the maximum of efficiency.

My stay at Wildeshausen during pre-summer weather

I organized a barbecue.

was a very pleasant vacation, although I tried to be as help-ful as I could. I had bad news that my leave was cancelled indefinitely, because I was not on the list to go to Burma from here. So I spent some time in Oldenburg and finally learned that we would all be going home on August 1.

I went on a long run from Sulingen to Quackenbruk with French displaced persons who were being evacuated by air. I had a TB case in an advanced stage. He actually coughed up about a quarter of one lung in my ambulance. It almost made me sick, but he lived through the trip to the airstrip.

As I drove along the roads, I noticed that about three-fourths of the farming was being done by women. The predominance of women was evident everywhere. They had a hard winter coming. The horrors of Bergen-Belsen were gradually fading from my memory and not too soon to suit me. There was little I wanted to remember about that place.

Sergeant Perry, Pike, Scotty, Dick, Job, and I drove to Bremen for a look around. It was a terrible sight—about 90 percent gone. The calorie count for citizens here was about twelve hundred calories a day. My heart ached for the people in the cities who were hungry all the time. The people on the farms might have been a little better off.

Everyone knew that Germany bombed the churches in London. You didn't see in *Life* magazine what the Allies did to the churches in Germany. Most were reduced to rubble. But in wartime there is only black and white, never any gray area. The enemy must be all bad and the winners all good. War is like that.

[From My Diary]

Sergeant Perry shot a little deer several days ago so last night we barbecued it out in the open and had a little picnic. It was my idea and the first barbecue I had ever done. The meat was delicious with big slabs of special rye bread that the German officers got fresh from the bakery every day. It rained but after a wetting shower it cleared off. We came back about 9 p.m., drank the sergeant's scotch and told stories until about 2 a.m. We are being relieved so we will soon say goodbye.

Went to a nice restaurant in Eindhoven and had eggs, fried potatoes, tea, butter, sugar, milk, white bread and strawberries that were all from the black market. It cost $10 U.S. Upon finishing my meal, I was presented with a bill by a rather nice-looking waitress. I paid the bill and she brought me back my change and remarked in a happy mood, "Here's your fucking change." She thought nothing of using such a word since Tommies had been there for several months and they use that word in almost every sentence. I was just about floored. I wish I could have seen the expression on my own face.

Belgium

We were now living in an old insane asylum, as they called it then, in Louven that still had about twenty inmates. The city was old and quite large, with a population of about fifty thousand people. There were plenty of cafes and plenty of food to buy, so no one was going hungry.

Collins and I were on our way to London to see about a job with UNRRA—the United Nations Relief and Rehabilitation Administration. I was awaiting my release from the AFS Ambulance Corps, but in the meantime I was trying to plan something that would bring in enough money so that Georgie and I could get married when I got back. Civilian life would soon be upon me.

Our Belgium Trip

The sunset was beautiful on this longest day of the year, June 20. We squeezed our way into an officer's section on the train and were quite comfortable traveling to Lille where we changed trains for Calais. We stopped at Ghent to take on some more "chums," British soldiers on leave. It was a large city with the outskirts pretty well chewed up by the war. Belgium had houses about eight feet wide and two stories high and no windows on either side. In one of the main squares there were three-story buildings, which once housed the early guild associations. Best known were societies of merchants and workers. There were also religious, military and social guilds, which flourished between 1100 and 1500. When it was evident that only the rich could become the guild merchants, the journeymen as they were called, formed guilds of their own. This was the beginning of the modern labor unions.

It seems almost impossible that I will be in a Red Cross officers' hotel tomorrow night with all the luxuries I can ask for.

REVERIE

I am letting my mind drift back two years, when Georgie and I met. Thinking about going home has stirred up a lot of feelings about seeing her again. Just think, we wrote letters back and forth furiously in that short whirlwind romance, which has not been culminated but has probably brought about a better understanding—one for the other. Short romances are fun though because they leave so much unsaid and undone that they become, shall we say, mysterious. We both hold back enough in our letters to keep each other interested.

We are now in London. I will take a good look around, and maybe Georgie and I will both go to London some day. Spent the next day sightseeing, passing Saint Pauls; Parliament; the Tower of London; Westminster Abbey; and the National Gallery, where I saw Rembrandt's works. Collins, again, played the great tour leader.

In my state of limbo, I felt London was a dreary, dull, grey-looking city even on a sunshiny day. The land of the "frozen face." People don't smile much. Perhaps I was being hard on the English who had just been through hell in a war that came directly to their shores. I needed some cheering up myself and couldn't get it from these British.

Later Collins, John Root, and I went to the Haymarket Theatre and saw *Hamlet*. Coffee was served right at our seats in the theatre. Later we had roast wood pigeon at the Buttery restaurant.

We went to the UNRRA offices and planned to go to Brussels to await our release from AFS before signing on. After I told Georgie I was coming home, now I had decided to sign with UNNRA. I wondered if she would forgive me. Our contract would pay about two or three thousand dollars and a large clothing allowance. If I had come home right away, I would have had no money. By staying over here for a while I could save up some money so Georgie and I could get married. I planned to tell her I would have to take my chances that she would still be there when I got back!

My decision to sign with UNNRA didn't materialize. I received a letter from Georgie who made it clear that she expected me to be home as soon as I could gain passage. I sensed that she found it difficult to wait for me much longer. The letter that I had expected to mail never was posted.

So after staying near the so-called white cliffs of Dover, actually rather dingy, we traveled to Calais where Collins and I went to a bagpipe concert presented by Scotsmen in full dress. Then on to Paris where Collins and I spent our first leave in two years.

In Paris we stayed at the St. James Hotel on the Rue de Rivoli, just opposite the Tuileries. Collins, Barbour, Barrel, C. Y. Keller, Clifford, Ecclestone, and I went to see the play *Arms and the Man* by George Bernard Shaw. The next day I had lunch with

Simone Sclar and her mother and brother. She then took me to all the historical points of interest on the Left Bank. Had dinner at the hotel and then to the theatre to see *Love in Idleness,* which had many digs in it about the English.

The next day I met Collins at 1 p.m., and we went for a long sightseeing walk visiting the Grand Palais; Invalides; the Eiffel Tower, where we looked down on all Paris; Trocadero; and then to our starting place Arc de Triomphe. Had dinner with Collins and his mother. Later the guys went to the Bal Tabarin to taste some Paris nightlife.

One night we all went to Pigale and wandered up and down the street experiencing the carnival. Since I had heard that no one visiting Paris should miss the topless women dancers at the Follies Bergere, I secured a ticket for $3.20. Quite risqué for this small town guy to be sitting alongside the cat-calling inebriated servicemen on leave who sat as close to the stage as they could so they wouldn't miss anything!

I was getting lonesome for Georgie, so I went shopping for Tabu and Lucien Le Long perfume to bring back to her. As I walked in Luxemborg Gardens and around the Sorbonne, I saw GIs with their "taxi girls" queued up in front of hotels waiting for vacancies. Everything seemed to remind me of the love I was missing.

Traveled to Rambouillet and stayed a few hours at a 17th century chateau and then came back to Versailles, such a thrilling place. They say the palace began as a modest hunting lodge built by Louis XIII. Louis XIV hired the best architects, sculptors and landscape gardeners, spending probably over $100,000,000 to complete it as a palace—this seemed exorbitant even in the 1940s. But it didn't stop there. Later, rulers added even more rooms so that the palace was more than half a mile long and had enormous wings attached. The Room of Mirrors was known around the world. The grounds were laid out as formal gardens. Even though it was beautiful beyond description, I realized that it probably was the symbol of the power and opulence that the French people thought was enough! It all ended in a bloody revolution. I expect that the French people, who finally took over the palace, realized a great deal of tourist trade from the opulence that was once only for kings to enjoy.

I went to the Comedie Francaise and then I saw Ibsen's *Peer Gynt.* Imagine, after the horror and the degradation and terror that I had experienced for months, here I was living in luxury in Paris. Even with all the excitement, I personally felt like I was floating about aimlessly at this point. I knew that I had to find myself and discover a real purpose for my life. I would soon be heading back home to a place that I had not seen or experienced for two years. What would be my fate? How would I fit in?

At Sea Again

In mid July, after a very rough ride, I finally arrived in Brussels and then on to Antwerp to board the ship S.S. *William Benan*. C Platoon is together again—Robert Barrel, Whitfield Bell, Chan Keller, Art Ecclestone, Tom Barbour, and myself. At sea, we passed by Walchern Island and saw the flooded area. There were many ships in the channel with only their masts above water—a graveyard.

I was feeling very strange. I didn't see how I would ever be able to live a regular life again after the life I had left. I had heard a lot about anxiety neurosis—I guessed I was having a dose of it.

While mulling over my life, I remembered a fellow in one of our reserve sections who started a conversation with me as follows: "I'd like to kill a man just to find out how it would feel, what sensations I would experience." He craved new experiences and new sensations. He would shock himself on the ear to see how he reacted to electricity. He would burn himself to see if he felt different sensations on different parts of his body. Within limits he did everything imaginable in his quest for new feelings.

The conclusions I drew after discussing him with some of our more rational characters was that he would come to a horrible death. He would become a murderer and die by the hand of the law or become an incurable dope addict and die from an overdose of some narcotic. I never knew what became of him as we were like two ships passing in the night. I was just fortunate that I didn't have the life that he appeared to be living—on the edge. And I couldn't wonder what would happen to him. I had to concentrate on my own postwar life and hope that I would find what I had dreamt about in my foxhole overseas.

REVERIE

Every turn of the ship's propeller brings me closer to my love. Every hour brings me closer and closer. I have a funny feeling—a weak kneed feeling, an empty feeling in the stomach like you have when you ride on a roller coaster. I am thinking about the changes in my family since I left two years ago—new nieces and nephews. My friends Lewis and Evelyn Brownell have a child, Helen. My sister Josephine is expecting a child. So much has taken place while I have been gone. Will Georgie notice changes in me? Will I see changes in her when I can be with her at last?

Homecoming

I awoke on the morning of August 5 to find myself in the good old U.S.A.—Richmond, Virginia, to be exact. What a feeling! I felt a little afraid of the life I was to go back to. I had recuperated somewhat from the stress of my wartime duty by being assigned light duty at the TB hospital and later during my leave in Paris, but after I was given passage home, I was on my own. There was no GI bill for AFS ambulance drivers. There was no counseling to relieve the trauma of what we had been through. I began civilian life by returning to my parents' home in Selah, Washington, by train from New York.

It was a warm August day in Chehalis where Georgie had been waiting two years for me to come back from the war. She had spent her summers working at various jobs, which supported the war effort—the Seattle Port of Embarkation, the Federal Housing Administration, and Boeing Airplane Company in Seattle and later in Chehalis.

One day when Georgie was busily drilling holes in wing panels for the B17 bomber in the Chehalis plant, the whistles blew and an announcement came over the loud speaker at the plant, "The war is over. You can all go home." And they all did, never to return again. Everyone burst out onto the streets shouting, "It's all over." For Georgie this meant a little extra vacation before resuming her teaching career when fall rolled around. For me it meant relocating from the war zone and the concentration camp to civilian life without any money, job, or completed college education.

Georgie knew I was coming home but she didn't know just when. I called Georgie's mother who told me that she was spending the day at the Lewis County Fairgrounds helping her brother-in-law prepare an agricultural booth displaying his beautiful ripe peaches.

In those days, I couldn't get on a cell phone and call Georgie, so I headed for the fairgrounds and wended my way through the agricultural exhibits until I saw her, with her back to me, putting the last peach on top of a pyramid of fruit. She turned around to see me approaching. There was a hint of embarrassment because she was not warned beforehand in time to shed her bandana and work clothes for something she considered more presentable.

The years of wondering how we would act were now rolled into one moment. As her vibrant brown eyes met mine I stood paralyzed. Finally I blurted out, "Aren't you going to say something?" Georgie was shocked at suddenly being in the same space with me. As I looked at her, dressed in her casual clothes as I had envisioned her, all my worries about coming home penniless and wondering what I would do to make a living melted. Georgie had written me about a dream she had in which I had come home unannounced and surprised her. Maybe I took her up on that and decided that was the way she would want it. Whatever the reason for my surprise return, it was not an embrace and "fade into the sunset" occasion.

Neither of us knew what to expect or what to do. We had spent two years becoming better acquainted through our letters. Now we were not confined to letters slowly making their way across the ocean, which was no longer between us. We were standing face to face. All the romantic dreams were now real. Each of us faltered as the moment of reality was upon us. We didn't know where to begin. It was to take more time to feel comfortable in ourselves and comfortable with each other. All the loving things we had written to each other were still on the printed page. The words we wanted to say were frozen. There was a lot of catching up to do, and we now had the time and space to do this catching up. It was time to walk toward each other, touch each other, and be together in real life, making up for the two years we had been apart.

We spent a few days of visiting and reconnecting. Georgie, being from a family of more formal upbringing where love was seldom expressed in public, did not put her arms around me in front of her family. But with every touch of her hand, I could feel her emotion.

I established my place of residence in Seattle with my sister. I had no money for traveling down to Chehalis for dating and so took Georgie out infrequently. I had to make what I had go a long way until I became permanently employed, so I didn't approach the subject of marriage right away.

Georgie's sister, sensing we needed time to ourselves, offered us her car to make a trip to the ocean. We were almost shy of being alone together, but we desperately needed the time and space that this trip would allow us. Without even making reservations, we headed toward Long Beach and stopped at the first motel we saw, registering as Mr. and Mrs. Phillips. Young people reading this today will chortle over this pretense. In those days, staying at a motel was suspect if the couple weren't married. Motels didn't want to encourage prostitutes using their establishments! In our case, the manager wouldn't have had any worries about us. Georgie slept in her slip under the covers and I slept in my clothes on top of the covers with a blanket thrown over me. The tension was high I can tell you.

Georgie's educational colleagues probably were making bets as to when she would be married. Christmas vacation was approaching, but still no wedding announcement. I did spend Christmas with Georgie and her family. Her first Christmas gift to me in person was a fine leather shaving-bag. I had a strange sensation about receiving such a nice gift after having lived so frugally overseas. I asked her to return it and get the money back. I was not aware of Georgie's feelings, only of my reluctance to accept this gift that was out of character for me, the war returnee who had lived out of an ambulance for most of two whole years.

This first Christmas away from the battlefields and the chaos of destroyed cities brought up feelings of not belonging back home with civilians who had not experienced what I had. I was somehow a misfit. It brought back wartime memories of making tree decorations of crumpled colored pictures from magazines when we were in the war zone. It brought back memories of my childhood without wrapped presents under a tree. It pointed up to me the importance of becoming settled and saving some money so Georgie and I could think of marriage.

After Christmas, I returned to the milieu of my sister and her friends. On New Year's Eve I was invited to an ultra liberal party in Seattle. Georgie had waited two years to celebrate New Year's Eve with me and was thoroughly disappointed and hurt when I did not plan something for us to share. But I was caught up in my own need to belong and my own sense of well being. I was too insecure at that moment to align myself completely with the woman who had waited for me to come back from overseas and who had a career and money saved, everything that I didn't have. My contacts for work were found in the shipping industry in Seattle where my sister lived.

Return to Italy by Liberty Ship

On January 2, 1946, I got my seaman's papers and signed on to the Liberty ship *Fernafold M. Simmons*, being loaded with wheat which was to be given to Italy. Brent Milnor, whom I had worked with at the shipyards before the war, let me know about the position. He had signed on earlier as bos'n (boatswain), who is the crew member in charge of the working crew on board.

Now I was once more determined to work hard and save enough money to ask Georgie to marry me. While still in port I filled in as cook after our cook was let go. I had been doing the second cook's work, the third cook's work, and the scullery man's work. The good side of all this is that I got the pay of the ones who were not around. I thought that working hard and getting dead tired would make me want Georgie a little less, but it didn't. I wanted her as much as I ever had.

After Georgie and I said our goodbyes, I went uptown to buy barber shears, clippers, and comb. I anticipated making some extra money on the trip across the Atlantic. Brent bought some items to sell to the Italians, even though I tried to convince him to give them away to the poor people when we got there. The rest of the crew went ashore to tie a load on before we set sail into dangerous water with mines left over from the war.

[Letter to Georgie]

I am thinking about what we will do after I get back. I could buy a car when we reach New York and drive home from there. If the trip lasted until June, you could come east and meet me and we would be married there and have a nice trip across country for our honeymoon. Am I dreaming too much?

We finally cast off at 5:30 a.m. on January 22. I had seventy-six hours for the week, twenty-one and a half hours in overtime. I was now an ordinary seaman doing ordinary jobs such as tying up the ship when it came into port, stowing line and ship's gear, helping trim the rigging, and getting the booms ready for discharging cargo. I chipped old paint and put on new. I steered the ship on night watch and also stood lookout on the bow of the ship. The remainder of the time I stood by in case of emergency and went at a run if the mate blew his whistle.

Before the end of my first watch, we dropped the pilot at Port Angeles and faced heavy weather all day with water washing over the deck, drenching us. The plan was to be in Balboa, Panama, by February 6. When we passed Santa Barbara, we could see Catalina with the pelicans sitting in the water looking so darned wise. Got lonesome sitting on the hatch cover listening to the ship carpenter's radio. It must have triggered my dreams that night, dreams of my love back home.

Brent and I cemented our friendship on this trip, and when he learned that I was writing to a schoolteacher, he said, jokingly, "If you marry a schoolteacher, she will try and make a schoolteacher out of you." He gave me several other reasons for not marrying a schoolmarm. I included the following four in my letter to Georgie:

> School teachers are too exacting, paying too much attention to details.
> After teaching more than one year they are "old womanish."
> They always want their own way.
> They are narrow-minded and petty.

I asked her if I should believe any of it and admitted that the first and third descriptions might apply to her. Then I began pondering what Brent had said. I heard enough to begin thinking about my attachment to Georgie. It didn't stop me missing her or wishing I could be near her or dreaming of her. I thought I'd better warn Georgie that being at sea warps and distorts a person's powers of reason. A person is subject to many crazy thoughts. As Brent says, "Never make any important decisions on board a ship."

Still I had to admit that I was planning to marry Georgie after this trip. Later Brent and I were talking and I mentioned my plans to get married. His response, as he burst into a big guffaw was, "Kunkel, you will never be able to settle down. You, like me, have seen too much and not enough of this world to ever want to stop traveling and seeing new places."

In my diary I wrote, "Dreamed of my sweet last night. Seemed she was running from me but finally stopped or I caught up and she embraced me so hard with her arms and legs I couldn't have gotten away if I had tried. There was more to the dream but some things have to be left unspoken."

Arrived in Balboa on February 8. Got shore leave with Brent. Watched a parade of young kids dancing to music. It made me want to dance, and I had to restrain myself from grabbing one of the olive-skinned beauties with the flirting eyes and joining in the festivities. I bought two billfolds and the pair of maracas that Georgie wanted. Indulged in some good coffee, ice cream, and a few beers before slumming in the Cocoanut Grove district. The street where most of the prostitutes lived was deserted since the end of the war. They had come from all over—Colombia, Jamaica, Costa Rica, Brazil, and Ecuador. They told me that the "Gringo" was despised by the Panamanians. They hate our guts, took our money, and spat on us. Nevertheless, we decided to go into a bar that wasn't as run down as most. We ordered some green beer, and no sooner had we sat down than two "Blue Moon" girls came over and plunked themselves down beside us and asked us to buy them a drink. Brent, knowing the score, told them to scram. You see, if you bought them a drink, you got charged a dollar for their drink, which is colored water. And before they had swallowed it they would have clapped their hands, and the waiter would set another round of drinks on the table. It turned out to be very expensive if you got roped in.

Brent bought whiskey and rum to sell to the drinkers on board. Someone stole Brent's billfold and seaman's papers and passport. What a sorry lot returned to the boat! We dropped anchor after going through the locks, took on some stores, and are now on our way in seas that were getting heavier all the time. I was a much-envied man since getting so many letters in Panama from my love. It had taken a long while for me to digest them and try to respond to them. We were back to communicating by letter again.

One little boy came out to the ship on one of the "bum" boats and entertained us. He would stand on the bulkhead and dive into the water after nickels we would throw in. I am sure the water was twenty-five or thirty feet deep. The older boy said he always played hooky from school when a ship came in. We fed him until his little belly was stretched skin tight and hard as a football.

Valentine's Day got me to daydreaming about the past. I wrote Georgie about the other Valentine's Days that I spent away from her. The first was in Manipur at a little camp we called Khongkhang. I received a Valentine from her with a nice lipstick kiss that had the most delicious smell. Then last year I was in Faenza, Italy, living in an old building with a leaky roof and sleeping and freezing alternately on an old brokendown stretcher. Georgie sent me another lipstick print. But none this year. No matter. From now on I planned to have a big, tasty genuine kiss on Valentine's Day.

I was beginning to get a perspective on Georgie's thinking since I returned and sailed away again. She said she would be willing to go on teaching for two or three years. I asked her if that wouldn't be a high price to pay. She would be spending a critical stage of her life teaching and soon would be too old to have children. I thought that every woman wanted to be a mother. I planned to talk all this over with her when I got back.

Many of the crew brought enough liquor on board to get very drunk, resulting in T.A.R. F.U. That stands for "Things are really fouled up," to use a more polite word for the letter F. (I would spell it out, but we received kid-proof software when we bought this computer, and it only printed XXXX for the F word.)

I got to the point where I wanted to get away from it all, so I went back to the fantail and climbed up into the big gun tub and lay down on a

Refurbished Liberty Ship

folding cot and escaped into the vastness of unreality. How wonderful to be alone for a while. I lay there for a good half hour enjoying the moon, the stars, the fleecy-gray clouds, and the gentle roll and pitch of the ship. After all this mayhem, I had time to reminisce about the islands which are so beautiful surrounded by a tropical blue sea. The city on St. Thomas sits back in a small cove and climbs up the side of a steep mountain, probably a thousand feet high. Earlier in the day, the city appeared so colorful with red-tiled roofs and white walls of the buildings against the grayish green of the hillside. In my thoughts I wasn't alone—my love was sharing the moments of peace and tranquility with me.

Our food was running short due to waste in the galley. It hurt me to see so much good food thrown into the sea when only two years ago I was hungry and would have gladly eaten the food thrown away here. Thinking of such conditions reminded me of the poor around the world and the need for labor legislation to benefit the working people. Swede and I often talked about these ideas. He was smart and had read Spinoza, Nietzsche, Kant, Paine, Marx, and Engles. But he seemed to have lost faith in everything, often suffering from depression, and talked of committing suicide. He revealed that he suffered from sterility caused by gonorrhea. I thought, "Will I be one of those seagoing blokes who can't face the life that was dealt to me or, as Georgie might say, can't face the consequences of decisions that I make for myself?"

At last we were on our way again. Everyone was sober and the weather had calmed, even though we got big swells from time to time. Occasionally, there was a rattle of dishes that went skating from the tables onto the deck. The steward's department had improved and I could at last sleep at night without tossing with sweat.

[Letter from Georgie]
Dearest Norman:

It seems like months since you were here. Today we gals at school were discussing Yosemite National Park. What a beautiful place for a honeymoon! It is supposed to have marvelous scenery, waterfalls, everything you could ask for. But New York is in my mind right now. I even bought a pair of white shoes to save for this spring and summer. Hope you're not mad at me still! That would be terrible if I don't hear from you until March sometime.

I AM WITH YOU

L OVING YOU
O NLY YOU
V ERY MUCH
E VEN WHEN YOU'RE MEAN!

Y OU'RE FAR AWAY
O VER THERE BUT YOU
U NDERSTAND

Letters from my love are unsettling even with their assurance that I am still loved. Georgie asked me about the pajamas we bought for me in Seattle. "Well," I told her, "I washed them and they shrunk down to your size. I will give them to you when I get back, at least the upper half. The lower half I don't think you would be needing very much!! For this crack I think I almost deserve to have my face slapped."

It is easy to joke about something that is on my mind almost continuously, especially when I am on watch and thoughts creep into my head while I am sitting here at the wheel.

I wonder if Georgie will ever completely understand me. I'll always be kidding her, and she will always be taking it seriously until I tell her later that I was only kidding. I reminded her that she told me she would never let me go again after I got back. In my next letter I wrote:

> Remember, I once said that if you wanted me you would have to take me by the hand and drag me along with you. I will probably never get the initiative to drag you along to the preacher. I'll probably get cold feet and back out right at the last minute. Honey, you'd better mean that as a threat. Never let me go again. If you do, I'll be going and you will never catch up with me. You will always be waiting just to say goodbye like you have been doing for nearly three years.

Took a nap for a couple of hours and dreamt that I was running down the street with the maracas that I bought Georgie, keeping time to a rumba and dancing wildly. Then while I was shaking the maracas, one of them broke and I found myself in a very bleak, dimly lighted room. It was cheerless and very lonesome because my roommate was not there. It seemed that I had never been so blue and lonesome. I awoke with my back raw from sliding first one way and then the other. You see, I sleep crosswise of the ship and every time it rolls, I slide four inches one way and then four inches the other.

[Letter to Georgie]

> Tonight the heavens belonged to me, my own jewelry store! I was picking stars for you like I would diamonds if I had millions of dollars to spend. The two I selected for your earrings were Sirius and Canopus because of their brilliance and sparkle. I picked them because they have a lot in common with your eyes. Then I chose Venus for the ring on your finger because of its size and newness in appearance when you see it the first thing in the evening and the last thing in the morning. Then for your crown, the last thing, I chose Jupiter, Regal, Betelgeuse, Mars, and Saturn. For your necklace and bracelet I picked the hundreds of small brilliant stars, of which there are so many, and which can only be seen here out in the open sea away from the lights of port cities.

> As I sit and look at you bedecked in these beautiful star diamonds, in my imagination I see a smile on your lips. You are smiling because you are happy and you love me and because you know I love you beyond all stretches of the imagination. Now this song starts ringing in my ears, "I Can't Begin to Tell You How Much You Mean to Me."

> Brent and I were pipe dreaming again tonight and we dreamed up something that sounds pretty good to us, but I know it will not sound good to you. We plan on staying on this ship for a short trip to Europe when it gets back to the States, if that time is before April 20th. In the event that we do make another trip with it, we would get a week's leave and go to St. Louis, Missouri, to see some of Brent's friends and on to St. Joseph to see my aunt and uncle. On the other hand, if the ship gets back after April 20th we will come to the West Coast and land in Seattle as quickly as we can and get

on a ship to the Orient. By the time I return from that trip I should have enough money for us to get married. We could even get married before I go to the Orient. The captain says we will be back before April 1st, making it a short trip when we all expected it to last four months.

[From My Diary]

The mate saw me cutting the messman's hair. He told me he would give me an hour's overtime if I cut his hair, which almost covers his ears. My reply was, "Since when have you been authorized to dispose of the company's overtime to use as you see fit?" Yes, our first mate, who made clear at least $400 a month plus what he could graft, was asking me to cut his hair for one hour overtime (85 cents) when the lowest paid crew member paid me a dollar without giving it a thought. I thought, "Well, his hair can keep on growing till it gets to his shoulders before I'll ever cut it."

We are about 800 miles from Gibraltar. Anticipation of getting that near was interrupted by rough weather with 30-foot waves breaking over the boat deck and flying bridge. They are hitting abeam. A big wave hit us, smashing the two lifeboats on the port side and breaking the ceiling vents, which let water pour in. The water was ankle deep on the main deck. We then changed course and ran with the storm until we had all the boats securely tied and the ventilators fixed. Finally back on course but the captain says we are two days behind schedule. The rest of the day we just tossed like a cork. It has calmed finally, but another storm is expected.

We have had the wind and the sea behind us all day and overnight. It makes steering hard but we are sure piling up the miles, making back some of the lost time. We began guessing when we would be in our destination, Naples. This will be the first time I will have arrived there by ship. When I left in that Liberty ship bound for Marseilles last year I remember how beautiful the harbor was with Vesuvius in the background. George Collins and I stood on deck until we could no longer see Naples, Vesuvius, the isles of Ischia or Capri.

Heard on our radio that we are heading for Messina, Sicily as our port of call, rather than Naples. That is a tough break for all of us who were looking forward to Naples. At least the poor people in Sicily will welcome the clothes I have to give away.

March 1st we passed through the straits. It was misty and cloudy with "The Rock" looking like any ordinary rock. There were traces of habitation even through the mist. The mate says he is thoroughly disgusted about us giving grain to Italy or anyone else in this world. There is still animosity about what Italy did during the war. "Did they ever do anything for us?" is the typical question I'm hearing. The mate does not associate himself in any way with the working class of which he is one. Evidently he cannot identify with the poor people there. And yet most of these youngsters on board say they believe in Christian ideals and say they go to church. They say they believe in the United Nations, but if you ask them if they have read the charter or offer it to them they say it is a "crock of shit."

It is Saturday in the Mediterranean. "Sparks" has Glenn Miller tuned in. I dreamed of my love last night. I would sleep for fifteen minutes in one position and wake and turn and sleep fifteen more in another position. During all this restless sleep I was dreaming of my love and me. It was very odd. I would awaken and remember I had just been dreaming and when I would fall back to sleep, my dream would continue from where it had left off. It seemed that Georgie and I were just about ready to be married—but not actually married. It seemed that her mother and sisters thought it was all right if we didn't wait until after we were married to have sex. They said a day or two didn't make any difference. The irony of it all was that although we could have stepped over that line we had been afraid to cross so far, we didn't. It seemed as though we were living together but on a platonic plane. The dream just stopped with no ending or anything settled.

Latest report is that we will be in Messina Bay, Italy, at 1000 hours tomorrow, March 6th. The bay is mined and we will have to proceed slowly. Our steward department has decided to do a little better job in keeping the mess and galley clean since the captain got mad and insisted they shape up. Too little, too late. The damage has already been done and we will never recover what was wasted or sold on the black market!

Messina had a population of 200,000 before the war. I wonder how many are left and what condition the docks are in. Granted, they have had two years in which to rebuild but probably did not have the materials to do so.

The captain says we will only be in port about five days. I think he is being a little optimistic if he thinks 10,000 tons of wheat can be unloaded in five days. I doubt that.

We docked and were met by a starving, destitute mass of people who were really not much above animals. They were barefooted on the cold cobblestones and were only partially covered by their tattered rags, which had been clothing once. How terrible! It just tore my heart out to see my own brother human beings existing in such squalor and poverty in this world of plenty. I am going to give away all the clothes that I brought for these people and I may even give away the six pounds of wool yarn that I was going to sell.

It is not safe to be out after dark. Gangs of kids beat you up and strip all the clothes off you. No lie! If you are able to walk after you are beaten and stripped you are lucky. Already our carpenter got rolled and our second engineer got rolled. There may be more by morning.

When we started unloading this morning, hundreds of hungry-looking people swarmed around the gates hoping to get a chance to pick up some of the spilled wheat. I have seen cities more thoroughly destroyed in Germany and France and Holland, but not cities with people starving like these. A man came up with a picture of his wife telling how good she is in bed and that she can be had for the night for two packages of cigarettes or the equivalent in soap, food, or any other commodity. Cigarettes seem to be the basis for exchange. They bring $30 a carton in U.S. currency.

Three crews worked round the clock unloading this loose wheat. There are 300 men or more working and about three times that many outside the dock gates hoping they would get a job unloading. Guys are bringing prostitutes aboard. Brent and I went ashore tonight with Sammy as our guide, bodyguard and interpreter. He is a good kid, about 17, and smart as a whip. Went to Messina's best nightclub, which wasn't much. Sammy got us two girls to talk with and dance with. Had a good dish of ice cream for $1. Left there at 9:30 and met Jim Heaton and Brandt. Both have guns. They protected us after Sammy went. Shooting was going on all night – robberies, gangs.

It was March 8th and I became Chief Steward. My first day in my new job was a headache, physically and mentally. I haven't eaten a meal all day. It is 2000 hours now and I have been going since 0600 this morning. I am trying to teach old dogs new tricks. The Chief Cook cannot read English and the rest have little education.

We went to Reggio, Italy, today to unload the rest of the wheat. People heard we were coming and stayed up all night waiting for us. This will be the first U.S. ship in there since the war. The purser is crazy, a maniac! He is selling our penicillin to the guys who are coming back from shore leave with venereal disease. Our old cook from Seattle has VD so I called for an examination. After we spend four or five days here, we will return to Messina and let him off there. Five guys on board now have VD. I wrote to Georgie that if I didn't have her I might have been one of those fellows. This faithfulness is really paying off for me!

An Italian reached into my porthole last night and tried to steal my blankets! The world is upside down! The only improvement is that now I am an officer and can fraternize with the other officers instead of trying to stay out of the way of the drunken seamen. We went to a private home of some high-class Sicilians for some dancing and singing which lasted into the night.

Looking forward to going back home, I have purchased 10 bottles of champagne for a little party when I get back. I also bought a pistol, an Italian Beretta. We have orders to go back to Messina for some stores and then to Oran, Algiers for sand ballast and then to Hampton Roads, Virginia. Orders can be changed though en route.

Brent and Sammy went to Rome. If I hadn't become steward I could have gone with them, but my job requires me to prepare for going back to the U.S. by getting the largest storeroom in some sort of order and counting and sacking my soiled linen and preparing more menus for the coming days. It is really quite a job keeping 40 men happy with their work by feeding them well.

Yesterday when I went to town I saw many starving old women and children looking between the cobblestones for grains of wheat dropped from trucks hauling it to storage warehouses. I shopped for some souvenir bottles of cognac, several pieces of pottery, a gallon of olive oil, some books and magazines. I have given out all the clothes that I brought along to give away knowing that there would be extreme poverty everywhere.

We heard on the news that the U.S. was loaning 50 ships to carry grain from Russia to France. We may be one of those 50 ships. The captain is sitting with crossed fingers now awaiting further radio reports. If we do get pressed into that shuttle service, we will turn around tomorrow at Gibraltar and start back toward Odessa. They can keep us in this service until January 9, 1947, by the contract we signed. We will have to stop at Gib anyway to drop off two more of the crew. One has an abscessed knee and the officer's messman has a hernia that has broken loose.

It is 0830 hours on March 19th. The old Rock is shining in the sunshine just off our starboard beam. Dropped the hook here in Gibraltar. The doctor came on board to look at the two guys and he said it would be all right to take them along with us. It is now 1800 hours and we are on our way again. According to "Sparks" we will be in the states on April 5th and paid off by April 8th.

I bought some handkerchiefs for my nieces today from the Spanish that came out to our ship in little boats. I gave them all the leftovers from dinner and they in turn gave me for my kindness a bottle of perfume (Tabu), a bracelet and a bottle of brandy.

The sea began hitting us broadside so I didn't get much sleep. Now that we are nearing New Orleans, I am very busy taking inventory of everything on the ship—beds, chairs, food, chemicals, stoves.

Beecham, the messman, went completely crazy just now. He was going to jump overboard but was caught before he made it. He is being held down now by four men. We may have to put him in a straight jacket and lock him in a room before we reach New Orleans. We did tie him in bed last night and this morning he seemed quite rational and stayed that way all day. Tonight he had another spasm and we had to tie him down again.

We picked up the pilot on Sunday, April 7th and began our trip up the river through beautiful country. We will be in New Orleans, USA, before dark, dropping anchor in the Mississippi, twenty minutes by train from the city. There are over 100 ships tied up here in the river and 275 ships in port waiting or loading cargo. The doctor is aboard now checking everyone out.

The city is big and living inexpensive compared to Seattle. I went ashore to taste food not cooked in our galley, Greek food to be exact. There were lots of slot machines in the restaurant, but I wasn't interested in that. I had come in for the purpose of calling Georgie. My premonition that she wouldn't be home was correct. What a letdown for me and probably for Georgie when she got home and learned that I had called from New Orleans. I also picked up the mail and had two letters from my love.

We are still waiting for clearance and our payoff so we can all leave. The Italian cook ran away without immigration clearance, costing the captain 1,000 smackers, which the captain had put up for bail. Oh Me! Can't get any work out of anyone. My department is really in shambles. I am still awaiting some stores that I must stow before I leave. As soon as we get our pay, Brent and I are jumping the train to St. Louis.

My last chance to write Georgie was a postcard from the Mark Twain Hotel with an inset showing the cocktail lounge. (After 55 years, I looked at this card Georgie had saved and she had circled with an exclamation point the word "rest" which I said I was having after so many hours on the train. I still had to learn what to say to Georgie about drinking since she is a teetotaler. In her mind, I was living it up instead of rushing back to her side. Maybe that is why I sold most of the bottles of champagne I brought back.)

I had time on this trip to talk with Brent about signing up again. Since I had been promoted to chief steward, I could get more money on the next trip. But I didn't want to test Georgie's patience, so at the end of the voyage, I came back home.

Finally, Talk of Marriage

Having earned a stake on this Italy trip, I was feeling more capable of opening up to married life. We had discussed marriage in the past, but never until now had we both agreed on it at the same time. Georgie told me that she felt an urgency to finally take me up on my written proposal I sent with her ring in 1943: "Consider yourself engaged." This homecoming was different from my World War II homecoming. We couldn't stay away from each other from the time we came together again. We spent all our time deciding to get married and making plans for the special event we had envisioned for so long. Georgie wanted to go to Olympia to get our license and to visit her uncle to ask him to "give her away," since her father was not living.

After obtaining our marriage license on April 22, 1946, we waited only the required three days and no longer. We were both feeling that it was now or never! Can you imagine inviting guests, getting our clothes ready, contacting a minister, ordering a cake, asking the wedding attendants to take part, and arranging for a photographer all in three days? It was a little easier for me. All I had to do was go back to Seattle to get my good clothes ready, while Georgie, her mother, and sisters, (Sarah and Grace) all began a whirlwind effort to make the wedding a reality. In our personal haste to become "one," we over-looked the fact that out-of-town relatives might need more time to prepare to attend. Consequently, neither Georgie's oldest brother nor my own mother and father could come to this hastily-planned event. We didn't think at the time how this would affect the communication between my folks and my bride, who was the one traditionally responsible for the wedding.

Georgie and I talked about how many children we wanted to have. Georgie said, "I want eleven children like my mother had." I was astounded and suggested that she be fitted for a diaphragm. Just one more chore for Georgie to fulfill in the next three days! Later Georgie learned that there were some states that would not allow a doctor to fit a woman with a diaphragm unless she could produce a marriage license. This was just one example of the discrimination that existed in those days. We were both to learn how many more examples of sexism would be uncovered when Georgie began to call herself a feminist in the 1970s.

Now Georgie was centering on our marriage and our life together. Our last piece of planning was to meet briefly with the minister of the Methodist Church, who was reluctant to perform the ceremony since we hadn't planned ahead for counseling sessions with him. He warned us, "No couple for whom I have performed a wedding ceremony has ever divorced." When he was late to our wedding, Georgie's sister Grace called to remind him of the important event. It might have been a Freudian slip, since I don't think he really had his heart set on performing a wedding ceremony for two people who appeared to him to be rushing into matrimony. He didn't realize that early in my two years overseas I had

Our Wedding Day

proposed to Georgie by mail. We had also experienced two years of exploring each other's deepest thoughts by mail. Yes, we were ready.

At last it was April 25, 1946, our wedding day. Georgie's maid-of-honor was her friend, Lorraine VanHoy, who had asked her to sing at her own wedding later that same month. Neither Georgie nor I realized that it would have been the traditional thing to ask Georgie's sisters Grace and Sarah to be matrons of honor. I expect they were so anxious to get Georgie married off at last that they didn't mention this oversight!

Georgie's Uncle Ray was supposed to give her away. but the minister neglected to include that part in the ceremony. She has always been glad that she wasn't given away by one man to another man in marriage. As her Aunt Arta played the wedding march, Georgie came down the stairs in her white formal (that came in handy since she didn't have time to buy a wedding dress), a veil, and white bible borrowed from one of her friends who had just been married. But before she could reach the bottom of the stairs, the phone rang and on the line was the Superintendent of the Chehalis Public Schools, where she had applied for a teaching position. Her sister asked, "What shall I tell him, Georgie?"

Georgie replied, "Tell him that I am too busy getting married right now to discuss it." Then she proceeded on down into the living room where I was waiting for her, along with her attendant and her brother, Harvard, who was my best man.

Afterward, the small gathering shared the tiered wedding cake placed on the dining room table covered with a crocheted tablecloth handmade by Georgie's mother and a vase with her mother's tulips as the centerpiece. One of Grace's friends, a professional photographer, took our wedding picture. I had a rather scared look on my face thinking about the responsibility of it all, but Georgie looked radiant holding her orchid, which she considered a must for any wedding.

Georgie proved to be a free spirit. She had always yearned to be the center of attention, but never had the nerve, she said, until she had me by her side. After our wedding, she changed into a bright red going-away suit! Only once before in her life had she been dressed all in red. It was when she was about six years old. Her Nanny took her downtown and bought her a red felt coat and hat. This was the outfit she wore one Sunday when the family took a trip to visit their old homestead at Riffe, Washington, which was then being rented out. When they started through the pasture, Georgie's sisters taunted, "That bull is going to charge you. They always charge anyone wearing red." Georgie said she was so terrified she ran back to the car and stayed there until everyone was ready to go back to Chehalis. She never chose to wear red again until our honeymoon.

Our wedding night was spent in Aberdeen, after having a Chinese dinner in a rustic, small town cafe. We wondered why the waiter asked if we were just married and then realized later when Georgie changed into her filmy nightgown (which I didn't think she even needed) and rice fell out of her hair. After the second night at Lake Quinault, amongst the great moss covered trees of the rain forest, we stayed at Georgie's aunt's place, but since she had only twin beds we slept in just one of them since Georgie couldn't bear to sleep alone.

It was a real adventure for Georgie to travel on to the Empress Hotel in Victoria, B.C., the massive old building looking like a medieval castle, and then to cross on a ferry to Vancouver, B.C. for another night in the big city. Before coming back to Chehalis, we visited my folks in Selah so they could finally meet my bride.

Later in the month, Georgie and I traveled in the back of a pickup truck with Lorraine Van Hoy and her husband-to-be all the way to Goldendale, Washington, where her folks lived on a farm. They had prepared everything for Lorraine's wedding. Georgie wore a lovely pink jersey formal with a flounce at the waist when she sang "I Love You Truly" and "Because" in the little country church. As Georgie said, "A singer isn't always honored in her own hometown, but when she travels across the mountains to appear in a wedding, all the young men stare at her in awe and all the women look at her in envy." I will never forget the image of my love standing there dressed so beautifully and singing so well.

Many a time later on in my travels, I would hold that memory in my thoughts. I was to sail away again soon after our marriage on a ninety-foot fishing boat, one of a fleet of fishing vessels to be presented to the Chinese through the UNRRA program. This was the United Nations Relief and Rehabilitation Administration that I had contacted in Italy earlier. Details of this six-month adventure can be found in the Afterword.

PART SIX: REMEMBERING

Speaking Out About the Holocaust

After years of burying my memories of Bergen-Belsen, I learned that John Spellman, Washington's governor, was hosting a commemoration of the Holocaust at the state capitol in Olympia on April 29, 1984. As one of the liberators of the Bergen-Belsen Concentration Camp, I decided to attend. On stage were survivors of the Holocaust and liberators who had served in the U.S. Armed Forces.

After the ceremony, I walked about looking for people with nametags that might connect them to the camp that I helped to liberate. Suddenly I spied a woman with the nametag, "Laura Varon, Bergen-Belsen Survivor." I had never before met a Bergen-Belsen survivor. At the camp itself, I was helping evacuate those who could not speak because they were so emaciated. Those who were able to walk had already been evacuated before I arrived. I moved those who were dying or who were so starved and ill that they could only lie and stare up at me. Few had the energy to

With Bergen-Belsen Survivor, Laura Varon

talk. They had no homes to go to, so I was never able to keep in touch with them.

Meeting a survivor of Bergen-Belsen was incredible. We were stunned to find each other. We shared what we remembered about that terrible camp. This meeting provided closure for that experience of so many years before. Since that time, Laura Varon has written her story of the Holocaust, *The Juderia: A Holocaust Survivor's Tribute to the Jewish Community of Rhodes.*

In her story, Laura tells about her move to Bergen-Belsen. She was living alongside others with dysentery, typhus, and a host of other maladies. She says she was "bullied and brutalized" just as others were. There was no work to do at this camp. It was as if the Nazis had "organized this place as a final collection point for those of us who had somehow survived." There was no need here to expend bullets because disease and starvation would eventually end lives. It was just as she had given up and was preparing for death that the soldiers came to the barracks. After feeling that she would like to be left alone to die, she roused enough to watch them as they raised their hands "in a taut salute."

Now she and I were in the same room. The years that I had wondered what happened to those women were now at an end. I finally knew that many of the women were alive and well. Well, physically, but not ever to shed the terrible memories of the camp.

Laura told me of another woman who had also been at Bergen-Belsen, Stella de Leon, who died before I could share this book with her. She bore the tattooed number A24348.

The "A" stood for Auschwitz where she was first held before being transferred to Bergen-Belsen. She remembered when her sister, who was in the camp with her, got up to get water and stumbled over bodies outside. Then, just weeks before liberation, her sister died.

It was after making contact with these survivors of Bergen-Belsen that I determined I would tell my own story. From that time on, I began to speak about my experiences at high schools and elementary schools, sometimes on the same platform with Laura or Stella.

After I told my story at a local high school, one young woman wrote me a thank-you letter. She said that my story stirred up in her mind a

With Auschwitz and Bergen-Belsen Survivor, Stella de Leon

personal story. She had to leave her country when she was age fourteen because of a religious war in Azerbaijan. She herself was an Armenian living there. Before they fled, she was riding on a bus with her mother, and a Muslim fellow found that an Armenian woman was on the bus. He began treating her badly and finally threw her out of the bus while it was still going fifty miles per hour.

My story helped her reach into her own past. She was full of questions such as: "Do you blame the German people for what they did? Do you hate them for it?" These questions have always been difficult for me to answer. Hatred resulting in dehumanizing other humans, and finally using violent means to exterminate them, doesn't happen in a vacuum. There must be deep-seated prejudice passed on from generation to generation to affirm a dictator such as Hitler who determined to rid the world of Jews and others whom he singled out as inferior.

Recently I saw the documentary interview of a German woman in her eighties, Traudl Humps, who, as a much younger woman qualified to become one of Hitler's personal secretaries. She began her interview with dignity and assurance and told about meeting Hitler for the first time. He appeared to her as a mild manner-ed, polite man. She was welcomed into the "inner sanctum" of his personal dwelling. Those serving Hitler in this capacity often ate dinner with him and talked of mundane subjects. They were cautioned not to ask questions of a political nature or to ask about the war, but to provide a homelike atmosphere while he was present.

With Henry Friedman, Early President of the Holocaust Survivors in Seattle, Washington

She said that he didn't appear to have an erotic nature, nor did he appear to be capable of personal love. He seemed like two persons, one ordinary and calm and the other the fiery speaker at the podium with the charisma to stir up a huge mass of people.

As the questioner dug deeper into feelings about serving such a monstrous leader as Hitler, she broke down with, "I now feel guilt and shame." It was not until Hitler retreated to the bunker with his staff, furnishing them with cyanide in case they were captured, and went into his inner quarters to take his own life, that she realized that he had abandoned her and the others. It was not until later that she learned the details of Hitler's war, including the horrors of the concentration camps.

I remember conversing with some people at an informal social gathering. I said, "I cannot blame ALL the German people for the sins of the Nazis and their sympathizers." I was then verbally attacked by a woman who could not accept that there were any "good"

Germans. And yet there are stories of Germans coming up to the fences around the concentration camps offering food. There are stories like the one told about Schindler who began as a greedy wartime factory owner and ended with compassion toward those he could save from extermination. Then I am reminded of what Elie Wiesel, a survivor of a concentration camp, said, "Tell those who need to know that our pain is genuine, our outrage deep, and our perplexity infinite."

It is difficult to say what I, myself, would do, if my life were threatened in a police state where any dissident talk or action could be met with death. When does one sacrifice one's life for what one believes in? Certainly, my life was threatened many times at the front when my job was to pick up the wounded, even when the troops were retreating. Every time my ambulance was rocked with the exploding enemy shells, there was the chance that one would have me singled out.

I have begun to realize that hate and blame is debilitating to the human spirit. Those survivors of the death camps who could shed the gnawing hatred somehow released themselves from torment. But I do not blame those who have not yet shed this hatred. Looking back at the horror beyond words that I personally witnessed at Bergen-Belsen, I can understand those who still hold onto such hatred.

Once we flew Lufthansa Airlines back from Europe. A survivor of the Holocaust heard about this and said, "How could you fly on a German airline after what the Germans did to us?" It was difficult to answer her angry feelings. Rev. Dale Turner wrote a column in the *Seattle Times* in September 1993 that summed up what hatred does to the person harboring hatred. It was entitled, "Hatred, Like Acid, May Harm the Vessel in which it is Stored." He brought out that holding on to enmity, hatred, and vindictiveness is symbolically like storing acid in a vessel that can be corroded.

From this I learned that it is healing to end differences early on and not to hold hatred in one's heart. Psychology has always taught that we are the ones who control our own feelings and how we will act upon them. It is hazardous to our own health when we harbor vengeance inside ourselves or blame others for what we feel.

As you can see, I have worked through a great deal of emotion in putting all these experiences and memories into perspective. Telling the story, even though it has not stopped my terrible grief over the women inmates at Bergen-Belsen, has helped cement the fact that the Holocaust was a true period in history and not just "too horrible to contemplate that it could have ever happened."

Appearing on the Oprah Valentine's Day Show

In 1989, a few years after I started speaking about the Holocaust, Georgie drew upon her writing expertise to enter an Oprah Winfrey essay contest. The topic: "Why My Husband Should Be Husband of the Year." In this essay she wrote about my involvement in helping people, including the women survivors of Bergen-Belsen Concentration Camp during World War II.

After sending in her entry, we went on a trip and when we returned, Georgie retrieved messages from the answering machine. The first one announced, "This is a message for Georgie Kunkel from the TV station that held the Oprah Winfrey essay contest in your area. Out of 400 essays submitted, you have won the contest for the Northwest area and soon you will be contacted by the Oprah Winfrey producer." The next message was, indeed, from the producer who gave us information about our trip to Chicago to appear on the Oprah Winfrey Valentine's Day Show.

So many people have asked about this essay that I thought it would be appropriate to include it here.

WHY MY HUSBAND SHOULD BE HUSBAND OF THE YEAR
By Georgie Bright Kunkel

From the first time we met at the Trianon Ballroom in Seattle, I knew that this man was caring, honest, and warm. He came way over to the corner where I was sitting alone and when I saw his dark eyes meeting mine as he bent over to ask me to dance, I was filled with a kind of magnetism.

We didn't have much time to get acquainted because Norman was soon to go overseas to serve with the American Field Service Ambulance Corps as an Ambulance Driver attached to the British and then later with the U.S. Occupation forces in Italy.

For two years our letters traveled slowly back and forth. As the letters kept coming, I knew that I must wait for him. I never once thought that harm might come to him even though he was hospitalized several times with jungle illnesses.

His letters indicated a strong caring for family and a wish that his mother not know that he was in the hospital and he made me promise not to worry her with bad news. I felt rather special that he had trust in me.

When the war was over, he brought back all the letters I had written on onionskin paper rolled up and stored in a protective can and after we married we stored these along with the ones he had written to me over this two-year period.

Just recently, we got them out to put them into chronological order and to transcribe them to send to the AFS Archives in New York. Memories brought back by re-reading them have cemented the strong feelings I have about him as the selfless, sharing person that he is.

For example, when we looked through the letters about Bergen-Belsen Concentration Camp with the descriptions of the agonizing task he had of sorting the living from the dead, I realized how much humanity he expressed and how deeply he cared for others.

Over the years, my husband has been a balancing influence in my life. We have shared everything. I helped him by giving him encouragement during the hard times he had working his way through the remainder of his college education without benefit of the GI Bill which was denied to those not in the U.S. forces. He supported my struggle for my Masters Degree after we had four children and during the women's movement we spent our 25th wedding anniversary at a national women's conference with time also for marching in a peace demonstration in San Francisco.

My husband devoted his life to his family and to the children that he encouraged in the elementary school where he taught for 25 years. Although he was encouraged by his supervisors to get his principal's credentials, he chose to remain in classroom teaching.

Even today, he gets letters from former students telling him how much he has meant to them. Our own children, two grown sons and two grown daughters, know that their father would do anything to help them and he has done so.

Now that we have eight grandchildren and one more on the way, I realize even more how much he enjoys being married and sharing with all these offspring—no matter what age.

From my husband I have learned many things. He taught me to be more affectionate than I had ever learned to be in my immediate family with their more reserved Maine heritage. He has been willing to risk whatever it takes to make our life more fulfilling. He has shared with me the choice of religious commitment and has never given way to complaining.

My own developing sense of humor was nourished by my husband's down-to-earth Missouri wit. Nothing he says is dull. When he talks about someone being poor he remembers what his folks always said, "They don't have a pot to pee in or a window to throw it out of." Yes, he's down to earth.

Last year Norman completed several weeks of devastating radiation treatments that temporarily left him depressed and lacking in vigor. He never gave up but kept plugging and now he is resuming his life with some limitations but with a sense of survival no matter what the odds.

I still dream about him as a young man full of vigor and I think of him as my young lover. It will never change because we have found love, trust, and delight in each other's company.

He has given me backing in my urge to write. With his encouragement I completed a cartoon book called, "Grandma's Sex Secrets" about senior sex! Nothing is impossible.

Sure there are times when we disagree and when circumstances give us a jolt, but we are survivors and we intend to cherish each other for years to come.

Our children recently gave us a Forty-second Wedding Anniversary Party. Who but a creative, loving husband would celebrate a year that few other couples celebrate.

"Why wait until we're fifty years married," he said. Those are my sentiments too. Why wait until my husband is any older to appreciate him in writing.

Truly, Norman is the HUSBAND OF THE YEAR and will be for me as long as we are both together.

Our appearance with Oprah Winfrey on the Valentine's Day Show aired in 1989.

After Georgie read the essay on the show, Oprah asked me if I had anything to say to my wife. I responded with:

Dear, you were brought up as a kind of free spirit believing that you could do anything that you set your mind to do and you have. You were also brought up believing you could make a difference in changing things that you thought needed to be changed. I think together we have done quite a lot to make the world a better place for all of us to live in.

We now watch the video of this show every year on our anniversary. We shared the video at our fiftieth wedding anniversary when Georgie wore her gold skirt made from the sari material I brought from India during World War II and her silk brocade vest made from the obi material I brought home from China after we were married. Georgie sang a love song that she wrote for me. She called it "You Looked at Me" in memory of the first time I looked into her shining brown eyes at the Trianon Ballroom in Seattle in 1943 before I left to go overseas during World War II.

After this exposure on a nationally televised program, I was to receive letters from many people who had never known that I had been through the Bergen-Belsen experience. I was beginning to get even more closure as I was asked to tell about my experiences at Bergen-Belsen. I had met survivors of this camp, but I had never shared my memories with any of my AFS friends who had been with me overseas.

Even though AFS reunions held in New York had been financially prohibitive for me after we were first married and started raising our four children, Georgie later urged me to attend. She said, "We can find the money for you to attend alone." So I contacted an AFS friend, George Collins (now deceased), who had also been a liberator at Bergen-Belsen. Even though we had shared this horrendous experience, neither of us spoke of it. After returning from the war, he had resumed his interest in

Georgie wearing silk brocade "obi" vest from China and skirt made from sari material from India.

architecture, becoming a professor at Columbia University. Our time together, between AFS banquets and such, was spent talking about architecture and once visiting an old structure which had a special ceiling that he wanted to photograph.

In October 1992 I was invited by the Northwest Regional Office of AFS to be specially recognized with four other AFS drivers: Arnold Motz, Ken Proctor, John R. Kociencki, and John Hodel. Only one of these drivers had been anywhere near Bergen-Belsen. He came to the camp to bring our monthly stipend of $25.

For several years I had only brief contact with the AFS, which had become the student exchange programs involving countries all over the world. During these years, the local AFS produced a video of the student exchange programs including a very brief mention of the AFS Ambulance Corps. Exchange students and volunteers in the AFS student exchange program had little knowledge of AFS Ambulance Corps drivers who served in

World War II after sowing the seeds of the corps during World War I. This was to change in the years to come. As World War II AFS drivers began to disappear from the World War II driver roster, there was a sense of urgency to record their personal stories.

From Left: Arnold Motz, Ken Proctor, Norman Kunkel, John R. Kociencki, and John Hodel

The Holocaust Memorial Museum

To add further closure to my Bergen-Belsen experience I must tell you about the special experience of attending the opening of the U.S. Holocaust Memorial Museum in Washington, D.C. This museum was charter-

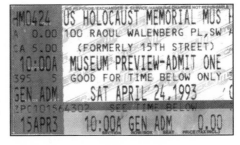

ed by a unanimous Act of Congress supported by the Carter, Reagan, Bush and Clinton admin-istrations, and built entirely with private funds. It is a national institution for the documentation, study and interpretation of Holocaust history, and this nation's memorial to the millions of individuals murdered during the Holocaust. While Jews were the primary victims, Romani (Gypsies) and the handicapped were also targeted for destruction. Millions more including Poles, homosexuals, Jehovah Witnesses, Soviet prisoners of war, and political dissidents were persecuted and murdered.

The day before the dedication, on April 21, 1993, I was one of many liberators who were honored at the Tribute to Liberators and Rescuers at Arlington National Cemetery Amphitheater. The U.S. Army Band played for the processional and the presentation of flags of all the liberating countries. When the flag representing the British Army was presented, it brought a lump to my throat. Never before had I been so honored for my participation in World War II.

Colin Powell was on stage with John S. D. Eisenhower, the son of Dwight D. Eisenhower, who had commanded the U.S. forces in Europe during World War II. Harvey M. Meyerhoff, Chair of the U.S. Holocaust Memorial Council, presented Eisenhower Liberation Medals to the Fighting Forces of the Commonweath of Nations, the Fighting

British Flag Representing the British Second Army which Liberated Bergen-Belsen

Forces of the former Soviet Union represented by Russia, and the Free French Fighting Forces.

It was General Eisenhower who gave authenticity to the Holocaust by personally visiting a concentration camp and viewing the horror with his own eyes. When he spoke out about this, we thought no one could dare refute it. But I was to learn very soon that there are people who do refute it. This has only made me more willing to tell my story so more and more people will know what really happened in the concentration camps during World War II.

A stirring reading "America Remembering," written by Chaim Potok, was presented by Liv Ullmann, the only woman taking part in the tribute. Potok brings to mind the massive impact of the Holocaust upon the victims and the valor of the rescuers. "Let it never lead us to despair and defeat . . . and let it stir in us the firm resolve that the horrors it unveils do not signal an end to our determined advance toward a just world . . ."

Following the tribute to liberators and rescuers at Arlington National Cemetery Amphitheater, I was invited to tour the halls of the Pentagon. I wasn't sure I wanted to visit a place symbolizing military might after having seen what military might destroyed during World War II. However, as we went through the long corridors looking at models of aircraft carriers, paintings of important events in the life of this country and the presidents who led our country throughout its history, my wife noticed a special poster. It was probably the one that may have influenced her sister Anne to become a part of the Army Nurse Corps during World War II, serving in field hospitals in Africa and France.

Now we were ready to attend the U.S. Holocaust Memorial Museum dedication ceremony. It was held in an outdoor area behind the museum. People had come in their best clothes, not expecting to experience this celebration outside with rain coming down. As they walked to their chairs, their name-brand high heels sank into the D.C. mud.

Laura Varon, a Bergen-Belsen survivor, had come through security to enter. When she saw the area surrounded by a chain-link fence and the crowd of people sitting on a lawn beginning to ooze mud, she asked if she could go on out for a while. She had to compose herself before coming back into conditions that reminded her of the concentration camps she had lived in for so long before being liberated.

As we sat in our seats waiting for everyone to clear security, we could hear shouts and cries of people marching on the street outside our fenced area. As the sounds became clearer we heard, "It never happened." and then "The Holocaust is a lie." A woman sitting near us told a story about being hidden from the Nazis during the Second World War because she was Jewish. On hearing the approaching sounds of denial, she became so upset that she left her seat and walked through the mud to the fence calling to the demonstrators. A mounted park police officer came up to her, dismounted, and led her back to her seat. Those who were demonstrating had never believed the eyewitness testimony of General Eisenhower, nor did they believe what the survivors and liberators represented as they told their stories here at this dedication ceremony. Nevertheless, I personally can testify to the degradation, torture, and killing that was brought upon those who were interned at Bergen-Belsen. Once I started telling my personal story of it all, I vowed never to let people forget.

The presidents of both the United States and Israel gave importance to this ceremony while stirring accounts of rescue and survival were presented. Stephania Podgorska was only sixteen years old when she was left alone with her six-year-old sister after their father died and their mother and brothers had been forcibly taken by the Germans to work at a labor camp. For over two years she successfully hid thirteen Jewish men, women, and children in the attic of her apartment in the Polish city of Przemysl. After the war she married Josef Burzminski, one of the thirteen she saved.

William J. Lowenberg fled to Holland with his family in 1936. In the fall of 1942 they were arrested and taken to Westerbork concentration camp. Separated from his family at age sixteen, Lowenberg is a survivor of other Nazi camps, including Auschwitz and Dachau.

Met with Arthur Fiedler while in the Washington D.C. area. He was an AFS Driver who served with the British Liberation Armies.

Elie Wiesel, born in Romania, received the 1986 Nobel Peace Prize and was the founding Chair of the U.S. Holocaust Memorial Council. You have undoubtedly seen the haunting picture recorded at Buchenwald in 1945 when Wiesel was found lying in a fourtiered bunk with starved survivors who were so emaciated that they could not move. This picture, along with Wiesel's terrifying account of the Nazi death camp in his book, *Night*, will remind generation after generation of an infamous period in so-called modern history.

When Wiesel was liberated from Buchenwald, he imposed a ten-year vow of silence upon himself before trying to describe what had happened to him and over six million other Jews. When he finally broke that silence, he had trouble finding a publisher. "Such depressing subject matter," said Robert McAfee Brown who wrote the preface for the Twenty-Fifth Anniver-sary Edition of *Night*.

After this electrifying program, which was punctuated by stirring remarks from our own U.S. President

Livingston Biddle, Pedro Velez (*AFS World Magazine*), Eleanora Golobic (AFS Archives)

Clinton, Jessye Norman sang "America the Beautiful" leaving the audience in reverent silence.

When the New York AFS office learned I would attend the dedication ceremony, they sent representatives to seek me out before the program began. My wife and I were huddled under an umbrella when I heard my name being called. I looked up and there stood Pedro Velez from the *AFS World* magazine, Eleanora Golobic of the AFS archives, and Livingston Biddle who had served as an AFS Ambulance Corps Driver and who had also served as chair of the National Commission for the Arts under President Carter. He served with the AFS as captain during World War II and was decorated with the European-African-Middle-Eastern Campaign Ribbon for outstanding and conspicuous service with the Armed Forces under difficult and hazardous combat conditions. I felt honored to be present for this historic occasion and to be interviewed for a special article in *AFS World,* "Remembering the Holocaust."

Laura Varon and I were in touch that weekend and went through the museum together at a special showing the day before the public was admitted. As we began our walk, we entered a high-ceilinged hallway covered with pictures of smiling individuals. These were the images of Jewish people before the terror began. Each room we entered brought us further into the degradation and final torture and murder during the extermination period of Hitler's Nazi Germany.

Bergen-Belsen Concentration Camp: A huge pile of leather from inmates' shoes. The soles were discarded, and the leather uppers were then sold.

There were scenes of shoe soles left in huge mountains on the grounds of the concentration camps. The leather tops had been cut off and sent away to be sold. There were display cases full of the things that were taken from the concentration camp victims—jewelry, watches, eyeglasses, and any number of other objects. The most precious were hoarded by the S.S. troops in their palatial living quarters. There was an actual reconstruction of the rough wooden bunks where dozens of people had slept on wooden slats.

One of the greatest ironies of all was a replica of the gate at Auschwitz, which had the German inscription in ironwork: ARBACHT MACHT FREI meaning: WORK WILL MAKE YOU FREE. How insidious and monstrous was this greeting to a people who had not known freedom and who could not work for it nor hope to save their own lives. Those who walked in long lines before the Nazi masters were at the mercy of the selection process:

To go to the right and cer-tain death or go to the left and perhaps have more time to live in forced labor camps.

As one walked further into the museum, the light was dimmer and the air colder to represent the con-ditions of an actual death camp. Turning a corner into a smaller alcove, we were shocked by a replica of the furnaces which con-sumed the dead and, as one

Replica of the Furnaces into which Bodies Were Thrown

survivor reported, also the living. Another report stated that a Jewish man who was ordered to feed these furnaces, went mad and never recovered from the tortuous choice he made in order to live by obeying Nazi orders.

As I neared the exhibit of Bergen-Belsen, the camp I had helped liberate, I had a sensation of great sadness. I had never seen such a vivid account of the place. Laura Varon, Georgie, and I just stood there silently. There had not been one word spoken by anyone as throngs of people walked slowly through this place of memorial. An eerie silence had fallen over all who shared this special day. My wife, who has seldom broken down in public before, felt nausea and hurried to the exit to get a breath of air.

That evening we were invited to have dinner with Jewish friends of Laura Varon. It was a special occasion for all of us, to break bread during this Holocaust Museum dedication period.

Telling My Story As a New Veteran

In 1993 I was informed that I needed to document at least two months of service with the U.S. armed forces to become a bona fide veteran for the first time. The American Field Service had for years urged the establishment of regulations making AFS Ambulance Drivers veterans. I finally received my honorable discharge and medals representing the campaigns in which I served: India/ Burma, Italy and Germany, as well as the Occupation Army and Good Conduct medals *(see a picture of the medals in Appendix).*

Although it could not make up for the loss of the GI Bill and its benefits or the support services that I could have used directly after World War II, it did provide a sense of belonging with all those others who served in World War II. I now had a definite place in U.S. history.

After the Fiftieth anniversary of World War II, there was an urgency to meet the veterans and hear their stories. On October 28, 1995, I was invited to speak at the AFS International Evening in Ephrata, Washington where I met the exchange students in that area.

AFS International Evening at Ephrata, Washington,
with Exchange Students from Italy, Japan,
Slovakia, Germany, and Brazil

On April 30, 2000, I took part in the Holocaust Commemoration in Portland, Oregon, with Colin Gemmell Fred Burkhard Arnold Motz who were also AFS drivers during World War II.

At this commemoration I met Alice Kern, another survivor of Bergen-Belsen. She has written her story in *Tapestry of Hope*. Once again, I had another experience of closure as she shared her book with me and spoke to the gathering about her feelings of thankfulness for those who took her out of that misery and filth.

211

Alice had been at Auschwitz, Poland, but was moved to Bergen-Belsen. A lice epidemic broke out and everyone became diseased and malnourished for lack of adequate food. For some reason the lice didn't like her light flannel dress, but her fuzzy hair was lice ridden and she was depressed. This was so different from her life as a young girl, when she always saw life through rose-colored glasses.

The pile of bodies outside grew higher each day, and Alice, on the way to the outdoor latrine, wondered if her body would soon be on top of the pile. At last she became so weak that she sank into a coma. She thought, "Was this death?"

The deadly silence turned into loud shouting and the sounds of running and shooting. A door was flung open and a soldier wearing a beret looked inside. "I could see him fighting to control the horror in his voice at the sight that confronted him. Then a few more soldiers came in. One soldier came to me, lifted my head gently, and gave me a drink. With my eyes closed, I just let it happen. I was afraid to open my eyes and find out that it was a wishful dream. From a deep, dark and peaceful death, I was being rekindled like a fanned spark."

Alice was told not to eat any of the food on the premises because the Germans were suspected of poisoning all the food and water in readiness for their escape. Because the S.S. guards were surprised by the British storming the gates, no poisoning took place. Since I had not personally heard of this poisoning attempt, I can only guess that it had some basis in fact. Ironically, any food remaining on the grounds was probably contaminated after being strewn about in the filth of the camp. There was no need to further poison it. Poisoning was not the only danger involving food, however. After liberation, the inmates had to be watched so that they did not overeat, since too much or too rich food would be harmful until they could be conditioned to eating again.

In another instance during the liberation period in Germany, it was thought that a water tank attached to a hospital had been poisoned. However this story started from a German woman saying that she saw a person pouring poison into the tank. It turned out to be a water truck driver pouring in the regulation chlorine. History is the result of taking numerous stories and sifting out the facts that seem to bear out the truth. In the chaos of war and concentration camps, fear and terror often clouded the minds of survivors. One truth is evident nevertheless: concentration camp victims were threatened, beaten, starved, left in filth to be overcome with disease, and many were killed violently. No one who had been there could refute this. But there are some who still deny the evidence produced by eyewitnesses who have told their stories.

Alice observed the forcing of the Germans to carry the bodies and dump them into pits without wearing any protective clothing. She said that it gave her no pleasure to witness the tormenting of her former tormenters. She only wanted to live and forget.

When she had enough energy to move about, Alice looked for a washroom and was startled to look in the mirror and see a horrifying face, with two dark eyes deep inside a skull perched on a skeleton body covered only with a thin skin, staring back at her. She vowed to eat until she was plump and healthy once more.

As I read this story of Alice's camp experience and then looked at her in person, I could see a healthy looking, mature woman who had surmounted the agony of her past to continue on with her life. It gives me such pleasure to realize that many of the starved internees of this camp are now living full lives.

AFS Ambulance Refurbished by Hugh Gemmell, son of AFS Ambulance Driver Colin Gemmell. Pictured are Frederick Burkhard, Norman Kunkel, Arnold Motz, Colin Gemmell, and Hugh Gemmell.

After the commemoration ceremony, Hugh Gemmell, Alice Kern, and I were interviewed by *Culture* magazine. Gemmell spoke about his father's involvement with the AFS Ambulance Corps. Learning about this involvement for the first time spurred him to learn more about the AFS. In 1955 he found a rusted shell of a 1943 Dodge ambulance, the very same type his father had driven. Ultimately he bought it for $400 and with his five brothers, they set about to restore it in time for an AFS reunion in Williamsburg, Virginia, even down to hand painting their father's AFS Unit 567 insignia, an eagle they called "The Chicken."

It was Hugh who informed me of the British 8th Army Reunion to be held in Blackpool, England in June 2000. I had served with this army in Italy after my convalescence in Calcutta and then again in Cairo. My wife and I sat with British veterans, some of whom had served in the decisive battle at El Alamein. Winston Churchill once honored them with these words, "When, after the war is over, a man is asked what he did, it will be enough for him to say: 'I marched with the 8th Army.'" We were welcomed by the Mayor of Blackpool as we sat at the banquet table, sharing stories and looking about at the fewer numbers that had survived long enough to attend.

We extended our trip to visit some of the places that I had dreamed of showing Georgie sometime after the war. I had seen London, that had withstood the Nazi bombings, but now it was magnificent as it showed off the changing of the guard and the grandeur of Victoria Square. Paris was truly the City of Love and cerainly the

Georgie and I with J. Haywood and A. Davies, Deputy Chair of the 8th Army Veterans in Blackpool, England

City of Light, as the Eiffel Tower rose glittering and towering into the sky. Georgie saw at last the great Champs Elysees where I had walked on V-E Day.

Some years earlier, Georgie and I had seen Calcutta together. It was as I had described it to Georgie so many years before, except for increased automobile traffic spewing out exhaust amongst the bicycles, and people living in the streets. We both swam in the old Hotel Grand pool and luxuriated in our room. Georgie sensed a strong odor of mildew from the thick carpeting. Then I realized that the straw matting, that had once been a more appropriate floor covering in tropical climates, had been replaced so that the hotel could be considered Class A.

One morning we heard a commotion and went to the window. There down below were barefoot vendors with huge wicker baskets filled with the morning delivery of live chickens. Soon, those who needed to buy chickens were crowding around, paying for them, and carrying them off on their bicycles as they did when I was there in 1943-1944.

Georgie and I were beginning another period of travel as I was getting requests from groups who wanted to meet their AFS WWII Ambulance Corps Drivers. I was invited to speak during the Brazil National AFS Conference held September 7-10, 2000. Immediately on arrival at the conference hotel, I was interviewed by the local TV station at the conference site in Vitoria, just north of Rio de Janeiro.

All 190 participants at the AFS Brazil Conference took turns posing with me.

At last my wife and I could relax, unpack, and prepare for the evening's program. I could not believe I was actually in faraway Brazil, standing at the podium, telling about the AFS Ambulance Corps and its beginnings. I spoke about my wartime duty in bringing in the wounded, helping to repatriate citizens who had fled their homes as the Nazis attacked, and finally showed slides of the horror at Bergen-Belsen Concentration Camp. As I finished my speech, there was thundering applause and foot pounding like the adulation given to soccer stars such as the great Pele of Brazil. Group after group came up to pose for pictures with me. At age 82, I was gaining recognition as a part of AFS history.

I was able to meet the AFS Executive Secretary Paul Shay, who spoke about the vision and plans for AFS around the world. The intercultural students, as well as teachers, were gaining the opportunity to experience other cultures. There is now a renewed effort for AFS to become even more visible in the world, to recognize diversity, and to continue to provide a high quality experience for all of those taking part.

Eduardo Assed, Executive Secretary of Brazil AFS, acted as facilitator throughout our stay, making sure that my wife and I had reservations to sightsee in Rio de Janeiro, the place that I wished I had been able to visit during World War II. When in

Paul Shay, AFS Executive Secretary

India where tea was the British drink of choice, I dreamt about drinking the wonderful coffee in Brazil. Several nights spent on the beach at Ipanema gave life to the song my wife had sung so many years before, "The Girl from Ipanema."

On October 28, 2000, I was invited to speak at the Northwest AFS conference in Seattle, meeting the AFS volunteers and exchange students with their host parents. As a result of this participation, I was asked to present the Bergen-Belsen slide program at the AFS conference in San Antonio, Texas on January 20, 2001. I met President of AFS U.S.A., Alex J. Plinio, whom I would meet again later in Baltimore and also in Seattle.

In the lobby of the conference hotel was a World War I ambulance, *(see photo below)* loaned on exhibit by the Fort Sam Houston Museum. Yolanda Hagberg of the U.S. Army

Medical Department Center at Fort Sam Houston invited my wife and me to tour the museum, where not only World War I ambulances were on display, but World War II ambulances were stored as well. This fort is the center for the 5th Army Medical Division. I was attached with the U.S. 5th Army in Italy for the time required to qualify for veteran status.

Even after I thought my traveling days were behind me, I decided to make another cross-country trip, this time to Baltimore, Maryland, for what was announced as probably the last AFS Ambulance Driver Reunion. On September 19, 2002, my wife and I flew into Baltimore for a whirlwind few days. The morning after we arrived, (at 4 a.m. Seattle time!) I was asked if

I would come outside and stand by the two ambulances Hugh Gemmell had brought back to the reunion, so that the CBS interviewer could talk with me and others. A banquet was held for AFS officers and volunteers from all over the world. Here we met Alice Kern once more. She was to be the featured speaker at lunch. Soon we all heard her controlled voice telling the chilling story of her internment at Bergen-Belsen, after which she thanked all the AFS drivers in the audience for her liberation.

With Alice Kern and Howard Mayhew at AFS Driver Reunion in Baltimore, Maryland

AFS was to have some of its most momentous television and press coverage as the CBS Sunday news included a special on AFS and its beginnings. The Baltimore Sun also covered the reunion, featuring the meeting of Alice Kern, Bergen-Belsen survivor, with one of the liberators, Howard Mayhew, who had not heretofore spoken of his experience, not even to his own son.

At the drivers' buffet the final evening, a few drivers were brave enough to come to the microphone and tell some of their World War II stories. One story was about a situation in which some AFS fellows had stopped to skinny-dip when they realized that some enemy soldiers were coming near. They quickly took the soldiers into custody. Probably the first story reported of naked captors bringing in enemy prisoners.

Telling my story of Bergen-Belsen to colleagues at the AFS Driver Reunion.

I had experienced some difficulty speaking in the past few months due to a small stroke, which left me unable to think on my feet before a microphone, but I felt I had to tell as much of my story as I could. I began to falter when the memories of Bergen-Belsen welled up in me. My wife, who was sitting with a rough copy of this manuscript ready to share, came to my rescue. She opened it to a place, which is so heartrending to think about even yet. It was the letter I wrote in my fox-hole during the India/Burma campaign. I wrote it into my diary because I did not believe that I would last out the night since the Japanese had surrounded our position. This letter was a pouring out of emotion to Georgie, telling her how much she meant to me over the many months she had waited for me to come back home and wondering if I would ever see her again.

With Ward Chamberlain, Longtime AFS Driver Reunion Organizer

Meeting all the people who keep AFS vital and getting acquainted with the AFS drivers who had gone through the same hell I did was thrilling and like rolling back the clock to the 1940s again.

With all the experiences I have had during World War II and the wonderful contacts I have maintained with AFS people, I feel I have memories to last me into my next life! I have been able to attend two driver reunions, speak in Brazil, San Antonio, Seattle, and places throughout Washington State.

AFS History

Most of my presentations have included something of the history of AFS. The roots of AFS were nourished by Piatt Andrew. He had suffered a defeat in running for the U.S. Congress when he decided to become involved with the American Hospital in France. His first duty was as an ambulance driver. Within months he organized and directed an ambulance service that would serve virtually the entire French army until after the U.S. entry into World War I.

Several things made the ambulance corps successful. The first was the decision to use Ford chassis so all ambulances could be serviced with the same parts. The second was the loyal support of Anne Vanderbilt, who provided money and impetus for the ambulance corps to become independent from the American Hospital. Still another was Andrew's decision to pick Stephen Galatti as his deputy. After World War I, the AFS Ambulance Corps ceased to exist and Andrew died.

At the outbreak of World War II, Galatti immediately organized a section of ambulances and dispatched them to France under the command of Lovering Hill, who had been a section leader in the original AFS. After the French fell, the corps was offered to the British and was attached to the 8th Army in Egypt.

After the war in 1945, Galatti directed the transformation of the American Field Service into a student exchange organization of worldwide scope. As this new AFS Intercultural Program expanded, the focus on AFS history diminished somewhat. Only in the past few years has there been an urgency to connect with the early ambulance drivers and to listen to and record their stories.

My own history, stemming from a Midwestern heritage of hard working parents and older siblings, was further strengthened by my wartime experiences ending at Bergen-

Belsen Concentration Camp. What I have lived has taught me that life is too precious to waste in giving way to anger and hatred. It has given me the strength to carry on my life with the primary purpose of giving service. I would not have joined AFS in the first place unless I was wil-ling to do my part in helping to save lives.

I wondered how I could include a picture of

Steve Kunkel in Dad's Uniform   Norman Holding AFS Uniform

me in uniform. I certainly could not wear it as I was far from the slim young man who had signed up for the AFS Ambulance Corps in 1943, so I put on the cap and held my uniform.

Now we are looking forward to completion in April 2007 of the Bergen-Belsen exhibit in Germany at the site of the original concentration camp. I have donated my AFS uniform and my story of my experience in Bergen-Belsen to this exhibit as a part of the AFS Ambulance Corps section to be housed there.

Since reliving my wartime experiences, I have learned that life is fleeting. The time is now. I have also learned that no one is perfect and that we must cooperate with others, who are also not perfect, to improve life on our planet. It is easier to judge others than to have a positive life plan and live by it with room for acceptance of what others believe and how they choose to worship. I hope that for the rest of my life I will remember how much human misery results from greed and hatred. Focusing on the positive while at the same time working to make the world a better place is my goal. My wife and I believe in working together to achieve a society that does not leave anyone behind. This means that no one would be left to sleep in the street. This means that no one would go to bed hungry. This means that no young child would be deprived of loving care and education. We cannot change the world in our lifetime, but we can do our bit to improve our corner of the earth.

Choosing Peace

Several years ago my wife, Georgie, and I were named honorary chairs of AFS Greater Puget Sound. We were asked to prepare a talk, which Georgie presented at the spring meeting held in March 2003 with volunteers, exchange students, and their host parents in attendance.

The text of the speech follows:

Norman Kunkel and I wish to offer our thanks for being able to share with you today. We especially want to thank you students who have given up a year living in your own countries to be part of a U.S. family, experiencing life in the U.S. and bringing back what you have gained from this experience.

In these troubled times, such sharing with another culture is invaluable. But in times of political violence, anyone who ventures into areas of conflict may risk their lives. Today I would like to ask you to remember a young woman, Rachel Corrie, age 23, an Evergreen State College student (Olympia, Washington) who went to Gaza to challenge the Israeli occupation of the disputed territories. She stood in front of the military bulldozer and was crushed when it moved to demolish the home of a Palestinian doctor.

It was ten years ago that Rachel's parents, Craig and Cindy, and her sister Sarah and brother Chris along with Rachel, hosted Gustavo Ramas, an AFS exchange student from Brazil. He attended Capital High in Olympia while Rachel was in the 8th grade. This family has always supported AFS international peace and understanding. They are now grieving for their daughter who lived her life in this tradition of acting out her ideals.

It will take time for all the details of this tragedy to be investigated but in the meantime, a young person of deep conviction has lost her life. Her death has brought attention to the youth of the world—youth that have often chosen a high level of involvement in carrying out their beliefs. So many times, we see on TV and in the print media only the young people who break laws. It is up to all of us here today to spread the word that there are millions of young people throughout the world who are living their everyday lives in ways to model cooperation and warmth toward other people.

Let's not allow Rachel Corrie's story to die. She, and others like her, will serve as beacons of courage and hope so that we can all rise above the hysteria, hatred, and hopelessness that accompany terrorism and war.

AFS and its continuing programs of opening homes to visiting students from around the world is paving the way toward a future in which people will no longer say, "There will always be war." It is paving the way toward peaceful understanding around the world. Until worldwide peace is achieved, the thousands and thousands of AFS students and families and volunteers will continue to broaden the view into the peaceful world that we all hope for.

On a lighter note, let me leave you with an interesting happening that took place when Norman and I went to Baltimore for his AFS Ambulance Drivers Reunion in September 2002. One day we were told to dress in our best clothes and board a bus that would take us to the German Ambassador's residence. The German Ambassador had once been an exchange student in the U.S. and wanted to show his appreciation to the ambulance drivers who had been a part of AFS history. As we walked into the grand entrance, I spotted an enormous grand piano in the huge entry hall. There was no other furniture there. After all the others had gone on through to the patio for the reception, I stood and admired this glorious musical instrument. I was just exclaiming about the great sound that this magnificent piano would make when played, when the ambassador's greeter came toward me and said, "You can play it if you like."

Well, I sat down and played the

German Ambassador Wolfgang Ischinger invited Georgie and me to pose with him in March 2003.

song that I had written for Norman and had sung for him on our 50th wedding anniversary. Norman noticed I had not followed him out onto the patio, so he came back and as he approached the entryway he heard me playing his song. We will never forget this moment—just the two of us—sharing our song in the grand hall of the German Ambassador's residence.

I posed with a group of AFS Greater Puget Sound area exchange students at Orientation in 2002.

It all happened because my husband signed up for the AFS Ambulance Corps in 1943 and became a part of AFS history. And now we are excited to see AFS con-tinue on into the future, bringing exper-iences that have changed the lives of thousands of students all over the world. We salute AFS and know that even after we are gone, it will be spreading its message of peace throughout the world.

General Wesley Clark with Me at Senator Patty Murray's Veterans' Function in Tacoma, Washington

Alex Plinio, President of AFS USA with Norman at an AFS Meeting in Seattle

Kathy Rees and David Tremaine with Norman in 2002 at an AFS Student Orientation Retreat

AFTERWORD

UNRRA in China

Since we AFS drivers had been given information about the United Nations Relief and Rehabilitation Administration before I left Europe in 1945, I investigated this opportunity to make enough money to establish myself after returning from World War II. Major General Glen E. Edgerton, Director of the UNRRA China office, headed a program of ferrying two hundred (60- to 90-foot) fishing boats to China in order to rehabilitate their fishing industry. The U.S. funded this effort to the tune of several millions of dollars. I signed on as cook to sail on the MS *Ketchikan*, one of the fishing vessels captained by Doug Lance. In June 1946 we headed for China with eleven other vessels. It was our job to teach the Chinese about modern powerboat fishing techniques. These boats could do deep-sea fishing, which was beyond the usual fishing limits of junks in these waters.

Georgie worked at a summer job with the Federal Housing Administration in Seattle while I sailed across the Pacific Ocean. One day after getting to work, one of her colleagues handed her a newspaper report about one of the fishing boats, the *United*, which had sprung a leak and was having difficulties, even before sailing out of Puget Sound. In our letters written back and forth, I was to realize how this trip brought back the worry that Georgie had gone through during my two war years overseas, again in Italy and now once more in going to China.

At Guam, we had to keep a sharp lookout for mines, which had been laid when the Japanese were in control. As for typhoons, we were guaranteed forty-eight hours of good weather when we left Guam. After that, we had to hope for the best.

We reached Shanghai on August 8. There were no letters waiting for me and the place was much like Calcutta in India. There were about six million people, three million more than there had been six years earlier. The sidewalks were packed with sleeping and sitting people. They carried on all activities of life, even sex, right out in the open in front of the world.

[Letter to Georgie]

As you noticed, the letter preceding this one was addressed to "Bright" and then I put tape over that and put "Kunkel." I can offer no explanation at all. I'm very sorry, my sweet. This definitely goes to show that I have to settle down and get used to being married.

My greatest worry is whether you can see my point of view and whether you will wait for me, should I decide to stay here for a few more months and come home with lots more money in my pocket. It is our chance to have a home and some of the luxuries of life. I have already found some wonderful gifts to ship home to you, a camphor chest, some jewelry and two bolts of silk brocade material.

Little did I know when I wrote Georgie about all this that she would be angry that I was spending my money on such lavish things at the expense of my being separated from her.

During and right after a period of war there is always graft and wheeling and dealing. This was no exception. All UNRRA supplies were turned over to CNRRA (UNRRA's Chinese equivalent) and that was a government agency of Chiang Kai-Shek. CNRRA sold to the black market a percentage of the supplies received from UNRRA. Result: The people probably did not receive their share of relief or rehabilitation from these huge expenditures. I soon discovered that my pay was not what I had agreed to unless I signed a contract as a fisherman, which I did. Once again I was sacrificing time away from Georgie in order to bring home a nest egg.

Georgie showing off the mandarin jacket that I brought her from China.

[Letter from Georgie]

Sometimes I can hardly believe you will ever come home. It seems like years since you landed in Shanghai. How can they keep you so long? You know, I have a horror of waking up each morning. If I could only sleep like the Sleeping Beauty and not wake up until you come home. How nice that would be—but darn it—I have to live all those days until I see you. How many more lonely days and nights must I spend?

I skipped my 26th birthday as all day I was restless and unhappy and tried to forget it. I remembered all my other birthdays since I met you. My 23rd you were leaving for AFS duty, my 24th I received news that you were not coming home, my 25th you sent roses from Seattle but they didn't take your place. Life creeps on unsteadily without you, my love.

I wrote Georgie that I was sorry I couldn't be there with her to cheer and comfort her. I assured her that I would be there as quickly as I could be. I decided that I would terminate my contract when I got back from a fishing trip aboard the *John B* if I could get transport home. So after riding the waves out in the China Seas and fishing twenty-four hours a day, I tried to get all the necessary paperwork done so I could make the plan to leave on December 8. Many fishermen had quit and twenty more intended to quit. Things looked very bad, but the program continued in the same stumbling manner as usual.

The hardship and hard work we experienced out fishing for eighteen days was unbelievable. I was thankful it was over. But there was doubt in my mind about finding a position that would provide for a family after I got back home. I had already passed up the opportunity for shipping out that Brent Milnor had opened up to me and now I was leaving my contacts in UNRRA. I would be arriving in Chehalis in the middle of Georgie's teaching contract year without any networking opportunities in that small town. Since I had not completed my college education I could not gain from Georgie's contacts in education. But if I were not to lose Georgie, I needed to finally join her in making our marriage work.

[Letter to Georgie]
You mentioned knitting a "soaker" (wool diaper-cover for a baby). You have me on needles and pins! Are those soakers for someone else's baby? My dearest, darling wife, if they are not for someone else, please do not be so casual about it all! I really hardly know what to say. Please explain more fully what you mean by warning me beforehand about knitting. You have me biting my nails and about ready to go crazy. Write me, honey, or wire me via Mackay Radio if anything serious happens, OK?

I had a conversation with one Chinese fellow who spoke English. Since Georgie and I had already agreed on using contraception until I was better established financially, I asked him what the Chinese do to limit their families. He replied, "We just don't do it." Now I was wondering if that wasn't the best way after all.

I kept Georgie informed of the conditions here in China. The exchange rate was $2,500 Chinese to one U.S. dollar. A haircut was $1,250, rum and coke $2,500, women's silk stockings $24,000 and beer $33,000 a quart. Chinese silk was $8,500 a yard. Jade was a half million dollars for a small piece of good quality. I told Georgie that she could tell everyone when she gets the jade I am bringing home that it cost half a million dollars! My AFS check in Chinese dollars would fill a whole satchel.

There was no semblance of democracy. The Communists were only about twenty miles from us, sixty thousand of them. If you started talking about the political situation here with a Nationalist, he would just go off and leave you standing or politely tell you, "We don't talk about such things."

Although I wanted to make the most of my UNRRA employment, I realized that the situation was not what I had expected. An added impetus for my return was the absence of letters from Georgie after September 27. I did not receive any letters written later than that. Once more I was making the decision to go back home to assure that Georgie and I would be together.

Our flight was delayed in Hawaii overnight because of fog in the Los Angeles area. I stayed at the Royal Hawaiian Hotel, a deep pink stucco building which many years later I showed to Georgie during one of our Hawaiian getaways from the cloudy winter weather in Seattle. You can imagine the excitement when Georgie got my telegram that my plane would be landing at Ontario airport near Los Angeles.

[Telegram to Georgie]

PLANE ARRIVING ONTARIO
CALIFORNIA DEC 8. LOVE NORM

Georgie didn't waste any time asking for a leave from her teaching position to take a plane to LA. Since she grew up in a family of schoolteachers who never left their jobs unless they were sick or dying, she was breaking tradition to leave her students and take a cut in pay besides. I think someone was watching out for us because I stated in the telegram that I would arrive on December 8 without taking into account that I would be crossing the International Dateline. Since our plane was delayed a day in Hawaii the date on the telegram was correct after all.

Georgie's cousin had arranged a hotel room for us and also for a tour of the city. All we could think of was being together. After a day of sightseeing, including a walk through the farmer's market, we spent an evening at Olvera Street where we had our first taste of Mexican food. I was willing to try the fascinating burritos, tacos and interesting sugared delicacies, but Georgie was wary of anything that wasn't her usual meat and potatoes fare. I teased her a little about it. So while I was munching on a spicy bit of Mexican fast food, she was entranced by the Christmas decorations everywhere. There were colorful piñatas hanging from many booths and ornate statues of the Virgin Mary being carried through the street. Georgie brought back a picture book about *Pedro, the Christmas Angel*. Later on after we had our children, she made big sugar cookies cut to resemble Pedro to hang on the Christmas tree. This reminded us of our reunion after six months being apart so many years before.

Our time in Los Angeles was soon over. It was wonderful, but at the same time strange to suddenly be united with Georgie, wrapped in her arms, when we had only dreamed about it for the months that I was gone.

Time to Talk About Family

By Georgie Bright Kunkel

Norman received his BA in Education from the University of Washington in 1954 after our two sons were born, and was hired immediately by Highline School District just south of Seattle. His old friend Brent was right when he predicted that if Norman married a schoolteacher, he would become one also. When Brent learned that Norman was studying in education at the University of Washington, he wrote, "You will enjoy teaching." And then he added:

Graduation from the
University of Washington
in 1954

> Quite often I wonder where I would be if I had not gotten married. I enjoy my children and play with them every night. You can't beat married life. But what about those cold ships, those cold Liberties that lay unloaded, no smoke from the squat little stacks and their red lead showing above that gray Puget Sound? The forecastles are cold and damp and the steel decks ring hollowly. Then there are the cargo winches, when the ship is operating. Those winches bang around all night long and throw dust into your room. Then there are the drunks that file on board and sit at breakfast with a hangover. They can keep it all.

Men were a premium in the elementary grades and every elementary principal wanted at least one. People sometimes looked askance when Norman said he was a sixth grade teacher. They expected this six-foot-four-and-a-half-inch man to be a school principal or a least a high school teacher.

Norman taught at Gregory Heights School in Highline District in the Seattle area for twenty-five years and was involved in one of the first Outdoor Education Programs for elementary students. His class published the school newspaper, and he helped in landscaping the relatively new building. Now the building has been razed and a new building has been built on the property.

Now it is time to talk about the children.

Our family portrait: Norman holding Kim, Joe, Susan, Georgie and Steve.

The Story of Norman Joseph Kunkel, 1947-2001

Our son Norman Joseph, whom we called Joe, was born on September 16, 1947, at the little West Seattle Hospital, which was the second floor of a building at Alaska and California Avenue in Seattle. The doctor bill was $50 and the hospital bill wasn't more than $100. This was before we had any health insurance.

Joe was very active and physical from the beginning, although he loved to be read to. He grew up without television until he was ten years old. When he was old enough to join the Cub Scouts, I became his Den Mother. Joe had always been taught not to fight, but was constantly taunted by the school bully on the playground. Since Joe looked almost two years older than his age he was challenged by this bully who was older, but about the same size.

One day we got a call that our son had beaten up the bully. The teacher was almost celebrating the fact that this student had at last been beaten. Neither Norman nor I celebrated on hearing this news. It meant that our son had to take on this terrorizer all alone and was forced to fight when intervention by adults could have solved this problem much earlier.

As he got older, Joe was involved in swimming and track and played trombone in the swing band in high school. Joe loved outdoor life, once spending a summer on the Pribilof Islands in Alaska assisting an ornithologist in tagging birds. Another summer he worked in the seal harvest. He cherished an old shotgun that once belonged to his Grandfather Joseph and a rifle that Norman had given him and was proud of the deer he got most every year in Idaho. One year he killed a cougar and served it to us when we visited. He played a joke on me and said it was roast loin of pork. It worked.

Joe attained a BA in Education from Washington State University and began a teaching career. He became interested in studying to become a chiropractor and attained a Doctorate in Chiropractic from a college in South Carolina. After spending a few years building a practice in an outlying area, the local mill closed. Since it was the main source of employment in the region, Joe decided to return to education later attaining his Masters in Education from the University of Idaho.

Throughout the draft years during the Vietnam War, Joe had the trunk of his car fitted out with supplies in case he had to flee to Canada. He had heard me tell a story about my father telling my oldest brother, "I don't want a son of mine to become cannon fodder." This was our attitude as well. Ironically, Joe was never drafted.

After marrying Leslie Bren, they had five children. Curtis is a graduate of the University of Idaho. Jolie is married to Lance Taylor serving in the U.S. Navy, and they have three children: Joe named after his grandfather, Trevor, and Heath. Mica and Farron are working in the U.S. Forest Service in Idaho with summer work as forest firefighters. Travis, the last of the five children, recently began work at his first entry-level job.

Following his divorce, Joe joined a firm installing glass in Sun Valley, Idaho, and established residence with a new partner in Jerome, Idaho. Shortly after resettling, he was killed in a tragic motorcycle accident while coming home from a motorcycle road run to raise money for children.

This book was put on hold for a while after the shock of his death. However, an early draft of this book was sent to him before he died. He wrote on the margins of the manuscript, "I find a lot of Dad in me as I read through this story of his life." Joe had often served the Education Department in Idaho by reviewing the required written eighth grade exams. This expertise was evident in his editing of the manuscript we shared with him.

The Story of Stephen Gregory Kunkel

Nineteen months after our first child was born, we had our second child, Stephen Gregory, called Steve, who arrived on February 2, 1949. We always called him our groundhog baby. Steve was an active child, first walking like a bear instead of crawling, and then beginning to walk before he was ten months old.

Steve soon learned that he could sit back and observe what happened to Joe and learn from his mistakes. Since Steve was five in February before starting kindergarten in September and since he was not being totally challenged in school, his fourth grade teacher suggested that he be moved into the fifth grade in midyear.

When we hired a contractor to build our new home on our extra lot next door to our first little house, Steve watched our home go up, one step at a time from pouring concrete to framing and finishing. Since we had an agreement with this contractor that we would complete any jobs that our family could do in order to keep the cost down, Steve helped with daily carpenter cleanup chores. Our unfinished basement soon became a testing ground for his talents and over the span of just a few years he had finished our recreation room, basement bedroom, and bathroom.

Steve played the cello in the Seattle Youth Symphony Orchestra during high school and college under the baton of Vilem Sokol. There he met his first wife Joan Martin. He transferred to Garfield High School for his junior and senior years in a volunteer program to integrate this school which had a large minority population.

During the summers while attending the University of Washington College of Engineering, Steve worked on fishing boats going to Alaska. During the Vietnam War Steve was drafted. After nineteen months serving in Huntsville, Alabama, at a missile base, he was released after applying for the Army's "early out" program which allowed him to return to college to complete his BS in Engineering.

Steve gained experience as a builder planning and constructing our Whidbey Island vacation home on one of the few lots left on Holmes Harbor. He lived in an abandoned cabin next door until he could move into the house to complete the building.

He married Alice Shanley DeWalt in 1979. She has a Masters Degree in Education from the University of Southern California and a Masters in Organizational Psychology from Antioch University in Seattle, Washington. They have two children: Samantha, graduate of Seattle University, who lives with her husband Enarez Gonzales and son Isaac; and Farrah, who graduated from California State University at Hayward and is now attending Seattle Pacific University to complete her teaching degree. Steve is a Master Builder and has been in the general contracting business for over thirty years in Bellevue, Washington. He played in a string quartet for a few years and has been active in community affairs, now as president of Newport Hills Community Club.

The Story of Susan Ann Kunkel

After Norman was established as a teacher at Gregory Heights School, we decided on continuing our family and Susan Ann was born on June 16, 1955. Although I wasn't an accomplished person on the sewing machine, I did make outfits for the children when they were younger, even hand stitching a flower girl outfit for Susan after looking up appropriate garb in Emily Post's book on etiquette. Susan was so fastidious that even though she had a little white basket filled with rose petals which she was to scatter, she couldn't bear to litter the floor with them as she walked down the aisle.

Susan was precocious, speaking in sentences at an early age. She was a quiet child in the classroom much as I was in my school life, not indicating the active nature that was to evolve. She chose the cello to play in the school orchestra and showed skill in writing, never wasting words. After attending community college while working for a living, she completed an Associate Degree in Data Processing. This led her into the technology field at a time when companies were transitioning from punched cards to digital file storage.

Susan has remained active in church and political life, continuing her interest in gourmet cooking and travel. For several years she and her dad made fruitcakes on Thanksgiving weekend, wrapping them in cloth soaked in wine and putting them away to age so they would be ready for the Christmas season.

She had two sons, Gregory (now at Washington State University) and Kenneth (in high school), with partner Elmo Williams, Jr. (now deceased). In 1996 she married Dan Wilson, telecommunications specialist for Qwest, Inc. After a few years she landed a position as an Information Systems Manager in the Finance Department for the City of Tacoma. Susan is an avid reader and maintains an interest in the arts.

Our Family at Susan's Wedding in 1996. *Back row:* Mica, Steve, Curtis, Farrah, and Samantha. *Second row:* Kaz Waligorski (Kim's former husband), Alice (Steve's wife), Jolie Taylor, Kim Waligorska, and newlyweds Susan Kunkel and Dan Wilson. *Front row:* Gregory Williams, Farron, Travis, Kenneth Williams, Georgie, Norman, and Joe Kunkel.

The Story of Kimberly Jane Kunkel Waligorska

Kimberly Jane was born on February 11, 1959. One day I was called to substitute in the classroom very late in the morning when a teacher did not show up for work. I was told that I could bring Kim along in the baby buggy while I was teaching the class, awaiting the arrival of the regular teacher.

As our daughter Kim grew up, she showed creativity in many ways. She and Michelle Chan, a neighbor who lived across the street, would get together and make up games and play with dolls and put on little plays. She was active in sports, Girl Scouts, and Job's Daughters. Since Kim's birthday was in February and she was advanced for her age, she was able to enter a special program at a neighboring school in which her second and third years of school were combined. Kim chose the flute to play in the school orchestra and took part in recitals and in All City Orchestra.

During high school she worked as a babysitter and was employed at a local convenience store in the evenings. At age fifteen she went with her French class to France. She completed three years in science at Western Washington University where she was on the women's rugby team, which won a championship during her second year. Even before completing her BS degree, she was accepted by nursing school at the University of Washington where she then completed her degree, majoring in pediatric nursing. After she began her nursing career, she went camping often and loved to swim so much that she even swam in the freezing glacial stream at Glacier Park.

Kim is currently continuing her career in nursing at Children's Hospital and Regional Medical Center in Seattle. In the past, she mothered two children, Kara and Jesse, for about seven years when she was a partner to the children's father, John Martin. Later she was married to Kazimierz Waligorski with whom she managed a part-time travel business. After the death of John Martin in a motorcycle accident, she became even closer to her two "stepchildren." Jesse now has three children and Kara has two children.

Georgie and I posing with our grown children: Kim, Joe, Steve, and Susan.

****

Memories of the years we were active parents of four children are still with us. There were Christmases when Steve stayed up looking at the tree until late into the night on Christmas Eve. I had baked large cookies in shapes of schoolhouses, Santas, and even Pedro copied from the book bought on Olvera Street in Los Angeles after Norman came back from China.

There were the sounds of the trombone when Joe practiced for a swing-band concert and Steve drawing his bow across the cello and later Susan playing the cello. Flute sounds echoed in the house when Kim's older siblings had all graduated from high school. There were swimming and track events and shopping trips for clothes to replenish the wardrobes of fast growing youngsters. There were birthday parties for every birthday for which I made all the party favors and decorations.

Norman and I kept our teaching certificates current by taking courses after school or in the summer. We took time out for extended family get-togethers and carried on the tradition of family parties in our own nuclear family. We were both active in organizing the teacher's union in the district, and Norman was supportive in my involvement in the women's movement of the early seventies when Washington State passed its own Equal Rights Amendment in 1972.

We were early members of the Saltwater Unitarian Universalist Church and both served on the church board. As the children grew, we had more time to broaden our interests in our community. Norman volunteered for many years for the Northwest Environment Watch based in Seattle. After years of participating in various local chorale groups, I joined the Raging Grannies who sing parodies about changing the world so that everyone eats; is clothed and housed; and has a complete education, birth to death.

Salmon Catch at Westport, Washington
in 1964

Norman has not been on the speaking circuit in the past few years but has enjoyed activities such as tending to his azaleas and rhododendrons *(posing with the azaleas he propagated)*, swimming, attending important political meetings and church, reading, taking short trips, enjoying family reunions, and being my reviewer when I write articles for newspapers. He was my most important reviewer for my first book, *You're Damn*

Right I Wear Purple: Color Me Feminist, and we have collaborated closely on this book.

Extended family photo taken in 2004: *Back row:* Kenneth Williams, Kim Waligorska, Farron, Farrah, Curtis, Susan, Georgie, Norman, Gregory Williams, Mica, Alice, and Steve. *Front row:* Travis holding nephew Joe Taylor, Enarez Gonzales with Samantha Kunkel holding Isaac, Jolie Taylor holding Trevor (her husband Lance and their third child Heath are not pictured).

APPENDICES

1. Work Experience

2. AFS Ambulance Corps Service in Italy

3. Map of India/Burma Campaign

4. World War II Medals

5. Members of the AFS 567 Company who served at Bergen-Belsen Concentration Camp, Germany

6. AFS Ambulance Drivers Mentioned in *WWII Liberator's Life*

Work Experience

- Selling papers : 2 cents for the daily and 5 cents for the Sunday.
- Stacking empty boxes in a fruit warehouse for 5 cents a hundred.
- Picking hops for one or 2 cents a pound.
- Packing fruit in a warehouse for 35 cents per hour.
- Running peeling machine and turning apples on the kiln for 25 cents an hour.
- Digging sewer ditches for $44 a month in the WPA.
- Working in the mechanic shop, library and planting trees in the CCC.
- Cooking in Alaska for room, board, and $30 a month.
- Putting up Christmas decorations all over the Yakima Valley for 50 cents an hour.
- Packing orders in the catalog department at Sears Roebuck.
- Working as a shop clerk at Boeing for 65 cents per hour.
- Working in the pipe bending shop at Sea-Tac Shipyard that made destroyers.
- Clerking in a liquor store at 65 cents per hour.
- Making salads and washing dishes in a restaurant for meals in New York.
- Serving two years for the AFS Ambulance Corps during WWII for $25 a month.
- Longshoring on the Seattle waterfront.
- Cooking on merchant marine ships while in the Port in Seattle.
- Serving as a deckhand and chief steward on a Liberty Ship to Sicily and back.
- Serving on a 90-foot fishing boat from Seattle to Shanghai for UNRRA.
- Working in a Kraft cheese plant making cottage cheese in Chehalis, Washington.
- Working in a creosote plant in Seattle.
- Maintaining overhead transit lines for Seattle Transit.
- Working to put up utility towers in the North Cascades region.
- Serving as a part time supervisor at the Youth Service Center in Seattle, Washington.
- Teaching at Gregory Heights School in Seattle area for over 25 years.
- Serving as a supervisor for a boys' Job Corps camp in Lewis County, Washington.
- Working in Highline District maintenance during the summer months.
- Cooking on a tugboat and also on a cannery tender in Alaska during the summer.

MY PHILOSOPHY

As Studs Terkel reminds us, every job has dignity. Labor in itself is honorable. I witnessed the inequality and the class levels throughout my work life as well as during my war experiences in India, China, and while traveling throughout the world. I have always hoped for peace in the world, including equal access to needed goods and services for all people. The system that allows profit from labor and does not return an equal portion to the worker is dishonorable. Until all disenfranchised groups can work together to gain what is their right, there will always be isolated political movements, each trying to get a larger piece of the pie. As history has taught, no country on an imperialistic path has escaped revolution. Hopefully, the citizens of this country and the rest of the world will wake up to this fact before it is too late for peaceful resolution benefiting all citizens.

N.C.K.

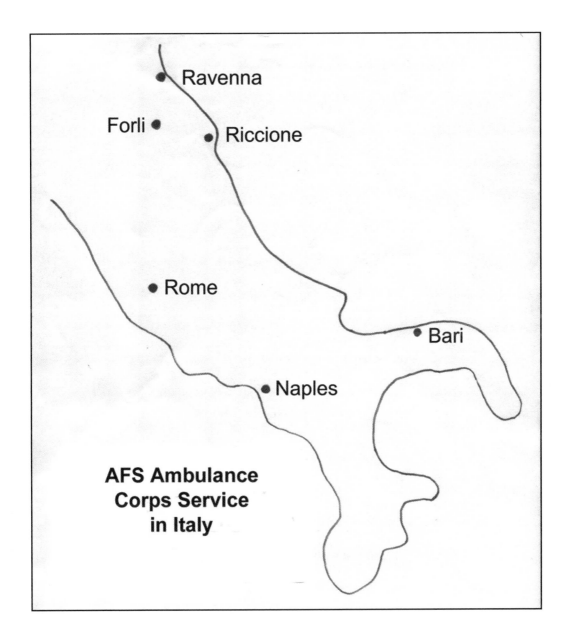

Ravenna

Forli

Riccione

Rome

Bari

Naples

**AFS Ambulance
Corps Service
in Italy**

Map of India/

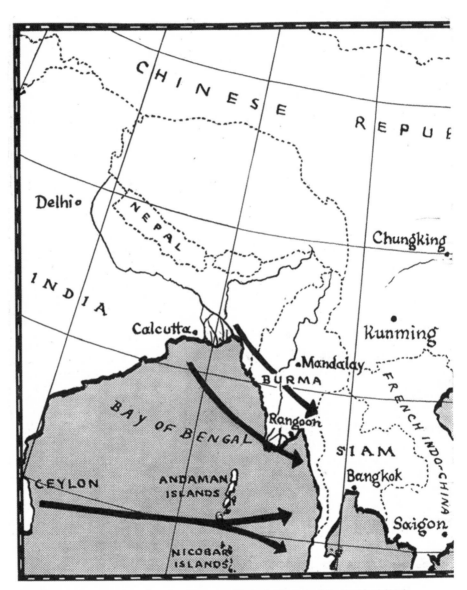

THE BURMA CAMPAIGNS have been no side-show. They have been an integral and a vital part of the over-all Allied strategy in the war against Japan.

The first objectives of the Combined Chiefs of Staff in this theater were (1) to crack the Jap's land bastion defending his "co-prosperity sphere" in South East Asia, (2)

Burma Campaign

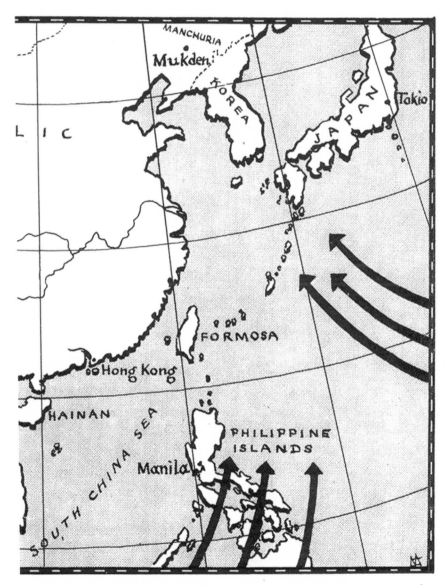

to reopen communications to China from India, and (3) to crush the Japanese armies in Burma.

Their long term objective was the tighten-ing—towards an ultimately throttling grip —of the offensive ring round Japan and her ill-gotten Empire: a ring whose steel spikes were Nimitz, MacArthur and Mountbatten.

AFS Patch andWorld War II Medals

Top left to right:

1.   European, African, Middle Eastern Campaign

2.   Good Conduct Medal

3.   Germany: Army of Occupation

Bottom left to right:

1.   U.S. WWII Medal

2.   American Field Service WWII Medal

Members of the AFS 567 Company who served at Bergen-Belsen Concentration Camp, Germany

C PLATOON

Bell, Whitfield Jenks, Jr. ....CM 47
Chapin, Wallace Arey ....CM 87
Clarkson, Bayard Delafield ....CM 90
Cole, Eugene Maurice, Jr. ....CM 92, IB 60-T
Collins, George Roseborough ....ME 26
Du Pont, Paul Henri-Berthold ....CM 92, IB 60-T
Elberfeld, Richard Bradford ....IB 2, CM 91-T
Feddeman, Frederick August ....IB 2, CM 91-T
Fuller, Warren Graham ....ME 26, CM 93
Keller, Chandler Young ....ME 26, CM 93
Kunkel, Norman Clyde ....IB 5, CM 92-T
MacLeod, Cameron, Jr. ....CM 96, IB 60-T
McMillen, Robert Trafford ....CM 92, IB 60-T
Meeker, John Royce ....ME 1, FFC, CM 86, IB 60-T
Murphy, Duncan Bassett, Jr. ....ME 4, CM 79
Wilson, Conrad ....CM 72

D PLATOON

Allen, Lewis Maitland, Jr. ....ME 32, FFC, CM 97
Applewhite, Robert Metzler ....ME 30, FFC, CM 94, IB 60-T
Bayer, Frank Arnold ....CM 86
Baylor, John Ransdell ....CM 86
Brawley, Arthur Leslie ....CM 68
Briggs, James Alexander ....ME 10, CM 88
Campagnoli, John Philip ....CM 86
Carter, Ralph Bidwell, III ....CM 86
Colvin, Donald Andrew ....CM 50
Congdon, William Grosvenor ....ME 20, CM 90
DeMone, Earl Fenwick ....CM 68
Dougherty, Joseph Francis ....CM 88, IB 60-T
Evans, John Marshall, Jr. ....CM 94, IB 60-T
Fogg, Joseph Graham, Jr. ....ME 32, FFC, CM 94
Gadarian, Harold Lance ....CM 86, IB 60-T

D PLATOON (continued)

Gallant, William Daniel ....CM 96, IB 60-T
Gilbert, Craig Philip ....CM 93
Greene, John Francis ....CM 75
Guenther, Jacob Jarden, Jr. ....ME 18, FFC, CM 92
Harvey, C. Tandolph ....CM 42, CM 92
Hazard, Gibson DeKalb ....CM 81
Henry, Charles Eugene ....CM 54
Hill, David Fentress ....CM 85
Hoffman, Edward Reingold, Jr. ....CM 92
Horton, Charles Henry ....IB 1, CM 89-T
Husted, John Grinnel Wetmore, Jr. ....CM 92, IB 60-T
Keen, Ian Walter ....CM 47, IB 60-T
Kendall, Bruce Douglas ....CM 92
Knowlton, George William, IV ....CM 43, CM 92
Leflar, Hugh Niles ....CM 92, IB 60-T
Lepard, Harold John ....CM 94
Martineau, Stanley Frederick ....CM 92
McGraw, Phillips ....CM 92
Mayhew, Howard Clifford, Jr. ....CM 96, IB 60-T
Meyers, Edward Raymond ....CM 86, IB 60-T
Mitchell, Dayton Thomas, II ....CM 68
Murray, Francis James, Lieutenant ....ME 24, CM 92
Prince, William Stevens ....CM 88, IB 59-T
Rich, William Alexander ....ME 28, CM 94, IB 60-T
Scott, Robert Gordon ....CM 81
Shethar, Norman ....CM 53
Smith, Arthur Carroll ....CM 92
Snyder, Thomas Stevenson ....CM 69, IB 60-T
Stryker, John Field ....CM 92, IB 60-T
Terrell, Howard Spencer ....ME 2, CM 93
Tilton, Henry Stephen ....ME 32, FFC, CM 94, IB 60-T
Tscherfinger, Robert Edwin ....CM 91
Wakefield, Willard Chester ....CM 86, IB 60-T
Waterman, Shelden Ward ....CM 75, IB 60-T
Waters, Melvin Earl ....CM 92, IB 60-T
Webber, Roger Babson ....CM 88
Willets, Chester Austen, Jr. ....ME 20, CM 81

D PLATOON (continued)

Young, Peter Cornell ....CM 86
Zukowski, Chester David ....CM 90, IB 60-T

RESERVE SECTION

Cole, Thomas Lionel Howard ....CM 82
Eisaman, Elmer Eugene ....CM 92, IB 60-T
Smith, Charles James ....CM 90
Smith, Donald Rhoderic ....CM 90

AFS volunteers who were present at Bergen-Belsen but not assigned to duty include:

Major Bertram Payne
Alan Willoughby
Carl Zeigler
Thomas Hale   CM 47, CM 97

AFS Ambulance Drivers Mentioned In
WWII Liberator's Life

Ainsworth, Joseph Rowan...................... IB 2 .... Illinois
Baars, James John Jr. .... IB 8 .... Washington, DC
Ball, _____ .... Enlisted when I did.
Barbour, Thomas, II .... ME 28 .... Connecticut
Barrel, Robert Larfeuil .... CM 56 .... Massachusetts
Barrett, John (Jack) White..................... IB 3 .... Connecticut
Baskin, Norton Sanford.......................... IB 4 .... Florida
Beeber, Nathaniel C. .... IB 4 .... New York
Bell, Whitfield Jenks, Jr. .... CM 47 .... Maryland
Bennett, Ralph Blackhurst, Jr............... IB 2 .... Oregon
Blair, Robert Fleming, Jr., Lieut. .... ME 27 .... Ohio
Boaz, Ralph Evans .... IB 26 .... Nebraska
Bragg, Donald Joseph .... ME 2, IB 5 .... New York
Brannan, George Edward .... IB 7 .... Illinois
Brown, William Banjamin .... ME 1, IB-T, IB 53..................... Ohio
Budinger, Fred Emil............................... IB 3 .... Illinois
Burkhard, Frederick Thomas .... CM 83 .... New York
Burton, Thomas Ashley .... IB 1 .... New York
Chapman, Ted
Cheney, Michael Sheldon, 2nd. Lieut. ..ME 4, IB 5, IB 53 .... California
Clark, Allen Williams, Jr.   .... IB 1 .... Massachusetts
Clark, Paul Francis................................. IB 3, CM 91-T, IB 59-T .... California
Clay, Buckner Woodford .... ME 4, IB 6 .... West Virginia
Clifford, William Carl............................ CM 96, IB 60-T........................ Ohio
Collins, George Roseborough .... ME 26 .... Massachusetts
Colvin, Donald Andrew .... CM 50 .... New York
Congdon, William Grosvenor .... ME 20, CM 90 .... Connecticut
Cosgrove, William Malloy..................... IB 3 .... Michigan
Crowley, John Rourke,........................... IB 8, CM 87-T.......................... New Jersey
Demarest, David Thompson................... CM 47 .... New Jersey
Desloge, Joseph John, Jr. .... ME 4, FFC, CM 94, IB 59-T .... Missouri
Devine, Thomas Franklin....................... IB 2 .... Ohio
Dignam, Frank Alexander...................... IB 5 .... Oregon
Dingman, Norman, Capt. .... IB 1 .... Kentuckey
Ecclestone, Arthur Greenhalge, Jr.......... ME 26, CM 76.......................... Massachusetts

Edwards, _____
Eggleton, William Lawrence Brere, III.. IB 5 .... Pennsylvania
Elberfeld, Donald Neil .... FR 4.. New Jersey
Evans, _____
Feddeman, Frederick August .... IB 2, CM 91-T........................... Pennsylvania
Fenn, Norman Dingman, Capt. .... IB .... Kentucky
Fiedler, Arthur... attached British Liberation Army
Fogg, Joseph Graham, Jr. .... ME 32, FFC, CM 94 .... Ohio
Fritzsche, Alfred, II .... CM 97, IB 59-T........................ Connecticut
Gemmell, Colin Roy .... CM 92, IB 60-T........................ Connecticut
Gilliam, Neil McDowell, Capt. .... ME 2, FFC, IB-T...................... Washington, DC
Graney, Patrick Clifford, Jr. .... CM 92, IB 60-T........................ West Virginia
Gray, _____
Grey, Robert Allen................................. IB 2, FR 8................................. Massachusetts
Griffin, _____
Guenther, Jacob Jarden, Jr. .... ME 18, FFC, CM 92 .... Pennsylvania
Hale, Thomas .... CM 47, CM 97 .... Massachusetts
Hamilton, Richard Truitt........................ IB 16, CM 92-T........................ Pennsylvania
Hendryx, Shirley Wilson, Jr................... IB 5 .... Indiana
Hill, Albert Donald................................ IB 2 .... Massachusetts
Hodel, John Charles .... ME 4, FFC, CM 53, FR 3-T...... New York
Horton, Charles Henry .... IB 1, CM 89-T.......................... Vermont
Hursey, George Herman......................... CM 87 .... California
Jefferys, Charles Norman, Capt. .... Syria FF, FFC, IB 1................... New York
Keller, Chandler Young, Lieut.............. ME 26, CM 93 .... New York
Knuepfer, Russell Norman..................... ME 4, IB 6 .... Illinois
Kocienki, John Raymond .... CM 92, IB 59-T........................ New York
Kornbrodt, Louis Theodore.................... IB 1 .... Oregon
Krusi, LeRoy Hines................................ ME 1, FFC, IB 6 .... California
Latham, J. Richard .... ME 1, IB 1, FR 4....................... Connecticut
Long, Chester Elliott .... IB 16, CM 91-T........................ Louisiana
Lutman, Donald Leo .... IB 1, IB 55 .... Ohio
MacGill, James, Lieut............................ ME 1, IB-T................................. Maryland
Marler, Frank McKinley, Lieut.............. CM 44 .... Ohio
Mayfield, Frank McConnell, Jr. .... IB 4, FR 8.................................. Missouri
Mayhew, Howard Clifford, Jr. .... CM 96, IB 60-T........................ New Jersey
McKinnon, Russell Albert .... CM 86 .... Massachusetts
Meeker, John Royce............................... ME 1, FFC, CM 86, IB 60-T .... New York

Miller, "Moon"..................................... Was in India with me,
                                                  one of 8 Millers in AFS
Moon, Gardner .... CM93, IB 59-T......................... Illinois
Moor, Daniel Weston .... IB 6, IB 53 .... Vermont
Morrill, Dewitt Crawford .... IB 7 .... Massachusetts
Motz, Arnold, Lieut.............................. ME 22 .... Oregon
Murphy, Duncan Bassett, Jr. .... ME 4, CM 79 .... Connecticut
Murray, Francis James, Lieut................ ME 24, CM 92 .... Michigan
Nemecek, Robert Buddy .... CM 88 .... Illinois
Null, Harold Miller................................ IB 1 .... Pennsylvania
Orth, William Tuttle.............................. IB 28 .... New York
Patrick, John R., Capt............................ ME 19, IB-T.............................. New York
Perry, William, Sgt................................. ME 5, CM 93, IB 48-T, CM-T.. Virginia
Proctor, Kenneth Arnold .... ME 30 .... Missouri
Roach, Alexander Joseph .... IB .... Michigan
Robinson, Robert Allen.......................... IB 3 .... Iowa
Rock, George Albert .... ME 13, CM 92 .... New Jersey
Ruppert, Karl... IB 2, CM 91-T.......................... Massachusetts
Searles, Harrison Lambert...................... ME 4, IB 4 .... New York
Shethar, Norman .... CM 53 .... Rhode Island
Smith, Francis Mitchel .... IB 5 .... Rhode Island
Smith, William Tucker.......................... IB 4 .... Connecticut
Spallone, Daniel Andrew Francis........... IB 3 .... Connecticut
Stewart, Peter Minnick.......................... IB 1, IB 45 .... Missouri
Sweetnam, William James .... IB 9 .... Massachusetts
Swensson, Hilding................................. ME 4, IB 11 .... New Jersey
Washburn, William Eugene .... ME 32, CM 97, IB 59-T........... Ohio
Waterbury, Robert Louis........................ IB 5 .... Ohio
White, Samuel Mervin .... IB 7 .... Rhode Island
Whiteside, John Burgess .... ME 4, IB 5 .... New Jersey
Wilhelm, John Caroll .... IB 3 .... Ohio
Wilson, Robert Paul .... IB 5 .... Connecticut
Wright, Charles McQuown .... IB 2 .... Tennessee
Wright, Mortimer Dickinson.................. ME 4, CM 56 .... Connecticut
Young, Thornton Claflin........................ ME 37 .... Massachusetts
Zeigler, Carl Frederick .... CM 88 .... Illinois